The Ile-de-France

THE ILE-DE-FRANCE

The Country around Paris

Marc Bloch

Translated by J. E. Anderson

Cornell University Press
ITHACA, NEW YORK

© 1966 by Ecole Pratique des Hautes Études
Translation © Routledge & Kegan Paul Ltd 1971

Translated from the French
L'Ile de France, 1913
republished in *Mélanges Historiques* 1966 (S.E.V.P.E.N.)

First published 1971

International Standard Book Number 0-8014-0640-4
Library of Congress Catalog Card Number 70-148715

Printed in Great Britain

Contents

list of illustrations   vii

chapter one
The Region   1
1 *The name Ile-de-France*   1
2 *The geographical characteristics of the Ile-de-France*   16

chapter two
The Local History of the Ile-de-France
before the Nineteenth Century   33

chapter three
Contemporary Local History and
the Ile-de-France I: Plan of Investigation   45
1 *Local societies*   45
2 *The tools of research*   51

chapter four
Contemporary Local History and
the Ile-de-France II: Problems and Results   56
1 *Local monographs: towns and villages*   56
2 *The earliest period: prehistoric and ancient times*   63
3 *The middle ages*   74
4 *The modern and contemporary periods*   100

chapter five
Conclusions   119

Notes   124

Index   179

Illustrations

Map of the whole region of the Ile-de-France   viii

Facing page

Beauvais: the Cathedral of St. Pierre   24
Beauvais Cathedral: the choir   25
The Seine at Mantes   40
The magnificent Château and grounds of Chantilly   41
Country road through Seine-et-Marne   88
The Château of Fontainebleau   89
Chartres: la Cathédrale de Blés Verts seen across the
cornfields of Beauce   104
Chartres Cathedral: the west front   105
Chartres Cathedral: the rose window in the south
transept   105

Acknowledgments

The illustrations facing pages 24, 40, 88, 89 and 104 are reproduced by courtesy of the Commissariat Général au Tourisme Paris. Those facing pages 25 and 105 are reproduced by courtesy of Dr Martin Hürliman.

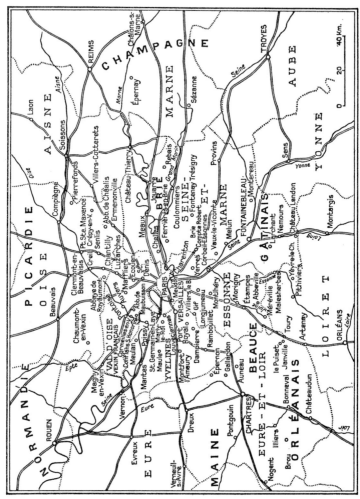

The Ile-de-France

chapter one
The Region[1]

The name Ile-de-France

When you come to think of it, the name of the region we are about to study—the Ile-de-France—has something surprising and intriguing about it. Why should a single province bear the same name as the great country of which it is only a part? And in particular, what is the origin of this word 'Ile', which would appear to be so unsuitable for a region that is not surrounded by any sea? The origins and vicissitudes of the names 'France' and 'Ile-de-France', in spite of some fine work that has been done on them,[2] are still not at all familiar; the problem we encounter on the threshold of this 'general review' is one that has been very inadequately solved, and still requires research. What follows would appear to be the more or less certain facts about the complicated history of these famous names.

France—*Francia*—is the country of the Franks. The Frankish people and the Frankish dynasties brought this name with them in the course of their migrations and conquests, across western Europe. At the beginning of the ninth century, at the time of the Carolingian Empire, the domain covered by the name 'France' was enormous. At that period the name was applied to that whole part of the Empire stretching to the north of the Alps.[3] When the Empire collapsed, the name France remained, to start with, attached to the two most important states, and especially the two most durable ones, amongst those which were formed out of its ruins: the kingdom of Charles the Bald and his descendants, and the one whose first sovereign was Louis the German. They were customarily distinguished from one another by the terms 'western France' and 'eastern France'. But eastern France soon came under the dominion of a new dynasty no longer Frankish, but Saxon; and it gradually lost the name of 'France'. Western France however kept it, and was the only region to keep it, becoming in fact the kingdom of France.

Such in rapid summary is what may be called in the widest sense the history of France. But alongside this broadest sense the word has always also had a more restricted meaning—that is, a more local one. It has always designated the region at the centre of the country subject to the Frankish kings; the region that appeared to be the most Frankish in character. Gregory of Tours, for example, applies it sometimes to northern Gaul, as opposed to the Auvergne, which had been only recently conquered and was often in revolt;[4] he sometimes applies it to the centre of northern Gaul and more particularly to the eastern kingdom belonging to Thierri and his descendants, the most thoroughly germanized of the kingdoms divided among the sons of Clovis.[5]

It is a well-known fact that the geographical vocabulary of the high Middle Ages, especially during the two centuries following the dismemberment of the Carolingian Empire, was extremely fluid and imprecise; and no wonder, for it was a faithful reflection of a society that was constantly in flux, and which did not succeed until quite late in the day in finding any lasting territorial framework. The name of France, like that of Burgundy and Lorraine, for example, was involved in this general uncertainty about all geographical terms. When the kingdoms of western and eastern France had separated, the habit grew up within each state of applying the name of France to a particular region. In the eastern kingdom, this was the country along the Main, what is nowadays called Franconia. In the western kingdom, the name France was used—as Gregory of Tours had already used it—for the whole of northern Gaul; and France was used in contrast to Burgundy, or Aquitaine, or the land of the Bretons. But as great feudal states began to develop in this northern Gaul, such as Flanders, Vermandois, Champagne, Normandy—all distinct from one another—the area denoted by the name France became more and more restricted. It became more or less confined to the region of the middle Seine, where it finally came to rest. Why did this region finally retain the name of France? The explanation is probably to be sought in the prodigious heights of fortune to which the family coming from a Neustrian count, Robert the Strong, managed to rise in the course of the ninth and tenth centuries. Robert the Strong's descendants, after more than a century of struggle, succeeded in taking the place of Charlemagne's descendants on the throne of Charles the Bald. Now it was in this district of the middle Seine that the Robertian family possessed its most important estates, at least since the days of king Eudes.[6] And it no doubt seemed quite natural to continue calling this district, from which the kings of France drew most of their power, by the same name as the kingdom as a whole.

Here are some examples of this use of the word 'France' in the early days of the Capetian dynasty. The abbey of Saint-Benoît-de-Fleury rose above the banks of the Loire about thirty kilometres upstream from Orléans. In a little treatise on the relics of Saint Benedict composed between 1011 and 1019, a German monk, Thierri d'Amorbach, wrote as he followed the fortunes of this abbey where he had stayed: 'to the east it touches on Burgundy, to the south on Aquitaine, and to the north on France'.[7] Now let us turn to another pious little composition, written at this same monastery of Fleury and about the same date, the third book of the *Miracula Sancti Benedicti*.[8] Its author —the monk Aimoin—places the village of Abbeville in 'France', a village whose houses even today are grouped at the edge of a small ravine on the plateau of Beauce, a few miles to the south of Étampes. A decree of king Philip I, drawn up between 1099 and 1108, shows that the towns of Mantes and Poissy, both on the Seine, and downstream from Paris, were considered at that time to be in 'France'.[9] Some sixty years later, a poet called Garnier, born at Pont-Sainte-Maxence, on the Oise, between Creil and Compiègne, wrote: 'Faire was my speeche for I was born in France.'[10] It is clear then that 'France' in the days of the early Capetians extended all round Paris, on both banks of the Seine.

The 'France' of which the administrative documents in the time of Saint Louis and Philip le Bel make so much, was far more extensive. The fact is that within the space of a century the dynasty's territorial power had developed to a remarkable extent. For example, in the account of the *bailliages* of France, drawn up on All Saints' Day 1285,[11] there are included, besides the *prévôté-bailliage* of Paris, those of Gisors, Senlis, Vermandois, Amiens, Sens, Orléans, Bourges and Tours. The word 'France' seems then to have applied to a wide area including, as well as the ancient demesne, a large number of territories annexed since the twelfth century by the Capetian kings. But not all of them. The monarchy's most important acquisitions—Normandy, the senechalsies of the Midi, and later Champagne—did not form a part of this France. These regions, which were great feudal states, kept their own individual institutions distinguishing them from the districts grouped together in administrative language under the name of France. The France of the administrative documents was the ancient royal demesne, only enlarged in size.

At the same period legal language gave the name of France a quite different and much more restricted meaning *Ad usus et consuetudines Francie, aus us et coutumes de France*[12] —there is no expression that recurs more often than these in legal documents drawn up in the thirteenth or fourteenth centuries in the region round Paris. The *coutume de France* was different from that of the neighbouring districts, for example the custom in the Vexin or at Orléans. It was followed in the district under the jurisdiction of the Court of the Châtelet at Paris, and in the *prévôté-bailliage* of Paris; and later it would be called 'the custom of Paris— the custom of France which is observed in Paris', as Beaumanoir had already expressed it.[13]

What were the boundaries of this France as the lawyers delimited it? It would no doubt be possible to discover them with some degree of accuracy, for many of the documents dealing with real estate in the thirteenth and fourteenth centuries in the Paris region have been preserved. By collecting all these passages and noting all the references to the 'custom of France' and the customs of neighbouring regions one could compile a legal map of the Paris region covering the period in question. It would then be interesting to compare those data for the thirteenth and fourteenth centuries with the lists of places governed by the 'custom of Paris' drawn up after the 'custom' had been codified.[14] This is a work that has never been carried out; we do not know the boundaries of the territory in which the 'custom of France' prevailed; but we at least know for certain that it stretched along the left as well as the right bank of the Seine. At the same time, however, popular usage (to which certain historians, neglecting the facts I have just adduced, have perhaps paid too exclusive attention) tended to reject the name of France for land on the right bank of the river.

If, as people have sometimes seemed to imagine, popular usage could be considered infallible in its geography, it would never have made the Seine a ruling factor in its geographical demarcations. The Seine is hardly a very broad river, nowhere does it meander through extensive swamps or flow through steep gorges; it does not in any way constitute a barrier. Furthermore, at least in the region with which we are concerned, the country does not usually change character much when one crosses from one bank to the other. Of course when it is a question of finding the boundaries of a small tract of land clearly defined by agricultural characteristics well known to the peasants and well expressed by them, we must make the most of all the evidence contained in popular language. But when it is a matter of delimiting an enormous region which a single person—particularly an uneducated person —would have difficulty in thinking of as a whole, and which was characterized by a complicated collection of geographical conditions, we should be wiser to distrust the information afforded by popular geography. In the limits thus popularly chosen, no doubt because of their obvious clarity, scholars are unable to find any true geographical validity. Ever since the high Middle Ages, a tendency had been noted in popular usage to give a particular name to the region between the Seine and the Loire—'from Mont-Saint-Michel to Château-Landon'— which is of all regions the one most lacking in unity. Writers or chancery lawyers from the ninth century onwards used as a label for this region the ancient word *Neustria*, not in its proper sense, which was much wider,[15] or the specially invented word '*Transsequania*'—the 'land beyond the Seine'. From then onwards the popular name

6

was perhaps the one most likely to crop up in the epic literature of the following centuries—the mysterious name of *Hérupe*, of whose etymology and origin we are completely ignorant. Towards the end of the Middle Ages the word *Hérupe* disappeared, but it survived in the adjectival form of *Herapois*, or *Hurepoix*.[16]

Hurepoix had the Seine as its northern boundary; and it covered all the left bank. The language of the right bank and the language of administrative documents always ignored *Hurepoix*, which never even made its way into the vocabulary of popular geography; and this language, as we have seen, continued for a long time to follow the ancient usage, which extended the name of France to both banks of the river. But common parlance, it seems, fairly soon ceased to apply the term to the left bank and reserved it for the right.

On this bank, immediately to the north of Paris, rose the abbey and fortress of Saint-Denis. The abbey and the fortress had been known from very ancient days as Saint-Denis-en-France. The expression *Sanctus Dionysius in Francia*, it is true, appears fairly late in the official deeds. The first passage in which I have come upon it is in a charter of Thibaud IV, count of Champagne, dated May 1226.[17] It was not adopted by the papal chancery until Gregory IX's time—for the first time in a Bull of 31 December 1227[18]—and by the chancery of the monks themselves during the period when Guillaume de Massouris was abbot, the first occasion being a charter of November 1248.[19] But chanceries in general never consented to adopt an expression till a long time after it had come into popular use. Take the poem called the *Voyage de Charlemagne en Orient*, composed either in the second half of the eleventh century, or about the middle of the twelfth.[20] In it we read that the Emperor, before leaving for Jerusalem, went to 'Saint-Denis-de-France' in order to

7

don his pilgrim's scrip.[21] The author of the poem lived in the region of Paris; he may even have been writing at the instigation of the monks of Saint-Denis; and it was no doubt from local usage that he borrowed the expression Saint-Denis-de-France. The juxtaposition of the saint's name and the word France was evidently a clear way of distinguishing the monastery near Paris from the other churches similarly dedicated to the martyr bishop.

But one cannot form any precise picture of the origin of the expression Saint-Denis-en-France without bearing in mind the following peculiarity of the language used by the *chansons de geste*. Saint Denis, as is well known, was the patron saint of France—I mean here the kingdom of France. Our ancient epic poets who sometimes called the kingdom 'France de Saint-Denis' represented their heroes as invoking the name of 'Saint-Denis-de-France',[22] no doubt in conformity with popular usage. This usage, probably fairly widespread, accustomed people to making a mental link between the two terms Saint-Denis and France. The expression Saint-Denis-de-France was originally applied to the saint himself, but the word France referred to the kingdom as a whole. Then the habit grew up of using this expression—first as Saint-Denis *de* France, later as Saint-Denis *en* France[23]—when referring to the most famous of the abbeys bearing the saint's name, and containing his tomb; at the same time people ceased to understand the term 'France' in the same sense as formerly. France in this expression was henceforward France in the restricted sense, that is to say the country north of the Seine. The first use of the word had prepared the way for the second. And the famous monastery, for its part, known by all as Saint-Denis-en-France, contributed to the assignment of the name France to the right bank of the river.

To the north of Saint-Denis, between the Marne, the

Seine and the Oise, there stretches a plain whose alluvial soil has made it one of the richest corn-growing districts round Paris. To the east and north a line of wooded hills and forests stretching from the Marne to the Oise breaks up the great flat fields where cereal-growing abounds. It is thus a plateau circumscribed by very clear boundaries—rivers, hillsides, and forests—and characterized by a crop for which its soil is remarkably well suited. It constitutes one of those regions of moderate extent that are popularly and strongly felt to be a unity, which sooner or later acquire a special name. In this particular case the name was France, the significance of which finally ended by becoming restricted to an area not much more than about forty kilometres square. At a quite recent period popular usage was still employing the word in this sense. To illustrate this last avatar of the name France, I need only refer to Gallois' work.

Bounded on three sides by watercourses—the Seine, the Oise and the Marne—'France' thus looked rather like a peninsula. Now the language of the Middle Ages did not make any very clear distinction between an island and a peninsula, and where we would say 'peninsula' people often said 'island'. The Cotentin which is bounded by sea on three sides, the County of Venaissin, bounded by the Rhone on the west and by the Durance on the south, was treated in the language of the Middle Ages as an island.[24] The Gauls, followed by the Greek and Roman historians, 'were accustomed to give the name of island'[25] to the peninsula formed by the Rhone and the Isère at their point of junction. The simple name France, as I indicated above, never ceased to be used in its localized meaning. But alongside of it, people soon began to use, and use more generally, the term 'Ile-de-France'. When did this word first appear? The first reference I have come across is in a passage of the second book of Froissart's *Chronicles*,

9

written in 1387.[26] It very soon became current coin. The Parisian priest who from 1405 to 1449 kept the curious journal known by the name of the *Journal of a Citizen of Paris*, and the Belgian chronicler Enguerand de Monstrelet, who wrote between 1422 and 1453, often used it. The first official document in which it has been noticed is a letter of the Duke of Bedford dated 7 August 1429.[27]

During the last centuries of the Middle Ages there was superimposed upon the ancient administrative districts of the *bailliages* and the *senechaussées*, a new administrative institution destined to last until the end of the *Ancien Régime*—the system of *gouvernements*. Among the lands grouped under the authority of the governor in command of the region round Paris the Ile-de-France was naturally included, that is to say the small area washed and bounded by the waters of the Marne, the Seine and the Oise. The first documents relating to the governors that have come down to us use the term Ile-de-France in the precise and restricted sense mentioned above; and they quote the Ile-de-France as one of the different districts under the Governor's authority. Here for example is how a charter of 31 December 1433 sets out the title of the celebrated La Hire: '*lieutenant pour le roy nostre sire et capitaine général deça la rivière de Saine, es païs de l'Isle-de-France, Picardie, Beauvaison, Laonnais et Soissonnois.*'[28] But the custom very rapidly grew up, it seems, of designating the *gouvernement* as a whole by the name Ile-de-France which, properly speaking, belonged only to a part of the governor's administrative district. This incorrect use of the term Ile-de-France is first of all noticeable in unimportant unofficial documents, then in the official documents themselves, starting from the last years of the fifteenth century. From 1519 onwards commissions delivered to the governors only carry these simple words: 'governors of the Ile-de-France'. The name Ile-de-France emerged in this

way from the narrow limits which had originally circumscribed it, and spread to an enormous region, approximately the area that had formerly been called France. Did
the memory of this ancient usage still survive at the time
when the Ile-de-France gained its wider meaning, and did
it have some part in this change of sense? We cannot tell.
The Ile-de-France in this enlarged form ceased to deserve
the name of island, which it nevertheless retained.

The boundaries of the *gouvernement*[29] of the Ile-de-
France, like those of all the *gouvernements*, often changed
and were always ill-defined. In 1789 it comprised thirteen
principal *bailliages*—Chaumont-en-Vexin, Beauvais, Cler-
mont-en-Beauvaisis, Senlis, Crépy-en-Valois, Villers-
Cotterets, Soissons, Laon, Melun, Nemours, Montford-
l'Amaury, Mantes and Meulan. To the south it only
extended some thirty miles from Paris. To the east it
ended about twenty miles from Paris, Meaux belonging
to the *gouvernement* of Champagne. To the north, on the
other hand, in the valleys of the Oise and the Aisne, the
frontiers of the Ile-de-France were more than a hundred
miles away from Paris. I must at this point refer the
reader to the excellent map of the *gouvernement* of the Ile-
de-France in 1789 drawn up by Longnon.[30] It clearly
shows that the boundaries of this *gouvernement* had not
been imposed on it by the requirements of geography, but
by the changes and chances of history. In what did these
changes consist? Many of them are outside our ken but at
least we have a fairly good knowledge of the history of
the Ile-de-France's northern frontier.

In the eighteenth century, as we have seen, Beauvais,
Senlis and Laon were part of the *gouvernement* of the Ile-de-
France. Now these towns and the country surrounding
them were considered in the Middle Ages to be a part of
Picardy, an enormous region whose unity—marked by
the resemblances between the various Picard dialects—

seems always to have been strongly felt by its inhabitants.[31] Even when the *gouvernement* of the Ile-de-France had approximately the same frontiers as in 1789, the memory of the ancient bounds of Picardy was still alive. It was to his good town of 'Senlis in Picardy'[32] that Henry IV announced his abjuration. In his great treatise on geography, the *Notitia Galliarum*,[33] which appeared in 1675, Adriene de Valois assigned to Picardy, along with the Amiénois, which certainly belonged to the *gouvernement* of Picardy,[34] five districts: the Noyonnais, the Soissonnais, the Vermandois, the Senlisien, and the Beauvaisis, which he knew to be part of the *gouvernement* of the Ile-de-France. The districts of Picardy were thus divided between two different *gouvernements*. Why was this? In 1435, by the treaty of Arras, king Charles VII had to cede to the duke of Burgundy all that portion of Picardy which is watered by the Somme. After this treaty, all that remained of Picardy in the hands of the French kings was too unimportant to form a separate *gouvernement*, and was attached to the *gouvernement* destined some few decades later to take the name of Ile-de-France. After the death of 'le Téméraire', the 'Somme cities' returned to the French crown, and were formed into a *gouvernement* of Picardy; but there was no restoration to Picardy of the towns and districts which had been incorporated in the Ile-de-France in 1435. Amongst these were Beauvais, Laon and Senlis, which, although Picard cities, remained in this way part of the *gouvernement* of the Ile-de-France up to the time of the French Revolution.

Are we then to adopt the boundaries of the *gouvernement* of the Ile-de-France as those of our study? In so doing we should only be following the example given by the *Société de l'Histoire de Paris et de l'Ile-de-France*, whose administrative council in its fourth session on 11 August 1874 decided to extend its work 'to all the former military

gouvernements of the Ile-de-France as it existed at the time
of the Revolution'.[35] But surely it is hardly necessary for
the historian of today, dealing with the life of a particular
region, to confine himself within the limits (which paid
little attention to geography) once upon a time traced out
in the administration of the *Ancien Régime* by events some
of which—such as the treaty of Arras—were of little
ultimate significance for the development of our national
destinies. It is not as if the *gouvernement* of the *Ancien
Régime* constituted a really living entity! Everyone knows
that with the establishment of absolute monarchy the
governors were without real power. Historical manuals
and atlases used to delight in dividing 'France of 1789'
into 'provinces' each corresponding more or less to a
gouvernement. Since the fine work done by Armand Brette,
there is no further need to criticize these obviously
artificial divisions. The *gouvernement* under the *Ancien
Régime* was only very rarely the framework of regional
life.

It would be equally mistaken to believe that in the
eighteenth century the name Ile-de-France applied
exclusively to the *gouvernement* of that name. Alongside the
gouvernement there was another administrative division,
and a very important one, with Paris also as its centre[36]—I
mean the *généralité de Paris*, that is to say the district
administered by the *intendant* of Paris. Now the *généralité*
too was sometimes designated by the title Ile-de-France,
not only in current speech,[37] but even (though this does
not seem to have been noticed hitherto) in official documents. In the year 1787 when provincial assemblies were
set up in the kingdom with the *généralité* as their framework, the one which met in the *généralité* of Paris was
given a name in the royal 'Regulations' that summoned it,
and by this name it continued to be called—'the Provincial
Assembly of the Ile-de-France'.[38] Its minutes of proceedings

again and again give the *Intendant de Paris* the title of '*Intendant* and commissary responsible for the province of the Ile-de-France'.[39] If we were to decide to adopt as the bounds of our study those of one administrative division under the *Ancien Régime*, why make it the *gouvernement* of the Ile-de-France, rather than the *généralité* of Paris, which was called a 'province of the Ile de-France'? But the boundaries of the *généralité*, although different from those of the *gouvernement*, were no more rational. One has only to look at M. Brette's map and notice in what an extraordinary way, in the Auxerre region, the frontiers of the four *généralités* of Orléans, Châlons, Dijon, and Paris are intertwined with one another!

In our times the description Ile-de-France, although removed by the Revolution from the political map, has not disappeared from common use. Scholars in particular often use it. But each discipline uses it in its own way and gives it different boundaries. For the geologist, the Ile-de-France is the extensive district at the centre of the Paris basin, whose rocks are the tertiary clays, in contrast to the older rocks belonging to the periphery of the basin. The geologist's Ile-de-France begins to the north near Coucy, and stretches southwards to beyond the Loire at a point where the sombre plains of Sologne die away. The Seine enters it near Montereau and leaves it on the far side of Mantes. The archaeologist's Ile-de-France consists of the region in which certain styles of ecclesiastical architecture developed in the Middle Ages; and the boundaries of this Ile-de-France, varying as they do almost from one scholar to another, never coincide—it need scarcely be said— with the boundaries of the tertiary deposits. The Romanesque or Gothic churches of the diocese of Laon mostly present characteristics which in the archaeologists' eyes define the architectural schools of the Ile-de-France, whether Romanesque or Gothic. But this diocese, being a

Picard region, would not be included by a philologist in the Ile-de-France, that is to say in the region where during the Middle Ages they spoke the dialect that was eventually to evolve into French.[40]

It is clear enough, then, that this single term Ile-de-France has carried many different meanings, both in the present and in the past. Must we then conclude that there has never been anything but confusion and perpetual instability in the use of this word? A closer examination will show easily enough what is common to all the various senses of the term Ile-de-France current since the time when it ceased to be applied only to the little district between the Marne, the Seine and the Oise. All the various Iles-de-France we have enumerated and distinguished may each have had different boundaries but they all had the same centre, which was Paris. No one ever thought of giving the name of Ile-de-France to any region from which Paris was left out. We shall therefore follow common usage in defining the Ile-de-France as the Paris region. Or better still, to show quite clearly that the region concerned only owes its unity to the vast human mass that overshadows the whole of it, we will borrow Vidal de la Blache's expression, and call it 'the country round Paris'.

Our study, then, will concern the country round Paris. But there will be no treatment of the city of Paris itself in the pages that follow. Paris deserves and demands a special study. Whether one deplores or rejoices in the fact, Paris on its own is 'a region of France'. It goes without saying that a fair number of works are concerned both with Paris and its surrounding districts; and I have not hesitated to refer to these below.

The geographical characteristics of the Ile-de-France

We have defined the Ile-de-France, but we have not so far delimited it. To fix the limits of our study and at the same time to get to know the region with which we are concerned, we must undertake a journey of exploration. We will cast round in a circle from Paris and we will stop at any point where a marked change in the character of the country, or some ancient regional frontier, or any geographical or historical detail, suggests a halt. But we shall not forget that one of the essential characteristics of the Ile-de-France is that it has no boundaries which constitute barriers.[41]

Our projected journey will be far from monotonous. In fact there is no region of France whose soil is more varied than the one we shall be exploring. The seas, lagoons and lakes of the tertiary period, the great meandering rivers of the quaternary era left on the Ile-de-France an infinite variety of deposits. Erosion and its subsequent effect on these deposits may well have eaten into them and carried them away in places, changing their distribution to such an extent that it is not always possible today to recognize the contours of these ancient areas of water, but erosion has not had long enough, or been strong enough, to obliterate their traces or to lay bare their deepest foundations. Its work has thus been incomplete and as it were fragmentary and has only resulted in bringing to light the diversity of these lands. Moreover erosion, as it attacked different kinds of terrain which offered varying resistance, penetrating more deeply in some places than in others, has moulded the Ile-de-France.

Our journey will not take us across any mountains; we shall rarely rise above 600 feet in height; but we shall frequently be going up and down hill. The relief of the

Ile-de-France is fairly varied, a fact which is largely due to the diversity of the rocks that compose it.[42] There is the limestone that forms the base of the plateaux, with the white splashes of hillside quarries from which the cathedral-builders drew their materials; there are the sands and gravels which carry the well-drained forests of Fontainebleau and Ermenonville; there is the clay overlying the hard, siliceous building stone (*meulières*) round whose pools the lush woodlands of Brie have grown up; there are the impermeable marls which prevent the water from welling up through the limestone masses and force them to gush out on the hillsides, marking a spring line half-way up the slopes by the long line of poplars; there are the alluvial deposits at the bottom of the valleys which carry the rich meadows and market gardens; there is the river-silt of the plateaux, bearing rich harvests. All this variety of rock and soil and this diversity of relief give the Ile-de-France the surprising variety and charm that are such a marked feature as one leaves the monotonous plains of the Somme or of Champagne and approaches Paris from the north or the east.

The variety of the scenery and the ever-varying contours are particularly noticeable in the country immediately to the south of Paris. The very thin limestone layer that used to spread over the whole of this country has been hollowed out and cut into by the watercourses, so that everywhere today there are valleys dipping down below the limestone level into the sands and the gravels; there are wooded valleys with steep sides, 'lonely spots' which attracted the Cistercians in the twelfth century, and later on the Jansenist solitaires. There are plateaux, fragments of one original vast plateau which covered the whole countryside, stretching between these valleys and sometimes running out beyond them into bold promontories, more than one of which in former times carried a fortress.

The limestone which forms the base of these plateaux is apt to crumble where it outcrops, yielding a porous rock near the surface, embedded in the clay, known by the name of *meulière*. This is often overlaid with *limon*, a rich and pulverized soil, free of stones which impede the plough. These loamy plateaux, though they grow splendid crops on a large scale, would no doubt be a little dreary and monotonous-looking but for the moisture provided by the impermeable clay which now clothes the surface near the *meulière*. Thanks to this there is no lack of vegetation nor of trees; and sometimes there are—as in Normandy—lines of apple-trees flanking the roads. In other places when the *meulière* is exposed or the layer very thin, the forest takes possession even of the plateau.

Towards the west both plateaux and valleys were formerly covered by one of the Ile-de-France's great forests, the forest of Iveline; but today cultivation has made large inroads upon it; though there are still huge stretches of forest in existence, and in the different areas the abundance of trees in the middle of fields recalls the one-time forest. Further west still, between the Seine and the Eure, the same steep, cut-up and varied country continues, and although only a hundred feet or so in height, it dominates the more fertile and more monotonous plains which open out on the left bank of the Eure towards Normandy, to which they really belong.

Of all the valleys to the south of Paris which dissect the limestone plateaux, none is more charming than the moist valley of the river Juine, a little stream whose waters run into the Essonne, a tributary of the Seine. On the left bank of the Juine, set in the midst of meadows, rises the little town of Étampes, its towers and steeples seen from afar seeming to blend with the tree-tops. Étampes is on the road from Paris to Orléans, watched over in former days by a great keep perched on the edge of the plateau.

The great keep which the local inhabitants call *la tour Guinette* kept guard for the king.

Let us follow this road to Orléans for a little while. After passing through Étampes, with the Juine on the left, its upper reaches bearing away towards the south, the road crosses the valley of one of the Juine's tributaries, the Chalouette, which flows from west to east; then it gently climbs up on to the valley's southern flank. Once past the summit of the watershed, one sees an entirely new countryside spread out before the eyes, with fields of corn and sugar-beet stretching out of sight over an almost flat landscape. This is Beauce. Beauce, as we have seen, is only the prolongation of the limestone mass which has been cut into by the waters to form the plateaux to the south of Paris. But the limestone mass in Beauce is very thick, and has completely resisted erosion; its surface does not break down into *meulière* and being very porous it does not hold rainwater near the surface, but allows it to filter down through the rock to a great depth.[43]

This Beauceron plateau, lacking springs, ponds and watercourses would doubtless be a stony desert like the *Causses* in the French *Massif Central* or the *Karst* in Jugoslavia, if it were not for the thick layer of loam overlying the chalk. This loam, improved by human labour,[44] produces the splendid cereal crops which are the special glory of Beauce and have made its fortune, earning for it the name of 'the mother of corn'.[45] It is also this that gives it a monotonous beauty when the corn is green and when it is ripe; but after the harvest it takes on the aspect of a rather dreary desert. Having no surface water, Beauce has no meadows and practically no trees. The 'ample' forest of Beauce felled by Gargantua[46] never existed except in the mythical world of Rabelais' heroes. Attempts at afforestation undertaken in recent times have not been successful, only showing how poorly trees thrive in this excessively dry soil. To reach water, you need not only to sink wells but to sink them to a great depth—an expensive operation. Wells are therefore few and far between, and it is round them that dwellings have sprung up and formed large towns. Other districts owe something of their pleasant aspect to the houses dotted about the country-side; but the scenery of Beauce lacks this charm, as it lacks also the beauty of trees. Moreover the very lines of this countryside are monotonous for the plateau (sloping very gently towards the south) has no noticeable contours, being marked only by almost imperceptible undulations. Only its edges have been cut into by the rivers. On the fringes of Beauce they have carved deep valleys down into the limestone, with steep sides, on whose ridges castles and fortified towns are perched. Above the green gorge of the Oeuf stands Pithiviers, the site of one of the first feudal towers to be built in the Ile-de-France during the Middle Ages.[47] Yèvre, with its four-square château flanked by four towers, commands the gorge of the Rimarde. And on the western fringe of Beauce, the town of Chartres, an ancient Gallic *oppidum*, rises above the valley of the Eure with the spires of its cathedral which stand out against the horizon of Beauce.

However rich it may be, this country without running water and without trees, evenly spread with its yellow coating of loam, is a dreary enough tract. 'O Beauce', exclaim a couple of often-quoted Latin lines, whose date and authorship I do not know:

O Beauce! Thou sorry land, wanting in sixfold measure:
Springs, meadows, forests, rocks, vineyards and
   orchards,
All are lacking in thy treasure.[48]

Nowadays you should ask the soldiers in the neighbouring

garrisons their opinion of Beauce when they carry out their autumn manoeuvres on the bare plateau after the harvest has been gathered in. You will hear the language and the tone of voice they use to describe this country in which 'you have to pay for a glass of water'. But the less attractive natural features of Beauce have combined with a fertility of soil marvellously suitable for growing cereal crops to give the Beauceron countryside a touch of originality and individuality that has always been popularly recognized. Beauce has never formed a political division on its own. However far back we go in history we shall always find it shared out between different governing powers. Yet the ancient name of Beauce, appearing for the first time in literature at the end of the sixth century but apparently Gallic in origin (if not more remote still),[49] has persisted down the centuries. In the Middle Ages it was used in numerous personal names. And even today the peasants understand it and use it in its exact meaning. Beauce is a perfect example of a 'natural region'.

In quite early days it was the corn from Beauce that provided food for Paris. During the Middle Ages there was a corn market on the island of *la Cité* called 'the Beauce market'.[50] Paris could never have grown and spread as extensively or as early without the good cornland of its surrounding districts, and of Beauce in particular. The history of Beauce is intimately bound up with that of Paris.

Let us now continue our journey along the Paris-Orléans road that crosses the plateau. Once Artenay is reached, there are trees to be seen round the villages; and as we advance southwards, a bluish line, which just now was only a faint suggestion on the southern horizon, takes on more definite features marking the appearance of forests. The forest of Orléans, once called the *forêt de Loge*, in which the Capetian kings delighted to go hunting, stretches to the south of Beauce over an area of clayey sand rather like the poor soil of Sologne on the left bank of the Loire. The quaternary watercourses deposited these sands on the edge of the limestone plateau. The forest extends in a narrow belt from east to west, broken in places—especially towards the west—by clearings. From north to south it is of no great depth: about ten miles at its greatest and only two or three where the Paris-Orléans road passes through. But from its extreme eastern point to the extreme western limit—from the neighbourhood of Gien to Coulmiers—it is more than forty-five miles; and further to the northwest, beyond a huge clearing, the forest reappears, following another belt of sandy subsoil, though now called by a different name: the forest of Marchenoir. Let us stop at the edge of this woodland for behind this long curtain of forest a new region—one might almost say a new world—opens up: the *valley of the Loire*.

On the western side, it would not be easy to assign any precise boundaries to Beauce. As you approach the valleys of the Eure and the Loire, the country gradually changes. The top layer of *limon* continues, but it no longer rests upon the Beauceron limestone which is permeable; it rests upon chalk, and there is a flinty clay mixed with the *limon*, an impermeable soil resulting from the decomposition of the chalk. The water is nearer the surface. Trees and meadows make their appearance; the fields are separated by thick-set hedges. As you approach Pontgoin, Illiers and Brou, the transition is complete. At this point Perche[51] begins, a green region full of copses which was once almost a forest.[52] The historical associations of Perche, and even its general aspect, link it rather with the western districts—with Normandy or Maine—and not with the Ile-de-France.

To the east, the transition is again gradual from Beauce

to a new kind of countryside, less uniform, more broken, and less fertile—Gâtinais.[53] If, for the sake of greater clarity one is intent on adopting tidy, though somewhat artificial, boundaries one could make Gâtinais begin at the valleys of the Rimarde and the Essonne. The same limestone mass that forms the Beauceron plateau continues on into Gâtinais; but a band of clay within this mass divides it into two distinct zones. In the whole of western Gâtinais the clay retains the water nearer the surface than in Beauce. In eastern Gâtinais, the soil is composed of the lower bed of limestone only, erosion having washed away the upper layer and the intermediate clays; for the sedimentary rocks being slightly tilted in le Gâtinais towards the east, have been more deeply eroded by the water than in Beauce. A long ridge running from Beauce-la-Rolande to just beyond Malesherbes, whose eastward-facing slopes are intersected by valleys, marks the eastern end of the upper layer of Beauceron limestone. At the foot of it the clays support a narrow strip of meadow and trees. Then, going further east, one sees the lower sedimentary limestone showing through, and the soil once more becomes flat and dry. Showing above the surface of this new plateau there are a number of knolls, fragments of the upper sedimentary rock, which have here and there escaped the effects of erosion. The loam which covers Beauce extends into Gâtinais, where it is thinner than in Beauce, and in some places even runs out completely. Formerly there was a startling contrast between Beauce, almost entirely corn-growing, and Gâtinais which, apart from its sterile stretches, could boast a good many crops entirely unknown in Beauce, namely, grass, saffron,[54] and fine vineyards[55] on the limestone hillsides. Nowadays even the poorest of the Gâtinais soils have been enriched and carry some crops; saffron and vine-growing have not disappeared, but have become less common.

To the east, the Gâtinais plateau is sharply cut into by the valley where the river Loing flows through small meadows flooded at the end of the winter season. We shall not cross the Loing valley, for beyond it there is well-watered, wooded country stretching as far as the Yonne, which must be studied as part of the Sénonais region. But let us follow the river downstream. No sooner have we passed the small town of Nemouis, nestling beside the water, than trees come into view above the left-hand river-bank. This is the forest of Fontainebleau, called *Bière* in the old documents, stretching away over sand and gravel laid bare by erosion at the end of the Gâtinais limestone plateau, whose detritus, carried down by wind and water, is spread over an enormous surface. A few patches of the limestone covering, also well-wooded, tower above the sandy stretches and look across to the romantic escarpments characteristic of the gravel country. At the foot of the heights on which the famous forest grows, the Loing flows into the Seine.

The valley of the Seine cuts into the western edge of a huge plateau which slopes away on the right bank of the river in gentle undulations as far as the Marne.[56] Brie—for this is the plateau's name—rests, like Beauce, upon a huge limestone mass overlaid in Brie, as in Beauce, by loam. But the two regions are very different in appearance. The Brie limestone is much mixed with marl, that is to say it is only moderately permeable; and it rests upon an impermeable layer of *marnes vertes*; moreover this Brie limestone decomposes near the surface to become *meulière* which, being spongy and mixed with clay, retains the water near the surface level. The result is that Brie is just about as moist as Beauce is dry. The smallest hole dug in the *meulière* soon becomes a pool. The rich *limon* covering the Briard plateau holds the moisture and forms a soil very suitable for trees. Certain documents from the early

Beauvais: la Cathédral de St. Pierre

Beauvais cathedral: the choir

Middle Ages describe Brie as forest[57] (*saltus, silva*). Perhaps it would not be wise to take them too literally. At a time when forests were badly looked after and left to the tender mercies of grazing animals who used them as pasture, and so were only moderately dense, common speech readily gave the name of forest to any country that was plentifully provided with trees, though we should not consider nowadays that it deserved the name, since the trees most probably never formed a continuous cover. Moreover, as has been rightly observed, it is still true today that Brie, seen from a distance, appears to be entirely wooded.[58] The fact is that there are numerous trees in the fields and around the farms. Here and there little groups of them form small woods, and even real forests, for in spite of all the clearings, the forest has not altogether deserted the Briard plateau.[59]

Relentless human labour has produced a wonderfully fertile soil out of the wet and heavy earth of Brie, though it has been necessary to drain it to make the most of it. Brie, like Beauce, is a district of large-scale farming but more attractive. Large farms are scattered about on the plateaux, and on their fringes, and round about the villages there are fine trees alongside the corn-ricks, like those that line the roads or form clumps in the fields, pleasantly breaking their monotony. There is often a forest to be seen on the skyline and the earth, which is always moist, sends up a slight mist that softens the light and the contours.

Eastwards, Brie extends as far as the chalky plains of Champagne, and overlooks them. The eastern slopes of the Briard plateau, facing the sun, are the home of the famous vines of Champagne. The whole eastern part of Brie has for a long time been firmly linked to the plains of Champagne by the bonds forged through commercial exchange; but the western part of Brie looks to Paris, and its furthest slopes are indeed not far from the capital. But where shall we set the boundary? History does not provide any satisfactory answer. During the Middle Ages the counts of Champagne owned a large part of Brie; so much so that at the beginning of the thirteenth century they added to their title as counts of Champagne that of counts of Brie.[60] It was only the chance accidents of feudal succession that fixed the frontiers of their Briard domains. Whilst Brie-Comte-Robert and the district of Melun always eluded their grasp, they were masters of the county of Meaux, to the north of the plateau, and quite close to Paris. We shall include in our study Melun, Brie-Comte-Robert, Meaux and all that portion of the Briard plateau which adjoins these towns; but Provins and Château Thierry cannot be included in this survey of the country round Paris. And as for fixing a precise limit, why be too insistent upon it, since neither nature nor history provides one?

Let us now leave Brie and cross, a little way downstream from Meaux, the valley in which the Marne, somewhat blocked by islands, and the canal running alongside, mirror the poplars on their banks in the apparently motionless waters. On the other side of the valley, facing Brie, is a plateau whose limestone base is likewise hidden under a layer of fertile *limon*. We have already discovered the name belonging to this plateau. Its southern slopes fall gently away to the Plaine-Saint-Denis, within sight of Paris; its rich soil grows the good wheat from which they once used to make the *pain de Gonesse*, dear to the inhabitants of Paris, This is 'France', or, if you prefer it, the Ile-de-France, in the restricted and true sense of the word.[61] There are a few knolls strung out east and west which look down on the slight undulations of this corn country —formed from material more recent than the limestone that lies at the base of the plateau—patches that have

somehow been spared erosion. It is on their slopes—
where impermeable clays have forced the water to the
surface—that the villages have sprung up; while their
summits, cutting into the sand or *meulière*, are given over
to forests, such as the woods of Cormeilles and Maffliers,
and the forests of Écouen and Montmorency, whose
bluish masses, seen against the hillsides, are the secret of
the rather solemn beauty that characterizes the peaceful
outlines of 'France'. To the east and to the north a series
of similar knolls mark the line of an ancient fold in the
landscape running from south-west to north-west. These
knolls are very close to one another, and stretch in a line
from the outskirts of Meaux to the neighbourhood of the
great forests that occupy the plateau itself above the Oise
valley round Luzarches, d'Ermenonville and Chantilly. It
can hardly be doubted that these heights—some of them
today almost completely bare—were formerly all covered
with woods. Linking up with the huge forests bordering
on the Oise, they formed a kind of afforested 'march' of no
great depth and perhaps never quite continuous.[62] That
was where 'France' came to an end; and we shall go no
further.

To the west, 'France' is bounded by the narrow valley
of the Oise which cuts through the limestone mass.
Facing the rather gentle slopes by which 'France' runs
down towards the river, there are on the right bank some
steeper slopes forming the edge of a new plateau, which is
composed of both limestone and loam—French Vexin.[63]
This plateau is topped by a few wooded knolls like those
at Cormeilles and Montmorency—the heights of Mont-
fermeil, Marines, Montjavoult, Rosne—and hillsides
covered by the forests of Arthies and Hautie. It is dissected by a few valleys; but these hillsides and valleys are the
only breaks in the vast uninterrupted stretches of field
upon field. French Vexin comes to an end by sloping

quite steeply away in whatever direction you take. To the north there is an intermediate bench that separates it from the green and fertile depression which, lying south-east to north-west, is called the Pays de Bray. At this point, between Vexin and Pays de Bray, some 150 feet below the former, and some 300 feet above the latter, there is a plateau, not more than eight miles wide and sloping markedly to the north, stretching away in chalky undulations under a top-soil of clay. This district, where trees are still very plentiful, was once covered by great forests, of which the forest of Thelle to the west is the last relic. It used to form a kind of preliminary forest screen in front of the wooded stretches of the Pays de Bray. Our journey will not take us beyond these woods, which used once to separate the two Gallic peoples, the Veliscasses and the Bellovaques, from the former of which the name Vexin is derived.

Westwards, French Vexin comes to an abrupt end above a deep valley whose slopes are dissected by numerous lateral valleys. On the other side of the valley there is a new plateau, very like French Vexin, with the same extensive fields of corn. Nevertheless the valley of the Epte—the name of the river that has carved its way like this between the plateaux to join the Seine—marks one of the clearest regional boundaries in France. By the treaty of 911, signed at Saint-Clair, on the banks of this same little stream, between the Frankish king Charles the Simple and the Norman Rollo, the Epte was fixed as the limit of the land conceded to the sea-king, the land that was to become the duchy of Normandy. In former days the banks of the Epte witnessed a constant series of relentless wars. But even when Normandy had been joined to France, the memory of the ancient frontier persisted. Even today it continues in the language of administrative geography (the Epte being the dividing-line between the *départements* of Eure and Seine-et-Oise) as it does also in popular speech.[64] And lastly, to the south French Vexin comes to an end, above the winding valley of the Seine, in a 'long line of hills',[65] with villages built of white stone on their slopes. These hills, often wooded on their summits, face across the river valley to the hills and woods of the country between the Seine and the Eure described above.

In the midst of all those plateaux, that have been more or less carved up by erosion and whose different aspects I have tried to trace, the Seine and the Marne, followed by the Seine and the Oise, flow together. As the crow flies, their meeting-points are hardly more than about twenty miles apart; but owing to the meandering of the Seine the distance by river is about double. The erosive effects of the rivers, and especially the long and wavering detours of the Seine and the Marne, whose meeting-point has several times shifted its position, are enough to explain the topography of this central region, the heart of the Ile-de-France. The alluvial deposits have formed terraces along the valleys, or spread out in wide layers over the soil of the plains of Villeneuve-Saint-Georges, Saint-Denis and Gennevilliers. The Marne and the Seine have by their changes of course cut so deeply into the plateaux that they have broken off whole fragments of them. This plateau detritus is the material from which the isolated hills in the middle of the alluvial plains have been formed, like the steeply sloping Vaujours and Créteil, or that fine amphitheatre of high ground which overlooks the right bank of the Seine from Villemomble to Passy, carrying on its flanks more than half Paris.

These rivers[66] of the Ile-de-France, which have thus moulded the countryside through which they flow, are one of the region's sources of wealth and charm. They have hollowed out valleys whose moist bottoms are occupied by meadows and gardens. The slopes composed

29

of various rocks and dissected by the river-beds are gay with bank upon bank of flowers rising one above the other, each adding its own distinctive note of colour to the landscape. The twists and turns of the valleys are such that each slope provides a fresh and varied feast of colour; and they wend their way pleasantly through the more uniform plateaux, opening up views that are subtly and constantly changing. The rivers themselves never dry up and they seldom flood in a dangerous manner. The calmness of their waters make them incomparable waterways. The smaller watercourses such as the Essonne, the Juine and even the Bièvre, which have now come down in the world, used once upon a time to carry a great many boats. The great rivers especially, which all seem to converge on Paris—the Oise from the north, the Marne from the east, the Seine (belonging to Champagne upstream and to Normandy downstream), the Loing, further away and yet still fairly close to Paris, passing on its course to the Loire —all these have served as links between the Ile-de-France and the surrounding provinces. Together with the vast open plateaux with their straight roads, only broken by fairly thin strips of forest, they have served as lines of communication bearing a ceaseless traffic between the Ile-de-France and the neighbouring regions.

The climate[67] of the Ile-de-France is intermediate between the coastal climate and that of the eastern provinces, which is on the verge of being continental. The Ile-de-France owes to the effects of the seaboard the mildness of its winters and its rainfall, which is fairly evenly spread over the whole year; but the already very considerable difference between the winter and summer temperatures, and the less frequent, less regular, and, in sum-total, less abundant rainfall than on the coast, gives the region the feeling of being no longer very close to the ocean. The fig-tree, which thrives at certain points on the

Channel coast because it needs above all a mild winter, is also to be found in gardens in the Ile-de-France. It is next-door neighbour to the vine which likes sunny and not too wet summers, such as are to be found in the central and more southerly districts of the Continent. Fig-trees, it is true, even when 'protected with straw and anything else that can guard them from the rigours of the climate'[68] only yield very moderate quality fruit; and the vines in the Ile-de-France, which once flourished there, find it difficult today to stand up to the competition of the Mediterranean varieties. The climate of the Ile-de-France is eminently suitable for corn-growing, and for forestry. Sown crops have won the day on a variety of soils which were formerly under forest. This struggle of corn versus trees is an important episode in the agricultural history of the Ile-de-France, though less important than was once thought, for a good deal of the cultivation was achieved simply on soil that was already bare and grass-covered. The close association of cornland and forest, rather than the struggle between them, was one of the features of the rural life of the Ile-de-France in time past, when the forest provided grazing for the farm animals, and where industrial crops were not, as they are now, in competition with cereals. But this close association is still today one of the characteristics of the countryside in the Ile-de-France.

Has one any right to speak of the 'scenery in the Ile-de-France'? I have alluded above to its variety and it is certainly difficult to imagine anything more different-looking than, for example, the flat landscapes of Beauce and the twisted rocks of Fontainebleau. Yet it may perhaps be permissible—ignoring rather special features—to try to sum up the common characteristics of so many of the scenes that have passed before our eyes. The limestone plateaux of the Ile-de-France, and the hillsides which sometimes crown them—themselves only fragments of

31

ancient plateaux—stand out in firm, straight almost horizontal lines against the sky, giving the scenes they frame a great feeling of noble simplicity. In this fertile Ile-de-France there are fields, gardens, houses everywhere, either scattered about the countryside or grouped together in large villages, eloquent of the human hands that have created them. But man, although he has pushed back the forest, has not destroyed it and often—except in Beauce— it appears on the summit of a hillside or strung out beyond the undulating plateau, its presence heralded by clumps of trees. The rivers, which are never torrents, have a gracious peace about them, or even a majestic calm. These landscapes of the Ile-de-France, harmonious, delightful, and a little solemn, from which the figure of man is never absent, are like the parkland of the seventeenth century, with their combination of trees, water, and large open spaces; shall we not admit that they deserve the name sometimes given them of classical landscapes?

Up to now we have journeyed through the 'country round Paris', the whole of which constitutes the Ile-de-France. Now I shall proceed to introduce the reader to its historians. In studying those who have sought to illuminate the past history of our region we shall find ourselves gradually uncovering this very past.

chapter two

The Local History of the Ile-de-France before the Nineteenth Century

Some of the abbeys in the Ile-de-France have had their historians from the Middle Ages onwards. At the end of the eleventh century the abbey of Saint-Florentin de-Bonneval,[1] on the banks of the Loire where Beauce and Perche meet, already had its chronicler.[2] In the course of the following century three monks, taking turns in a pious enterprise, wrote the history of the Beauceron abbey of Morigny.[3] But the *Chronique de Bonneval* can hardly be called a work of history, for it is in fact nothing but a catalogue of grants to the abbey. Its authors had no other intention but to make up for the silence of the monastic archives or to guard against their possible destruction, so that the monks should not out of mere forgetfulness forfeit any of their rights. The authors of the *Chronique de Morigny* were preoccupied above all with moral and religious ideas. The precentor, Thiou, wrote the first book so that the monks of Morigny who would later read it should be aware that in the early days of the abbey it had been troubled by the jealous fury of the devil and his angels; so that they might learn by this example to 'arm themselves against these monstrous enemies who remain in the house when we go out, watch while we sleep, and are not, like ourselves, subject to death'.[4] The unknown monk who composed the third book was nothing more than a hagiographer, who put forward as an example to the faithful the life of a certain abbot of Morigny, Thomas by name.[5]

The Renaissance was the first period to give us works of local history not inspired by religion or private interests. Curiosity about the past, a sense of local patriotism, and the notion that it is the mark of a good citizen to record in fine language the history of his city—such were the sentiments that guided the first writers to recapitulate the history of the towns of the Ile-de-France.

In 1597 a shoemaker, Noël Taillepied, produced a book entitled *Recueil des antiquitez et singularitez de la ville de Pontoise, ville du Vequecin François*.[6] It is a work more characterized by imagination than by a sense of history, but it has an interesting preface. In order to justify his undertaking, Taillepied recalls the memory and example not only of the historians of old, but also of Junius Brutus, Epaminondes and the Maccabees, 'and others without number who left nothing undone that might serve the interests of their country'. The same spirit inspired the *Histoire de Melun*, published in 1624 by a lawyer in the Paris *parlement*, Sébastien Rouillard by name.[7] Rouillard dedicated his book to the town of Melun, of which he was a native. Melun, his '*chère patrie*', his '*mere genes iarche*'. 'O city of Melun,' he proclaimed in this dedication,

I have for some years been at pains to bend all my studies to recover the story of your beginnings, now almost buried in the dust; to bring it back from darkness into the full light of day, and to give you an honourable rank among the most splendid cities of France. For by what other deserving deed, by what other signal achievement of spirit, could I show myself to be a true lover of my country? For this is an enterprise not attempted until today by any other of your sons.[8]

This Rouillard, who appears to have had connections with Justus Lipsius,[9] seems to have been a writer of very varied ability,[10] with rather hazy ideas, but thoroughly lively and intelligent. He would well merit some closer study and we shall find his name cropping up again further on.

In the same year that the *Histoire de Melun* appeared Jean de la Barre, a lawyer, who had been appointed provost of Corbeil by the favour of the minister Villeroy, died. La Barre left behind him in manuscript a history of the town he had administered, although it was not published until twenty-three years later. Historians of today still find it a useful source to consult.[11] But the best book of urban history written in the Ile-de-France during the seventeenth century comes from the pen of a Barnabite monk, dom Basil Fleureau, born at Étampes, and from 1662 to 1669 the superior of the college there. It is called *Les Antiquitez de la ville et du duché d'Estampes avec l'histoire de l'abbaye de Morigny*.[12] Like la Barre, dom Fleureau died without having been able to get his book published. The *Antiquitez* did not appear till 1683, sponsored by the town authorities, nine years after its author's death. Dom Fleureau despised—or perhaps knew nothing about—archaeology; he therefore did not give us the information we might have looked for about the town's monuments, which are nevertheless extremely interesting. He had very little critical judgment; but he was industrious, honest and accurate. The work he left behind has continued to be of the greatest help to all students in this field, and its value is increased by a number of supporting documents.

No history of the Ile-de-France as a whole has ever been written. Its unity was not obvious enough and its boundaries were too vague for anyone ever to have been tempted to try. But some of the districts that go to make

up the Ile-de-France have had their historians. As early as
the beginning of the seventeenth century Gâtinais had its
historian, a grand prior of the Gâtinais abbey at Ferrières,
dom Morin, who ruled this house from 1610 to 1628.
There was a chapel at Ferrières which marked the spot
where, one Christmas night, the divine crib had appeared
to Saint Savinien and his companions in a halo of light.
The Virgin venerated in that district was named Our
Lady of Bethlehem, and wrought miracles which Morin
recounted, neglecting nothing that could bring back to
the abbey of Ferrières its former prosperity, seriously
undermined by the wars of religion. Such was the object
of dom Morin's first works, which are only slim booklets.
In this way, no doubt, he conceived a taste for historical
research, and resolved to satisfy it by composing a much
larger work which would trace the fortunes of the region
of which Ferrières was the chief religious centre. This was
his *Histoire générale des pays de Gastinois, Sénonois et Hure-
pois*.[13] Dom Morin was just as unfortunate as la Barre and
dom Fleureau, for he died when only the first few sheets
of his book had been printed. His fellow-monks saw to it
that the *Histoire du Gastinois* was published, and it came
out in 1630. They entrusted the revision of the manuscript
for publication to a certain Claude Malingre, a Sénonois
historiographer, who made a pretty poor job of it. In
recent times M. Laurent, a more careful scholar than
Claude Malingre, has produced a new edition of dom
Morin.[14] But it may be doubted whether *L'Histoire du
Gastinois* really deserved reprinting. Even its modern
editor admits that it 'bristles with the grossest errors'.
Dom Morin was an excellent monk and a most active
man, but he was careless and somewhat naïve. A Sénonois
scholar one day hoaxed him in a rather cruel manner by
persuading him to insert in his work a reference which he
gave him written in an abbreviated form. Dom Morin did

not bother to decipher it, but let it be printed as it stood. But once the abbreviations had been written out in full, it was found to run as follows: '*Charron, de historia universali, in futilibus historiis nullis, pagina nulla, folio fracto.*'[15]

The history of some of the churches in the Ile-de-France was, as we have seen, written as early as the Middle Ages. The seventeenth century too had its local church historians. Sébastien Rouillard, whose name is already familiar to us, brought out in 1609 a history of the cathedral of Chartres. There is a very ancient tradition, still accepted by several good scholars, that the cathedral —surely one of the most splendid sanctuaries ever raised by the skill of the masons, sculptors, and glass-makers of a former age—occupies the site of an old pagan temple. According to this tradition there was, in addition to a sacred well still to be seen in the crypt, known as the Puits des Saints Forts and much venerated by the faithful, a mother goddess, whose type probably survived in the figure of the seated virgin before whom so many candles have been lit. According to the legend, the Carnutes, moved by the spirit of prophecy, had adored the Virgin Mother even before the birth of Christ. This is the explanation of the title given by Rouillard to his book: *Parthénie ou Histoire de la Très Auguste et Très Dévote Église de Chartres, dédiée par les vieux Druides en l'honneur de la Vierge qui enfanteroit.*[16] The *Parthénie* is of special interest to the historians of Celtomania. Some years later the cathedral of Chartres found a more accurate historian in one of its canons, Jean-Baptiste Souchet, whose work remained for a long time in manuscript form and was not published till the nineteenth century, through the good offices of the Archaeological Society of Eure-et-Loir.[17]

During the Middle Ages, the abbey of Saint-Denis-en-France had been an important centre of historical study. It was here that the official history of the dynasty took shape. But up to the seventeenth century no monk had undertaken to write the history of the abbey itself. The honour of being the first to take up this onerous task fell to brother Jacques Doublet, who brought out simultaneously with two publishers in 1625 his *Histoire de l'Abbaye de Saint-Denys-en-France*.[18] Accompanied as it is by considerable supporting evidence, this work remains the most completely documented account we possess of the most famous of the abbeys of the Ile-de-France. About the same period some of the great monastic establishments in Paris and its suburbs also found their historians. Dom Jacques du Breul wrote the history of Saint-Germain-des-Prés;[19] dom Martin Marrier that of Saint-Martin-des-Champs;[20] Jean de Thoulouse that of Saint-Victor;[21] father Ignatius de Jésus Maria that of Saint-Maur-des-Fossés.[22] Even the books which concern the strictly Parisian monasteries are of almost equal interest for the Ile-de-France, for amongst them were some of the largest feudal landlords of the Ile-de-France.[23]

But there still remained to be written the history of the Church in Paris, its bishops and archbishops, its chapter and the diocese as a whole. François de Harlay, who was made archbishop of Paris by Louis XIV in 1671, entrusted this work to an Oratorian, Gérard Dubois by name. Under the title *Historia Ecclesie Parisiensis* Dubois wrote an ill-digested and badly arranged book that is difficult to read, but full of facts and bearing witness to extensive work among the archives.[24]

The noble families of the first rank in the seventeenth century wished to follow the example of kings and churches and have their historians too. The books composed by the latter are also extremely valuable for local history; but it is as well not to have blind confidence in these works, which were inspired by family pride. We can at any rate congratulate ourselves on the fact that several of the great families whose history was closely bound up with the Ile-de-France had the happy idea of employing André Duchesne[25] to tell the tale of their glories, for he was one of the most patient and honest of the seventeenth-century scholars. The works he devoted to the houses of Montmorency,[26] Châtillon,[27] Dreux[28] and Broyes[29] are among the most useful sources that the historian of the Ile-de-France can draw upon.[30]

On 22 November 1630 a monk of Languedoc, dom Grégoire Tarisse, became superior-general of the Reformed Benedictine Congregation called the Congregation of Saint Maurus. This is one of the great dates in the history of French learning. Dom Tarisse was the real founder of the Congregation, and he did all he could within the community to encourage the development of historical studies. He thought, no doubt (as dom Tassin[31] says), that 'a monk who neglects the study of sacred literature will soon find the retired life quite unbearable and will return to the world'. The great monuments of learning produced by Benedictine scholarship are just as interesting for the Ile-de-France as they are for the other provinces—works like the *Annales Ordinis Sancti Benedicti* by Mabillon,[32] the *Gallia Christiana Nova*,[33] the *Art de Vérifier les Dates*,[34] and the *Monasticon Gallicanum*,[35] which dom Michel Germain undertook without ever being able to complete it. Along with some other historical fragments of his, we still possess a few of the precious plates. But these enormous labours did not cause the Benedictines to neglect local history, or—to call it by their name—*histoires particulières*. They would have liked each monastery in their Order to have its own history. Mabillon drew up an *Avis pour ceux qui travaillent aux histoires des monastères*,[36] which is admirably clear, balanced, and intelligent. As for the enterprise itself, the historian of today can only subscribe to what dom Tassin said in the eighteenth

39

century, in his *Histoire Littéraire de la Congrégation de Saint-Maur*.[37]

These local histories, based upon original materials, . . . throw light upon both the civil and the ecclesiastical life of the kingdom; they enrich our knowledge of the geography of the Middle Ages; they revive the memory of a whole number of places that have been forgotten; and most distinguished families can use them as a source for genealogical researches.

And dom Tassin added: 'Finally, they rescue from oblivion a multitude of great men and much instructive information.' And so the Benedictines wrote the history of a large number of the monasteries of the Ile-de-France. Saint-Germain-des-Prés, Saint-Denis, Chelles,[38] Maubuisson,[39] Saint-Martin-de-Pontoise,[40] Saint-Nicaise de Meulan,[41] Saint-Florentin de Bonneval,[42] all these had their religious and learned chroniclers. The majority of these works have never been printed. They were not meant for publication; they were meant to serve—and did in fact serve—as preparatory studies for the elaboration of more important works, such as the *Gallia*. The historian of today can go and consult them in manuscript collections. Some of the monastic histories composed by the Benedictines were, however, published; these were the ones whose ample scope made them of interest for the kingdom as a whole, and for the historian of the Church. In 1724, dom Bouillard brought out his *Histoire de Saint Germain-des-Prés*;[43] in 1724, dom Félibien his *Histoire de Saint-Denis*.[44] It is interesting to compare the latter with the work published almost a century earlier by Frère Jacques Doublet on the same subject. Compared with dom Félibien's work, which was the fruit of wise and methodical research, well-arranged, clearly written and

The Seine at Mantes

The magnificent château and grounds at Chantilly

luxuriously produced ('as satisfying to the eye as to the mind', says the reviewer in the *Journal des Savants* of 8 March 1706), Jacques Doublet's two ponderous volumes make a poor showing. Besides, in the course of a century, scholarly methods and the art of writing historical narrative had made undeniable progress. Unfortunately, dom Félibien published fewer documents than his predecessor; and this is why he has not completely superseded Doublet.

In 1704, Mgr de Bissy, who had succeeded Bossuet in the see of Meaux, decided to commission a history of the church to which he ministered. Since 1714, he had been abbot *in commendam* of Saint-Germain-des-Prés, the centre of the Congregation of Saint Maurus; and it was to one of the resident monks that he entrusted this history of the bishops who had preceded him, and of his diocese. He chose dom Toussaint-Duplessis, who was a good scholar. His *Histoire de l'Eglise de Meaux*[45] is a little lacking in clarity, but very reliable. The second volume consists entirely of supporting material, and is one of the most useful collections of documents we possess on the Ile-de-France, Champagne and Brie. Nevertheless the *Histoire de l'Eglise de Meaux* became the source of considerable embarrassment to its author. Desiring, no doubt, to pay court to cardinal Bissy, an ultramontane prelate of whom Saint-Simon said that he had 'sold his body and soul to the Jesuits',[46] he spoke of Bossuet in terms which many people found improper, coming from the pen of the official historian of the bishops of Meaux. The Meaux Chapter took up the cudgels against him, and a long polemical war of words ensued. This strange episode in the ecclesiastical disputes of the eighteenth century has attracted the attention of some scholars[47] but its complete history has not yet been written.

Dom Toussaint-Duplessis does not seem to have been a man to retreat in the face of polemical attack. In 1754

41

while a canon of Auxerre, the abbé Lebeuf,[48] who was already well known as the author of numerous learned works, issued the first three volumes of his *Histoire de la Ville et de tout le Diocèse de Paris*; dom Duplessis published a series of articles in the *Mercure de France* in which he attacked this work in the most vigorous terms.[49] In spite of these criticisms, which seem to have been partly prompted by a certain professional rivalry (abbé Lebeuf did not belong to the Congregation of Saint Maurus) and a measure of jealousy (for dom Duplessis had also written on the history of Paris, *Nouvelles Annales de Paris jusqu'à Hugues Capet*,[50] a work of second-rate value which had had only moderate success), and in spite too of the glib mockery poured upon his work by some wits who despised all learning,[51] the *Histoire de la Ville et de tout le Diocèse de Paris*[52] remains one of the most finished works ever devoted to the history of the Ile-de-France. I have ignored the first volumes, which deal with the city of Paris itself. The diocese is studied parish by parish and a description of places is given, along with their history. Abbé Lebeuf considered his work a contribution to a grand description of the whole kingdom, both geographical and historical, which he dreamed would one day be written, diocese by diocese.[53] The abbot had a thorough knowledge of the archives, or rather the cartularies, of the religious houses in the diocese, which are most certainly a source of priceless value for the historical geography of the region. He was both painstaking and precise and not without some critical sense. His style has been much criticized, but in my opinion its clumsiness has a certain distinction about it.

Amongst the not very numerous or distinguished works on local history left by writers from the latter part of the eighteenth century, it is interesting to note signs of the spirit of the time. A certain country curé in Beauce, abbé

42

Bordas (d.1772) devoted his leisure to writing a *Histoire sommaire du Dunois, de ses comtes et de sa capitale*,[54] which was not printed until the nineteenth century, under the aegis of a local society. Abbé Bordas was a rationalist priest: he expressly refused to recognize that Joan of Arc, 'that soldier-like girl', had any 'miraculous or supernatural mission'.[55] The *Histoire de la ville de Chartres, du pays chartrain et de la Beauce*,[56] by Doyen, appeared in 1786. It is prefaced by a letter from a patron born at Chartres, Brissot de Warville, the future member of the National Convention. The attention given to agricultural matters in this work would have astonished and shocked the historians of the seventeenth century. It certainly bears witness to the influence of physiocratic thought. Doyen was moreover a relentless opponent of scientific agriculture, of lucerne and clover and potatoes 'created by nature for the nourishment of beasts', though some wanted to use them 'for feeding human beings'.[57]

It is hardly possible to pass a general judgment on the local historical work carried out in the Ile-de-France under the *Ancien Régime*. How could one and the same appreciation cover both Félibien and Noël Taillepied, dom Guillaume Morin and abbé Lebeuf? All the same it may be worth while to attempt to give some indication of the value to present-day historians of works on local history written before the nineteenth century. More often than not, it must be admitted that what we ask of them is not so much history itself, as the material for history—learned dissertations on details of history or historical geography, lists of bishops or abbots, genealogical tables, supporting documents. It is difficult to give unqualified approval to the nineteenth-century scholars who re-edited books on local history composed in the preceding centuries, or had works printed that existed simply in manuscript. Here too one must beware of too hasty generalizations. The modern editor of abbé Lebeuf's *Histoire du Diocèse* rendered a useful service by putting this fine work, which had become scarce and expensive, within the reach of every library. But could the same be said of the editors of Noël Taillepied or the abbé Bordas? The learning expended in rectifying, by means of appendices in the new edition, the innumerable mistakes made by dom Morin would have been put to better use in writing a new book. The money spent on these new editions or reprints would have been better employed in helping to publish collections of documents, the lack of which is a sore hindrance in local historical research. Such a collection would, of course, have made many of the books published by scholars of past generations quite superfluous.

chapter three

Contemporary Local History and the Ile-de-France I: Plan of Investigation[1]

A study must first be made of the work accomplished by historians in the nineteenth and twentieth centuries. This is a work that is still unfinished and incomplete; it will be necessary to point out the gaps in it as well as the results achieved. It is nevertheless a large corpus of work, which could not possibly be catalogued in detail. The following pages will not attempt any complete bibliography of the Ile-de-France, nor even an exhaustive list of sources on special topics. I shall do no more than indicate some of the principal works bearing upon the chief problems.

Local Societies[2]

In the nineteenth and twentieth centuries people who were interested in the past history of the Ile-de-France, or the different districts included in it, formed societies for studying it in detail. The history of the societies I am about to sketch reflects, as though in a small but accurate mirror, the general history of historical research in France.

The first rallying points for scholars were the agricultural societies, most of which were more or less directly linked to the groups that arose out of the physiocratic movement. They have always made it a point of honour to welcome literary essays in their publications and, as a side-line, historical studies. But in the movement that concerns us here their part was never a very important one. Quite early on historians began to form themselves into specifically learned societies.

The first of the societies thus formed did not set themselves the study of local history or archaeology as their only, nor indeed their essential, aim. Their membership consisted of all who in a given town or region were interested in literature, art, or philosophy; they were in fact in the strict sense of the term provincial 'academies'. The preamble to the rules adopted by the *Société des Sciences, des Lettres et des Arts de Seine-et-Oise* in 1834 is thoroughly characteristic:

Besides the desire for purely scientific knowledge, the mind feels the need for some cultural education. This is a desire that must be satisfied, and one of which this Society fully approves. Its aim will be to elevate the mind, and to improve the judgment, by applying to special questions or periods the principles of pure philosophy, morality, legislation, literature and the fine arts, not forgetting those of history and archaeology.

And the *Archives scientifiques, littéraires et industrielles* brought out by this society from 1834 to 1837 do in fact contain a 'general course in literature'. Its *Mémoires*, of which the first volume is dated 1847, open with a translation of Horace, of course in verse.[3] Likewise, even among the local societies, inspired from the first by the desire to help historical study, there was hardly one whose publications were not open to literature. Only scholars whose research work has led them to examine the pages of a large number of issues of this kind of publication can know how alluring the genre of the fable—a literary pro-

duction that one might have thought long ago outmoded
—still appeared in the eyes of provincial poets. But all
these societies, including the *Société des Sciences des Lettres
et des Arts de Seine-et-Oise*, devoted an increasing share of
their work to the past history of the region, and this
rapidly became the preponderant element in it.

In 1836 a society was founded at Rambouillet which
went by the name of the *Société Archéologique de Rambouillet*.[4] To start with, it only contained nine members. It
would no doubt soon have foundered had it not been for
the zeal of a worthy scholar, M. Moutié, and the genero-
sity shown to it on several occasions by the duc de
Luynes. For ten years the youthful society had to confine
its activities to the insertion in local papers of articles on
the monuments of the region. Its very title showed that
the study of monuments held first place in the aims of its
founders; or rather, it was more a question up till then of
ensuring the preservation, rather than the study, of
monuments. It is well known what outrages the eighteenth
century, the Revolutionary period and the Restoration
had perpetrated against the Middle Ages. The anxiety to
prevent a recurrence of such acts of vandalism was the
first concern of those who founded the society of Rambouillet and all who were interested in the antiquities of
the nation. Evidence of this is to be observed in the
programmes of all the groups we shall see coming into
existence. In 1846 the *Société Archéologique de Rambouillet*
was able to publish a collection of documents, the first
of a long series of publications bearing as much on
history proper as on archaeology, which the historian of
the Ile-de-France often has occasion to consult.[5]

The *Société Archéologique d'Eure-et-Loir* owes its existence to the missionary zeal of Arcisse de Caumont, one of
the most ardent disciples of national archaeology, and a
great founder of learned societies. On 16 May 1856

47

Caumont delivered a lecture at the town hall of Chartres. The upshot of this was that some citizens of Chartres founded a *Commission chargée de l'étude at de la conservation des monuments anciens du département*, which was transformed a few days later into a *Société Archéologique*. Enlarging its programme still further, it announced its intention of concerning itself with 'all that existed before 1789 in the former provinces now making up the *département* of Eure-et-Loir'.[6] The *Société Archéologique d'Eure-et-Loir* continues to this day its equable and hard-working life.[7]

In 1864 the *Société Dunoise* was founded at Châteaudun. It proposed at first simply to set up an archaeological museum, but soon extended its activities to the study of Dunois history. In the same year the *Société d'Archéologie, Sciences, Lettres et Arts de Seine-et-Marne*, whose programme was rather similar both to that of the *Société des Sciences, Lettres et Arts de Seine-et-Oise*, and that of the specifically historical and archaeological societies, began an existence which was punctuated by long periods of inactivity.

In France, the last years of the Second Empire and the period after the war of 1870 were marked by a real renaissance of historical study. Many other minds were turned to scholarly research, which was from now on considered to be the necessary foundation for history. Out of this movement grew the most important of the societies we shall consider, the *Société de l'Histoire de Paris et de l'Ile-de-France*, which was founded in 1874. Among its founders are the names of men who were, or were soon to become, some of the greatest scholars of the day. To name only those who are no longer with us, there were Léopold Delisle, Giry, Longnon, and Gabriel Monod. The society has for choice dealt with the history of the city of Paris, but it has always made room for work on the Ile-de-France; and we have already seen that it extends the term 'Ile-de-France' to cover all the territory formerly under

48

the so-called military *gouvernement*. The society is relatively rich, for it recruits its members from among those who are interested in Parisian antiquities—a body of considerable size. It is well equipped for scientific work, because its headquarters are in Paris, which is an incomparable centre for study; and there can be no doubt at all —nor is it really surprising—that the *Société de l'Histoire de Paris et de l'Ile-de-France* rapidly established a position superior to that of any of the neighbouring historical societies.[8]

The same renaissance in historical study, attested in such notable fashion by the foundation of the Parisian society, also brought into existence a fairly numerous series of learned societies in the Ile-de-France. To mention only the most important, there were: the *Société Historique et Archéologique de Pontoise et du Vexin*, founded in 1877;[9] the *Société Historique et Archéologique du Gâtinais*, founded in 1885;[10] the *Société Historique et Archéologique de Corbeil, d'Étampes et de Hurepoix*, founded in 1894.[11] These societies differ from the majority of those formed before 1870 by virtue of their more precise and more exclusively scholarly aims, as well as by their better organized programmes of publication.

Two prelates, Mgr Guibert, archbishop of Paris, and Mgr de Bray, bishop of Meaux, made it their business to see that their clergy took some part in the revival of local history. It was owing to their efforts that the *Comité d'histoire et d'archéologie du diocèse de Paris* was founded in 1882, and the *Conférence d'histoire et d'archéologie du diocèse de Meaux* in 1893. These two associations were both full of promise, but only the second survived. Its bulletin has as its watchword a sentence borrowed from Mgr Baudrillart: 'The Catholic Church has no need of anything but the truth; and her stature is such that she can always bear to face it.'

The *Commission de l'inventaire des richesses d'art de Seine-et-Oise*, founded in 1878, owed its origin to a ministerial circular. It is in principle an administrative commission, whose members are appointed by the prefect. The intention was to organize similar commissions in all the French *départements*; but they have in fact only functioned in some of them. The above-mentioned commission changed its title in 1881, calling itself from then onwards the *Commission départementale des Antiquités et des Arts*. The volumes of proceedings and of memoirs produced each year since 1881 constitute a broad survey of local archaeology.[12]

The *département* of Seine-et-Oise has been the favourite hunting-ground for learned societies. Among the *départements* that concern us here, it is the one which possesses the most numerous and the most active societies. It is also the only *département* in which the various societies form a federation. Since 1902 the various 'learned, literary and artistic' societies of Seine-et-Oise have set up a permanent co-ordinating committee which sits at Versailles. It meets in conference from time to time, in one or other *département*. This learned federation has not so far produced any notable collective work which one might have expected of such a body.[13]

Historians are sometimes unjust to local societies. Certain irregularities, external peculiarities and oddities in their publications, which make them the despair of bibliographers, and more than this, the uneven quality of the work that they publish, has often caused us to forget the priceless services they have rendered and still render continuously to historical studies. By bringing workers in this field together they have both inspired and supported their individual contributions. They have provided many scholars with the material help without which they would not have been able to get their works printed. We owe them a great debt of gratitude. One must wish them a long life, and since it is in finance that—in almost every case—the shoe pinches, one can only hope they may have many and generous subscribers.[14]

The tools of research

No scholar has ever attempted the almost impossible task of making an inventory of all the manuscript documents relating to the Ile-de-France; but one scholar, limiting himself to the *département* and to examining certain collections of manuscripts only, did in fact undertake a similar labour. M. Lemaire, an archivist of the Seine-et-Marne, brought out in 1883 'under the auspices of the *Conseil général*', a book entitled: *Relevé des documents intéressant le département de Seine-et-Marne, conservés dans les bibliothèques communales de Meaux, Melun et Provins, à la Bibliothèque Nationale à Paris et aux archives des ministères des Finances et des Travaux Publics*.[15] It is an extremely incomplete collection. The task undertaken by M. Lemaire was immense, and for lack of adequate catalogues in the libraries or archives in which his researches were conducted, it was impossible to carry it through with full success. Scholars undertaking research on the history of the Ile-de-France should always consult the catalogues of the various repositories where there is a chance of finding relevant documents—especially those housing the archives of the Seine-et-Oise, Seine-et-Marne, Loiret and Eure-et-Loir *départements*.[16] The reader will find in this chapter some indication of the range of material at the disposal of research-workers in the archives I have just mentioned. My collection of notes was made possible by the extreme kindness of the departmental archivists. In the manuscript room at the Bibliothèque Nationale those who are interested in the history of Vexin can refer to a 'collection' specially devoted to this province. This collection, consisting of original documents (a few only), copies of documents and essays in manuscript, was made at the end of the eighteenth and during the early years of the nineteenth century, by a magistrate called Antoine-Joseph Lévrier, who died in 1823.[17]

Inscriptions, which are infinitely less numerous than manuscript documents, may be found listed not only in catalogues but also in a work which reproduces them in their entirety. The ancient inscriptions of the districts that now form the Ile-de-France will be found in the first part of volume XIII of the great *Corpus Inscriptionum Latinarum* of the Berlin Academy, published in 1899, while the Christian inscriptions earlier than the eighth century will be found in the two collections made by Edmond Le Blant.[18] In his *Collection des Documents Inédits* M. de Guilhermy started to publish a *Recueil des Inscriptions de la France du Ve siècle au XVIIIe*. The first part of this work—the only one to be published—is most relevant to the study of this region, for it contains inscriptions from the former diocese of Paris.[19] The work will be completed by studies undertaken by individuals forming volume IV of the *Inscriptions de l'Ancien Diocèse de Sens*, by MM. Michel, Quesvers and Stein,[20] and *l'Epigraphe du canton de Montford-l'Amaury*, by MM. Loisel and de Dion.[21] For a large part of the Ile-de-France, there is no collection of medieval and modern inscriptions available; this is a gap that needs filling.

It is not only inscriptions and documents from the archives that tell us the history of the past. Archaeological information is equally valuable testimony but it needs classifying if it is to be methodically examined. Numerous efforts have been made—though often of an intermittent and unco-ordinated kind—to put together collections of archaeological information on the Ile-de-France. These take a variety of forms.[22] In some cases they amount to no more than an attempt to give information about the monuments classified by the *Commission des Monuments Historiques*, for example the very useful *Statistique archéologique d'Eure-et-Loir* drawn up by M. Jusselin.[23] Other authors have set out to describe all the ancient monuments of a region, as M. Louis Régnier has done for the canton of Chaumont-en-Vexin,[24] and, for the canton of Écouen, the anonymous author of the *Répertoire archéologique* which was produced under the auspices of the *Commission des Antiquités et des Arts de Seine-et-Oise*.[25] Others again, without insisting on absolute completeness, but also without dogmatically excluding unclassified material, have listed all the most noteworthy monuments. This method—which hardly deserves to be called a method—has been adopted for instance by MM. Amédée Aufauvre and Charles Fichot in their *Monuments de Seine-et-Marne*,[26] and by M. Edmond Michel in the excellent book he has devoted to the *Monuments religieux, civils et militaires du Gâtinais*.[27]

A number of scholars have attempted to set up bibliographical registers not for the whole of the Ile-de-France (this framework, which would be too vague and too extensive, has never in fact been adopted) but for certain districts or certain towns in the Ile-de-France. These registers are of two kinds. Sometimes references have been compiled both biographical and bibliographical for authors born in a particular region, or connected with it by certain more or less definite links. Works of this kind —really bio-bibliographies—have been undertaken ever since the eighteenth century. In 1719 dom Jean Liron brought out his *Bibliothèque chartraine* or '*traité des auteurs et des hommes illustres de l'ancien diocèse de Chartres qui ont laissé quelques monuments à la postérité, ou qui ont excellé dans les beaux-arts'*.[28] This useful work was intended by the author to be the first volume in a *Bibliothèque générale des auteurs de France*, though no second volume was ever published. In the eighteenth century too dom Guillaume Gérou and several other scholars worked on a *Bibliothèque des écrivains orléanois*, planned on the same model.[29] In the nineteenth century M. Lucien Merlet followed up the work done by dom Liron. His *Bibliothèque chartraine* takes the *département* of Eure-et-Loir as its frame of reference.[30]

Other authors applied their efforts to collecting the titles of works bearing upon the history of a region, without concerning themselves with the character of their authors. In this way the *département* of Seine-et-Marne,[31] the cantons of Pointoise[32] and Magny-en-Vexin,[33] the *arrondissement* of Étampes,[34] have all acquired bibliographies. But these are only moderately useful, though they have meant a great deal of labour; for too much has been written of very unequal value on local history, so that no bibliographies of a non-critical nature can really be of much service.[35]

The current bibliography of the history of the Ile-de-France is covered by the periodicals issued by the local societies in the region. These all contain some bibliographical information. But special mention must be made of two excellent lists of current works—the *Bibliographie historique du Vexin et du département de Seine-et-Oise* compiled for several years by M. Louis Régnier in the *Mémoires de la Société Historique de Pontoise*, the publication of which seems unfortunately to have come to a halt;[36] and more particularly the *Bibliographie de l'Histoire de Paris et de l'Ile-de-France* produced by M. Vidier from 1898 to 1907, beginning as an annual and then a biennial appendix to the *Bulletin de la Société de l'Histoire de Paris*.[37] This work, very carefully and accurately drawn up, was a great help to all workers in this field, and it is to be hoped that it will be resumed.

Catalogues of documents, a corpus of inscriptions, archaeological or bibliographical lists, are after all the tools of scholars; and although there are some gaps, the supply is on the whole fairly adequate. What use has been made of these tools and what more remains to be achieved? Which of the problems presented by the history of the Ile-de-France have already been solved, and which ones still await a solution? This is the question to which we must now turn our attention.

chapter four

Contemporary Local History and the Ile-de-France II: Problems and Results

Local monographs: towns and villages

Let us imagine that a scholar wishes to work on the history of a French region, for example, the Ile-de-France. Often he is not attracted by any particular question or kinds of question, but simply by the desire to help unravel the past of his own country. He is confronted with a choice, and must in the first place decide the scope of his work and the form in which he will present his results. Often, and naturally enough, he prefers to write a local monograph rather than any other kind of composition. I mean by that the type of book in which the author treats the history of a town or village[1] in its entirety—in its political, economic, religious and archaeological aspects —either 'from the earliest times up to the present' or at least over a very long period. And it is generally his own town or his own village that he chooses. One can easily appreciate the reasons—and very good ones at that—that have led to the writing of so many books of this kind in the Ile-de-France. In order to give some estimate of them it will, I think, be helpful to examine separately the monographs dealing with towns and those dealing simply with villages. This distinction between town and village will no doubt not always be easy to draw in certain borderline cases. But in a general way it is clear enough, and corresponds to profound differences that exist between the two.

There are few books more attractive to read and to

write than a well-constructed work on the history of a town. But there are few more difficult to write, because of the great variety of knowledge demanded of the author and the singularly clear and perceptive mind needed for the precise narration on a subject like this. Must the historian record—I will not say all the events—but even all the important events that took place in his town? Surely not, for among these events there are doubtless some which occurred at this particular spot by mere chance, and within the general framework of urban history have no meaningful links either with the past or the future. To write the history of a town is not to relate a series of facts possessing no other unity but the unity of place. What, then, does the task consist of?

In the first place, the aim should be to trace the geographical and historical causes leading to the earliest settlement of the township at that particular spot, its further development, and perhaps even its removal to other sites. This is a delicate matter in which care is needed to avoid premature conclusions. Anyone observing the site occupied by the town of Pithiviers—an admirable defensive position on a promontory which is a continuation of the Beauceron plateau and overhangs a ravine—would at first glance conclude that it had been determined from the beginning by inexorable geographical necessity as the location of a town. But we have only to go four kilometres upstream to find at an easily accessible spot the few houses that constitute today the village called Pithiviers-le-Vieil. That was the former site of Pithiviers. The present-day town, which was for a long time called Pithiviers-le-Châtel, only dates from the troubled days of the early Middle Ages. The migration probably took place in the first half of the tenth century. The first Pithiviers, which became Pithiviers-le-Vieil, did not disappear, and retained its name. In other words the population did not all move, but the bulk of them no doubt betook themselves—or perhaps were transported by their feudal lord—to the new town downstream on the projection of the plateau, above the steep slopes running down to the narrow river then called the Essonne. It was an extremely secure spot, well protected by walls or palisades behind which the relics of a Breton king, king Solomon, fleeing before the Normans, found a safe resting-place. During the same period the people of Corbeil, leaving the right bank of the Seine, or rather leaving behind only a few houses which became 'le Vieux Corbeil', founded a new Corbeil in the 'peninsula' formed by the confluence of the Seine and the Essonne. There, entrenched between the two rivers, they too offered asylum to the 'holy relics' which the Normans had hounded from their resting-places. About the same time, no doubt, Étampes, whose first site had been in the valley of the Chalonette, at a spot since known as 'les Vieilles Étampes', withdrew to a place between the Juine and the steep sides of the plateau. Pithiviers scarcely grew any further, but Étampes and Corbeil, as a result of leaving the narrow quarters to which they had been confined by the constant threat of pillage, forged ahead to a new prosperity, which in the case of the second town continued and increased down to our own times.[2]

To write the history of a town would also mean to follow and describe the changes in its architectural appearance, and in the same breath the changes in its institutions, its economic development, the evolution of its habits and social customs. Above all it would involve showing—to all who have eyes to see them—the very close links between these different aspects of urban life, and the way in which its entire history is portrayed in its monuments, in the plan of the town, and in the whole of its material story. The embattled walls of the church of Notre-Dame at Étampes are still an eloquent witness to the struggles between the commune and the clergy.[3] Who could attempt to explain the industrial and commercial wealth attained by Chartres in the Middle Ages without taking into account a religious fact—that it was a great centre for relics and pilgrimages and a thriving cult of the saints? On the other hand, we see the expression of this fortune today brilliantly and magnificently embodied in the stained-glass windows which are the permanent memorial to the wealth and piety of the corporations of Chartres.

There is no single monograph on the towns of the Ile-de-France that could be held up as a model. But mention should be made of some useful works: the *Histoire de Chartres* by M. de l'Epinois,[4] the *Histoire de Meaux* by M. Carro,[5] the *Histoire de Melun* by M. G. Leroy,[6] the *Histoire de Corbeil* by M. J.-A. Le Paire.[7] No one since dom Fleureau's time has attempted a single broad sketch of the history of Étampes; but some excellent works produced by scholars of Étampes—especially MM. Léon Marquis and Louis-Eugène Lefèvre—would serve as preparatory material for anyone wishing to take up the Barnabite's task once again.[8] The urban history of Saint-Denis-en-France has not yet been written.[9] The destinies of the town of Saint-Denis were no doubt closely linked to those of the famous abbey. It is to this that it owed not indeed its beginnings, but at any rate its present name, which replaced the Gallo-Roman name of Catulliacus in the early centuries of the Middle Ages, and certainly a large part of its prosperity. The modern Saint-Denis is admittedly not much more than a suburb of Paris, a district of 'greater Paris'. Nevertheless alongside the history of the abbey, the history of the abbey borough, and alongside the story of the giant city, the story of its neighbour, the little town, would be a tempting and worthwhile theme for the pen of a scholar. Before being engulfed, Saint-Denis occasionally set up its trades as rivals to those of Paris; and it would not be without interest to trace the story of these rivalries and then of the fusion of the two towns.

Hundreds of villages in the Ile-de-France have had their historians. The *Conseil Général* of the Seine published between 1896 and 1903 an *État des Communes à la fin du XIXe siècle*. Every commune has its brochure containing, along with administrative details, a note on its history, by M. Fernand Bournon, who has taken the essentials from the great work of abbé Lebeuf. Someone has had the happy idea of including in each brochure, along with a sketch-plan of the commune, a reproduction of the corresponding section of the *Carte des Environs de Paris*, known as the *Carte des Chasses* drawn up between 1763 and 1774. *L'Annuaire d'Eure-et-Loir* has published,[10] and *L'Annuaire de Seine-et-Marne* still publishes,[11] studies on the various communes of these *départements*. Apart from these extensive undertakings, a large number of scholars have taken pleasure in sketching the history of the villages that abound in the fertile land of the Ile-de-France. What is one to say of this kind of work? In spite of the zeal displayed by their authors, they are only too frequently useless for purposes of general history, which is in the long run the only history that matters. The reasons for this are both practical and theoretical.

The historians who write such works are sometimes novices. Yet the task they have taken on requires an enormous variety of knowledge. One needs to be a geographer, or even a geologist, for a book like this almost always opens with a description of the village's soil. One needs to be something of a palaeographer to be able to read the ancient village charters without making

60

mistakes if—as may unfortunately be the case—they have not been published. One needs to be well versed in feudal law to understand them; one should be an archaeologist, to be able to give a correct description of the church, and in some cases, to be sure of not making a mistake about the prehistoric remains which can be found in so many places in the Ile-de-France. Then there is the complicated administrative machinery of the *Ancien Régime*, and the political life of the revolutionary period, both of them important to understand. And there are many other aspects I could mention. It is—one need hardly say—given to few men to have such wide and varied knowledge at their command. It is rare indeed to find a village monograph in which the historian, consulting it to clear up some special point that concerns him, finds what he is looking for.

Let us assume that the village historian has miraculously succeeded in avoiding any material errors in his book. Even if it is in this respect impeccable, does it deserve the grand name of a work of history? The restricted framework, the slower pace of village life as compared with that of the town, and the scarcity of documents, will hardly allow him to write a study of community life comparable to the great works of urban history. And what about the church? It will probably have been built by a master mason who did not belong to the village, perhaps from money provided by a distant *seigneur* who by an accident of inheritance had become the master of this piece of land or patron of the parish. In order to understand the Gothic features of the church at Larchant, on the western fringe of the forest of Fontainebleau, one must look not to Larchant but to Paris, to Notre-Dame Cathedral on which this more modest Gâtinais village church is modelled, because the canons of Notre-Dame were the lords of Larchant.[12] And what about the legal position of the

61

peasants? The documents relating to them in a single village are so few, so fragmentary and often so obscure that we shall certainly go astray in our interpretation of them unless we can compare them with others relating to the surrounding villages. How about the *cahier* drawn up in 1789? It was probably brought from the neighbouring town by some citizen. The peasants no doubt introduced considerable modifications into the model document that was set before them; but we shall not be in a position to understand the meaning and, so to speak, to catch the local flavour of our village *cahier* unless we can place it alongside those of neighbouring parishes. All history consists to some extent in making comparisons; and the truth is that the facts offered by the past life of a single village are too scanty and too thin for anyone to be able to understand them without comparing them continually with the facts provided by other villages in the same region.

Those who are interested in the local history of the particular corner in which they live would find greater inspiration if, instead of writing village monographs, they would widen the extent of their researches, but confine them to some specific aspect, with which a little study would soon make them conversant. For example, one might study the churches in his district, another its political life in the time of the Revolution; and these are obviously only two suggestions among many other possible subjects. Amongst those attracted by local historical research there are many owners of land with a knowledge and love of the countryside. Yet though we have many (perhaps too many) books embracing the whole history of a village, we have very few studies of the rural history—even in contemporary times—of the Ile-de-France. When people cease to turn out so many village monographs the energies that are at present running to waste will find a more profitable use.

Let us attempt something which we would like to see done by the scholars who are interested in the past history of the Ile-de-France. Leaving the monographs, let us examine one by one the problems presented by the history of the country round Paris at different periods.

The earliest period: prehistoric and ancient times

Man made his appearance at a very early period in the well-favoured lands of the Ile-de-France. We find him already there at the dawn of prehistory, chipping his flint tools. Archaeologists have marked out in this immense tract of time large-scale divisions which they call eras, and within these they distinguish a certain number of periods. The oldest of the periods in the remotest of these eras takes the name by which it is commonly known from a village in the Ile-de-France—the borough of Chelles, in the valley of the Marne, about the same distance from Meaux and the confluence of the Marne and the Seine. It has given its name to the Chellean period, the first one in the palaeolithic era, that is to say the opening period of prehistoric times.[13] Some of the most ancient relics of human industry that we possess consist of 'amygdaloid' axe-heads, which were discovered in the commune of Chelles among the bones of *Elephas antiquus* and the cave-bear. They were found lying in the gravel washed up by the river Marne—a broad river in prehistoric times.

The nameless peoples of the prehistoric ages—we can have no idea at all what they may have been called—and those who later succeeded them, perhaps called the Ligurians, have left plentiful traces in the soil of the Ile-de-France, such as chipped flint, polished flint and metal weapons and tools, dolmens and upright stones, and those holes hollowed out by the men of neolithic days in the

Beauceron limestone to serve as dwellings.[14] Numerous detailed studies scattered among specialist or local reviews give information about the discoveries of prehistoric remains made since the beginning of the nineteenth century at a great many points in the Ile-de-France. But what is needed is an inclusive work based upon a broad critical enquiry, studying not only prehistoric times in the Ile-de-France—for this would be an artificial frame of reference —but in the extensive 'Paris basin' of which the Ile-de-France is only a part. Such a work does not exist at present. When it comes to be written it will no doubt be valuable for prehistoric studies in general, but it will also throw a vivid light on what might be called the historical geography of the Ile-de-France. What land in the Ile-de-France, for instance, attracted the earliest human settlements? Was it the valleys or the plateaux? And of these last, was it rather the dry or the well-watered ones? This is the kind of question prehistoric studies ought to be able to answer but I do not think they have so far done so.[15]

When Caesar entered Gaul, the country that is today the Ile-de-France was occupied by Celtic-speaking peoples. This was the meeting-place for two large groups which Greek and Roman historians singled out from among the confused mass of nations with Celtic names. No doubt they represented two successive waves of a single invasion—the Belgae to the north and the Celts proper to the south. In the description of Gaul which opens the book that he devoted to the story of his conquest, Caesar explains that the Marne and the Seine marked the boundary between the Belgae, established on the right bank, and the Celtic peoples, who had settled on the left. This statement, it will be realized, was not strictly accurate; in fact the two banks more often than not belonged to one and the same people, at one place to the Celts and at another to the Belgae. Whatever Caesar—or

64

rather the Greek geographers from whom no doubt he took his information—may have thought about it, these rivers were not very suitable for forming the frontier between two ethnic groups. As we have already observed, the Seine is not a barrier, nor is the Marne. Yet Caesar made these rivers out to be the country's boundaries, and popular geography in the Middle Ages fixed the Seine as the northern boundary of *Hurepoix*. It is really rather odd to see the same over-simple or rather one-sided conception of the geographical function of rivers expressing itself in the same way in two such very different passages written at such different dates.

The region that later on became the Ile-de-France was not the property of a single nation during the Gallic period. It would seem that all the neighbouring peoples had been intent on pushing forward towards the great meeting-point of the rivers which forms its central focus. What were the frontiers? No ancient document gives us any help in tracing them. Yet we venture now and again to mark them on our maps, and this is because we think ourselves justified in supposing that they were the same as those of the dioceses. In the ecclesiastical organization of the Middle Ages the dioceses preserved the memory of the Gallo-Roman cities, and through these cities, the memory of the Gallic peoples whose heritage had come down to them. This may have been because there was in fact a territory belonging to a single people corresponding to each city; or (as we shall see by some examples) because such a territory served to provide two cities; or even that the territories of two different peoples were the basis of a single city. Such a method of analysis is only legitimate provided that not too much is expected of it. We must always bear in mind that we have no complete lists of the parishes in a diocese going back beyond the thirteenth century, and for some dioceses the oldest date only from the fourteenth.[16] It is obvious that in passing from the period of the Gallic peoples to the Roman city, from the diocesan city of the early Middle Ages to the periods of Philip Augustus, Saint Louis, or Jean le Bon, the frontiers may have undergone innumerable small modifications. It is certain that between the eleventh and fourteenth centuries the two parishes of Estouy and Courcelles-le-Roi passed from the diocese of Orléans to the diocese of Sens.[17] It may be argued that this was an isolated case but how are we to know? By mere chance this particular change has come down to us, because the list of the parishes in the diocese of Orléans in the care of a certain Arnould in the eleventh century, happens to have been preserved on a manuscript leaf in the Vatican. And it is more than possible that other chance events have robbed us of the knowledge of a good many similar changes. It is possible that a search among diplomatic documents might uncover some traces of this kind of case. Moreover a study of the administrative districts of the Merovingian period—the *pagi* which were formed at the expense of the cities—has already led scholars to believe that the boundaries between the dioceses of Paris and Sens, Chartres and Paris,[18] Sens and Meaux,[19] were readjusted during the first centuries of the Middle Ages. An examination of the ecclesiastical geography of the Middle Ages, supplementing the evidence of ancient documents, shows us in a general way what territory the Gallic peoples inhabited; but it does not enable us to trace their frontiers with any precision or certainty.

On the two banks of the Seine, between its two tributaries, the Marne and the Oise—of which it appears that only the former belonged entirely to them[20]—a small people called the Parisii were grouped round the straggling island settlement of Lutetin, no doubt one of the *oppida* on the heights of Taverny. It appeared to be more or less squeezed out of existence between the neighbouring great nations. To the west and south-west the Carnutes were occupying Perche, Beauce and both banks of the Loire. To the south-east the Senones were pushing forward from the Yonne valley towards la Brie, into le Gâtinais, and as far as the Beauceron plateau. These three peoples were Celts. And now for the Belgae. To the north-east the Suessiones, a powerful nation surrounded by subject peoples, were in occupation of both banks of the Marne; their extensive territory (*'fines latissimos'*)[21] stretched out over a part of Brie and no doubt the eastern part of the plateau which was later to be called France. To the north-west the Bellovaci were outside the boundaries we have fixed for the Ile-de-France. But to the west, on the far side of the Oise, the Veliocassi occupied the plateaux to which they have given the name le Vexin.

When Gaul had become a Roman possession the majority of the Gallic peoples kept their autonomy under the wing of the conquerors and became 'cities'. Certain modifications, however, took place in the region with which we are concerned, which seems to have been particularly important. It is difficult and even impossible to date them with any certainty. The Suessiones were no longer in evidence on the borders of the Parisii; two peoples who had formerly been vassal-states now broke off from this over-large nation—the Meldi in Brie and on the French plateau, the Silvanectes beyond the great forests bordering the Oise—and were given their independence by the Romans. The vast territory of the Carnutes was divided into two 'cities'. The western one kept the name Carnute, and later on transmitted it to the town of Autricum, its capital city, which was destined to become Chartres. To the south-west, over a part of the Beauceron plateau, and likewise over the Val de Loire and Sologne, there stretched the new 'city' of the Aureliani, carved out of the Carnute territory, round about Cenabum, which was to become Orléans,[22] On the western frontier of the Parisii the opposite took place: two peoples, the Veliocassi, though already occupying an enormous territory, and the Caletes, more to the west in the *pays de Caux*, came together to form a single 'city' stretching from the banks of the Oise to the cliffs along the Channel. We have no idea what brought about this last change. As far as I know the fact has never been explained, either because no scholar has made it his business to search out the causes, or more likely because no one has been successful in the search.

What became of the cities grouped along the middle reaches of the Seine in Roman times? What was life like in these towns? We can see—or imagine—them developing peacefully at first during the early centuries of the Empire around the sites of the Gallic settlements; then, during the invasions of the third century, retiring behind hastily-erected ramparts to easily defended spots, such as Chartres on the edge of its plateau, or Melun—like Paris—in its island situation.[23] What cults, what festivals, what crafts, what political institutions did they have? And in the country, what large proprietors were there in the *villae*? And most important of all, what was the history of Romanization in these areas? Its secret would perhaps be revealed to us by the proper names of persons, if it were possible to study them. None of these questions can be answered by anyone who merely consults secondary works. There are few devoted to the study of the Roman period in the Ile-de-France. And documents too, as I am well aware, are scanty. There are hardly any except those of an archaeological and epigraphical kind. Now the soil of the Ile-de-France seems to be very poor in Roman remains particularly as compared with other Gallic regions —the Narbonnaise, for example, or the Rhinelands, or even la Saintonge. The 'cities' of the Meldi, the Parisii and the Carnutes taken together only provide fifty-nine inscriptions for the corpus. It is absolutely essential to draw up for all 'cities' and towns and for all problems a list of what we can know, and a list of what we must accept as impossible ever to be discovered. M. Bonnard has recently drawn up a balance-sheet setting out the extent of our knowledge in *Chartres gallo-romain*.[24] It is to be hoped that others will follow his example. At the moment, I do not know anything of general scope and interest to recommend, apart from his work, with the exception of M. Pachtère's excellent book *Paris gallo-romain*, which bears very closely on the Ile-de-France[25] and along with it—though not at all in the same class—the Latin thesis of M. Dubuc, *De Suessonum Civitate*.[26]

If the Ile-de-France offers fewer monuments, bas-reliefs and inscriptions than many other French provinces to the scholar in search of Roman remains, it can at least show the best gift made to it by its conquerors—a network of ancient roads. But it is difficult to know exactly in what this consisted. It is obvious that the roads shown in the ancient itineraries are not the only ones of interest to us. There are many other Roman roads whose existence can only be discovered by an examination of the ground or sometimes by a reference in a medieval text; they too deserve to be studied by the historian of the Ile-de-France. But there is no comprehensive work to give information about them. If we wish to get to know them, we have to press maps into service, search through the archaeological reviews, the reviews of local scholars' work, the year-books of the *départements*, not omitting to extend our researches to works written before the nineteenth century, where clues to these roads, such as milestones, are sometimes mentioned, which are no longer visible today. The reader will find in the notes a bibliography on the roads of the Ile-de-France. I have made it as complete as I can; but I have no doubt that a good many gaps will be found in it, the information required being so scattered. Such as it is, I believe it may be of some use—and not only to scholars concerned with the study of antiquity.[27] The Roman roads have played a great part in history, stretching far beyond the period of Roman ascendancy over Gaul.

Consider the castles—very numerous in the Ile-de-France—built in the eleventh and twelfth centuries. Very many of them were sited near a road constructed by the Romans, because these roads were followed by the merchants who were successively—or rather simultaneously—protected, exploited and plundered by the lords inhabiting the castles. During the Middle Ages these Roman roads were followed by the pilgrims making their way to the great Christian sanctuaries; by the wandering minstrels, weaving into their *chansons de geste* the legends they had picked up in churches in the course of their travels, and even those tales which the remains of ancient monuments had inspired in the popular imagination. No doubt it was a Roman tomb placed, like the more famous tombs of Aliscans and the Appian Way, by the side of a road and near the gates of a town, that used to be shown as the '*Tombe Isoré*' on the road to Orléans, on the way out of Paris. Epic tradition had turned it into the sepulchre of a king of 'Conimbre', who was slain by William of Orange.[28] Yet the merchants and pilgrims of the Middle Ages sometimes turned aside from the roads the Romans had made for them. When the later history of the Roman roads comes to be written it will show where these détours took place. We know the precise line of the road that connected Lutetia (Paris) to Cenabum (Orléans). After crossing the valley of the Chalouette at the place where Étampes then stood, it ran due south across the plateau, on the line of the present-day villages of Saclas and Autruy. It is still followed by a secondary road at the present time, but the main road now runs further west, through Monerville and Toury. It changed its route a long while ago. The *Itinéraire brugeois*, drawn up at the end of the fourteenth century, already mentions Toury as one of the relay-stages between Paris and Orléans.[29] Let us now go still further back into the past. The abbot of Saint-Denis, Suger by name, in a book composed between 1144 and 1149 setting down the salient facts of his administration as abbot, thus describes the borough of Toury, with which he was well acquainted, having governed it as provost in his younger days: 'Toury, situated half-way, provides food for all pilgrims, merchants and travellers; it is a quiet spot, and offers peace and rest to all who are weary' ('peregrinis et mercatoribus seu quibus cumque viatoribus alimenta cibariorum *in media strata*, lassis etiam quietem quiete ministrans').[30] Why was the Roman road with its great flag-stones and its shorter route abandoned? None of the scholars who have noted this fact[31] has attempted to explain it. Let us, however, make the attempt. A short distance west of the road, between Saclas and Autruy, is the village of Méréville. A castle had been built there towards the end of the eleventh century, and the lords of Méréville to whom it belonged seem, according to Suger's account of the matter, to have been formidable bandits. These redoubtable barons had established their stronghold near the high road, which was no doubt still used by the merchants at the time when the castles were built. Was it not to avoid this den of robbers that the merchants changed their route and began to go further to the west? They would, it is true, find another castle at Toury; but as it was in the hands of the monks of Saint-Denis it would offer them a place of refuge. The line taken at the present time by the *route nationale* and the railway from Paris to Orléans may thus perhaps be explained by the necessities of a feudal age in which travellers were exposed to the risks of pillage. I venture to put this forward as a possible explanation but it cannot of course be more than a conjecture.

But we have other sources of information about the men who occupied the soil of our region in early days, quite apart from archaeological documents, weapons and tools, inscriptions and bas-reliefs, paving stones and concrete on the Roman roads, and apart from the literary documents. The very place-names, for anyone who can interpret them, are full of secret information. The two neighbouring villages of Lion-en-Beauce (*Lodunum* in Carolingian-period Latin) and Ruan (*Rotomagus*) go back at least as far as Gallic times, as is shown by their names, which reproduce those of two more famous Gallic towns —Lyons on the Rhone and Rouen in Normandy. Antony (*Antoniacus*) preserves the memory of the Gallo-Roman *Antonius* who no doubt possessed an estate there. A Beauceron village bears the name of Bouzonville (*Bosonis Villa*). The Teutonic name forming the first part of the word, and the very suffix *villa*, which was hardly used at all before the period of the great barbarian invasions, show either that Bouzonville belongs at the very earliest to the fifth century, or that it took a new name not earlier than the fifth century. The borough of *Catulliacus* became Saint-Denis because its fame and its fortune were due to the saint.

In order to study place-names, it is essential to know their ancient forms. The topographical dictionaries undertaken under the direction of the *Comité des Travaux historiques* aim essentially at providing a survey of these forms. But only one of the *départements* making up the Ile-de-France possesses a dictionary of this kind. The

Dictionnaire topographique de l'Eure-et-Loir, which came out in 1861, was edited by M. Lucien Merlet.[32] It is the work of a conscientious and accurate scholar, familiar with the local archives, but it is unfortunately already somewhat out of date. It was compiled at a time when a good many documents available today had not yet been published, and therefore it has considerable gaps. In particular, it does not give enough space to the forms of place-names and there is no attempt at any philological classification of names. I think there are topographical dictionaries in preparation for Seine-et-Marne and Loiret: let us hope they will soon be published. The *Dictionnaire des anciens noms des communes du département de Seine-et-Oise*, by Hippolyte Cocheris,[33] and the *Dictionnaire historique des communes et des hameaux du département du Loiret*, by Vergnaud-Romagnesi,[34] are more or less useless because they do not quote their sources. The historian of the Ile-de-France who either wishes to know the ancient form of a place-name, or meets a name in an ancient document and wishes to identify it, is forced, if the name does not belong to Eure-et-Loir, to search through the topographical tables nearly always contained in modern editions of medieval texts, polyptychs, cartularies, or collections of charters, and especially the registers of benefices and obituaries so carefully published by M. Longnon and his colleagues in the new series entitled *Les Historiens de France*.[35] As for the philological and historical study of names, only a very few research-workers have tackled it at all. M. Jacques Soyer has given us some most valuable 'Recherches sur les noms propres géographiques d'origine celtique de l'Orléanais'.[36] It is much to be hoped that this article will be the first of a long series. At present it is the only piece of work of fairly general scope and truly scientific method that has been devoted to this kind of question in the Ile-de-France.

But this is not because the 'toponomy' of the Ile-de-France does not present some interesting problems. Here is one that I would recommend to the notice of those with enquiring minds. I will choose to call it the Beauceron problem. Let us take a map of la Beauce and list the names of the inhabited places. It does not take long to notice that many of them are made up as follows: first a man's name, often apparently Teutonic in form, then one of the following words—ville (*villa*), or more rarely villiers (*villare*), or court (*curtis*). La Beauce is certainly not the only district in the Ile-de-France where names formed in this way are to be met with, but La Beauce has a higher proportion of them than other parts. In the canton of Janville, for example, fourteen out of twenty-two, in the canton of Anneau fourteen out of twenty-eight, in the canton of Malesherbes ten out of eighteen, in the canton of Méréville eight of the seventeen situated on the Beauceron plateau have names of this kind. They must of course be later than the Roman epoch; they would seem to date approximately from the Merovingian period. How are we to explain the fact that they occur in such numbers on Beauceron soil? Was la Beauce populated—or repopulated—in Merovingian times? I can only point to the problem. The important thing is to get a more accurate knowledge of the data in the first place, and above all to find the solution. The very singularity of the problem is a challenge to scholars.[37]

The middle ages

We should very much like to know the history of those oriental merchants, or brothers well instructed in the faith and coming from the heart of the great western communities, who were the first to teach the Gallo-

Roman cities of what was later to be the Ile-de-France the name of Christ, and to tell them of his sacrifice on the cross and his resurrection. The clerks of the Middle Ages thought they knew this glorious tale. This is more or less the form in which they told it. Three men called Savinien, Potentien and Altin, who came from Judaea, brought the new religion to the 'illustrious' city of Sens. They had heard its teachings from the very lips of the Saviour, for they had all three belonged to the glorious band of the seventy-two disciples. Then one of them, Altin, accompanied by Édoald, one of the Senones, visited Orléans and Chartres, in both of which they established churches. Paris on the other hand received its first pastor from Athens—Denis, a judge of the Areopagus who had been converted by St Paul. Before he died Denis chose two of his disciples who were to go to Rome to bring the news of his martyrdom. One of these messengers, Sanctin by name, returned to France and evangelized Meaux.

These were only legendary stories, with no other basis than the pious pride of the churches, who sought to link up their beginnings with the remotest Christian past. It is certainly true that the earliest bishop of Paris mentioned in history was called by the Greek name Denis; but when he died—as Gregory of Tours relates—in the reign of Decius, who ruled from 249 to 251, the voice of the great St Paul had been silent for nearly two hundred years. There are scarcely any obvious reasons for doubting that Savinien was the first bishop of Sens, and Potentin the second; but Savinien was certainly a contemporary of Constantine, or at the earliest of Diocletian. Some historians believe that there really was a Sanctin, bishop of Meaux; they identify him with the Sanctin who was bishop of Verdun in the fourth century. As for Altin, the 'saintly imitator' of Savinien and Potentien,[38] and the

75

deacon Édoald whose Germanic name does not fit a Gaul of the first century, what scholars would venture to affirm that they ever existed?[39]

We no longer believe in the errors spread by the partisan credulity of clerics in past ages. We scarcely possess any more certain information about the beginnings of Christianity in the Ile-de-France than they did. Most scientific work on this subject has only produced negative results; and the state of the documents is such that we should probably not be very hopeful of ever having much more information. The legend of Saint Sanctin has not yet been studied in a definitive manner;[40] but there is little hope that further study will produce much more than new information about the zeal displayed by the clergy in constructing an edifice of pious deceptions. It is improbable that Christianity penetrated to the Ile-de-France much before the period when the churches were becoming organized; but there is some difficulty in even being certain of the foundation-dates of the churches. The church in Paris probably took shape about the year 250; in Sens, Chartres and Orléans about the fourth century, perhaps in the time of the first Christian Emperors. The oldest bishop of Meaux on whom we have any reliable documentary evidence was a subject of the sons of Clovis, Medovechus by name, who appended his signature to the decrees of a Council held at Orléans on 28 October 549; but it is unlikely that he should be considered the first to govern the diocese of Meaux, for why should the city of the Meldes have been so long in acquiring a bishop? But we know nothing certain or even probable about Medovechus' predecessors.

The Christian Church borrowed its organization from the civil administration. As we have seen, the Gallo-Roman cities survived in the dioceses, but not without some vicissitudes. When Clovis' victories had placed the country that was already beginning to be called France under the rule of the Merovingians, that is when it was on the way to becoming the Ile-de-France, there was some danger that the unity of the dioceses might be disrupted. In 524, when Clodomir was dead, and his sons either assassinated or put into convents, his three brothers shared out the kingdom. The city of Sens was divided between Thierri king of Metz and Childebert king of Paris; the king of Metz got the town of Sens, the episcopal city, so that Childebert's subjects must have found themselves under the pastoral authority of a bishop who lived in Thierri's territory. This situation seems to have been intolerable to Childebert, and he founded a new bishopric in one of the towns of the Senones that had fallen to his share—at Château-Landon, no doubt, or perhaps at Melun. In the same way when three kings disposed of Caribert's heritage in 567, the city of Chartres was divided up, Gontran receiving a part of it and Sigebert the rest. Chartres belonged to Gontran. Sigebert then set up a bishop at Châteaudun, which had fallen to him in the division. But the church could not allow her organization to depend on the whims of lay sovereigns. The bishoprics of Château-Landon and Châteaudun only had a short life.[41] In the Ile-de-France, the dioceses of Paris, Chartres, Orléans, Sens, Meaux, and the enormous diocese of Rouen which stretched as far as the Oise, were a reminder up to the Revolution of the 'cities' of the Parisii, the Carnutes, the Aureliani, the Senones, the Meldi and the huge city produced by the union between the two peoples, the Veliocassi and the Caletes. As Sens was the metropolitan city of a province in the later days of the Empire —the fourth Lyonnais—and Rouen was the metropolitan city of the second Lyonnais, Sens and Rouen both had their archbishops. The Paris bishopric was not made an archbishopric until the year 1632; Chartres, Orléans and

Meaux, which had up till then been suffragan sees of Sens, now made up the new ecclesiastical province.

It is probable that at the beginning of the Merovingian period each city had its count in the same way that it had its bishop. But these early counties were soon split up, some dismembered in the partitions that were constantly breaking up the unity of the Frankish kingdom, others, unaffected by these, being no doubt considered too large to be under the effective authority of a single man in these troublous times. The county or *pagus*, as constituted under the descendants of Clovis, was, like the diocese, the heir of the 'city', but more often than not an impoverished heir, who had only received a part of the patrimony. Some of these counties included territory taken from two 'cities'. The geography of the *pagi* of the Ile-de-France is a complicated and obscure subject, which has still been only partly unravelled. They appear to have been as follows in Carolingian times.[42] Two of them, the county of Meaux and the county of Orléans,[43] had kept intact the 'city' territories from which they had sprung. On the other hand seven counties had been formed from the 'city' of the Carnutes: Dreux, Vendôme and Blois, which do not concern us here; le Dunois; the county of Chartres; le Pinserais, probably incorporating certain villages from the 'city' of the Parisii; and that enigmatic *pagus Madriacensis*, which was perhaps formed at the expense of both the Carnutes and the Eburovices, and may have owed its name to the village of Mércy, on the left bank of the Eure[44]—or alternatively to the village of Méré, on the right bank.[45] North of the Seine, Vexin stretched from the Oise to the Andelle. This fragment broken off from the 'city' of Rouen had preserved the Gallic name of the Veliocassi. The 'city' of the Parisii had given birth to two *pagi*, Parisii to the north, and the *Pagus Castrensis* to the south, with its capital at Châtres, the modern Arpajon.

Finally to the south-west there were three counties: Gâtinais, Étampois and Melunois—the remnants of the 'city' of the Senones—which were on the fringe of what we now call the Ile-de-France.

When the Normans had established themselves on the western bank of the Epte, Vexin found itself cut in two— with Norman Vexin on the right bank and French Vexin on the left. From the reign of Philip I onwards, French Vexin was swallowed up in the royal domain. After 916 all trace is lost of the *pagus Madriacensis*, which was perhaps partly absorbed into the state of Normandy. The *pagus Castrensis* also disappeared towards the end of the Carolingian epoch, but no scholar has ever taken the trouble to investigate when and why this happened. Towards the middle of the tenth century a new county was formed, upstream from Paris, around the reconstructed Corbeil. The county of Paris, since king Eudes' time under the rule of the Robertian family, l'Étampois and le Pinserais, which had perhaps been acquired at the same time as Parisis, together with Orléanais, which Robert the Strong already owned—these formed the very kernel of the royal domain that belonged to this third line of kings. Hugh Capet however had to hand over the county of Paris to one of his best servants, Bouchard le Vénérable, who already held Melun and Corbeil[46] in the Ile-de-France; but after Bouchard's death, which took place about 1007, Parisis reverted to the kings and was never again to leave their hands. Gâtinais was joined on to the royal domain by Philip I, and Louis VI took possession of Corbeil. The county of Meaux, with the rest of the Champagne state, of which Meaux had for a long time been only a part, was brought as a dowry to Philip the Fair by the heiress of the house of Blois. The other counties in the Ile-de-France were destined to survive till feudal times.[47]

It would require much patience, and a selfless devotion bordering on asceticism, to reconstruct—with some inevitable gaps—the list of counts who governed the different counties in the Ile-de-France, and to unravel the tangled skein of the county dynasties; and it would be a difficult task because of the poverty of the source material. It could, however, be amply rewarded by its results, which would throw a flood of light on the problem of feudal origins. We are relatively well informed about the counts of Paris; though the book devoted to them by M. Mourin[48] has no other claim to be remembered by scholars than that it inspired one of the most famous reviews in the *Revue Critique* during the heroic period of French scholarship;[49] but their history is too closely connected with that of the Robertian family for the author to have failed to take advantage of the labours of scholars who have attempted to throw light upon the beginnings and the rise to fame of this illustrious family.[50] M. J. Depoin has published a study on the *Comtes de Paris sous la dynastie carolingienne*, but its most interesting conclusions will have to be closely examined before being definitively accepted.[51] The counts of Gâtinais have been the subject of a good deal of well-directed research.[52] The counts of Chartres,[53] Corbeil,[54] and Vexin[55] have had their historians too. But the information that even the most diligent scholars have been able to glean about the counts' succession in any given county is so scanty, uncertain and obscure that it will only become really significant for our knowledge of feudal institutions when it is all sorted out, and comparisons are made. Then the composite work will shed light from one county to another.[56] Along with the study of the counts should go a study of the viscounts, who were first of all—like the counts—officials, and then became hereditary chiefs. This work would be assisted by some detailed studies based on material relating to the viscounts of Corbeil[57] and Étampes,[58] the viscounts of Gâtinais, who changed their title to viscount of Fessard,[59] and the viscounts of Vexin, who made themselves counts of Meulan[60] in the eleventh century. The history of the counts and viscounts of the Ile-de-France would no doubt yield new and accurate information about the transformation of public duties into patrimonial seigniories—one of the most frequently referred to, but least well known in its details, of all the changes that led to the development of the feudal system. And if by chance this information were not forthcoming, we should at any rate be in a better position to gauge the unavoidable extent of our ignorance.

But such a study ought not perhaps to be separated from the study of the simple seigniories—those that did not bring their holders any titles borrowed from the nomenclature of the various offices of Carolingian times, or at any rate brought them titles relatively late in the day, and more or less by usurpation. When did these words 'count' and 'viscount' begin to denote *seigneurs* who were not the heirs of Carolingian counts and viscounts? Which families took it upon themselves one after another to bedeck themselves with these titles? This would be an interesting subject for research. We know for example that the first of the *seigneurs* de Montfort to call himself comte de Montfort in the official deeds was Amauri V, in 1226; but his father, the illustrious Simon IV, conqueror of the Albigenses, was in current usage treated by his contemporaries as comte de Montfort.[61] This was no doubt because he was in possession of real counties, and was well-known to be an actual count; and people were pleased to call him both by his highest title and by the name of his patrimonial territory. Amauri had given up his counties but was far from wishing to give up the fine title of count. In this case we can pretty well follow the history of the title and easily discover the reasons for

81

its being used. But are the other cases analogous to the Montfort case? Or are they different? The historian of the feudal system in the Ile-de-France will have to find the answer.

The chief hindrance to a perfect knowledge of feudal history of the Ile-de-France is the paucity of documents. Of basic secular archives we have only those which date from very recent times. The lives of the great lay lordships are known to us only by chance, from information gathered here and there from the charters preserved in the archives of chapters or abbeys, and from chronicles, and from the thirteenth century onwards in the royal archives, though these are not at all complete. Hence scholars have not felt drawn to this kind of study. There is not much more to refer to than the following: a book—to be consulted with some caution—by M. André Thein on the lords of Montfort;[62] the useful works by MM. Richemond[63] and Estournet[64] on the lords of Nemours; by M. Devaux on the lords of Pithiviers,[65] by M. de Dion on those of Puiset;[66] by M. Moutié on those of Chevreuse;[67] and the works in which M. Depoin has sought so patiently—and sometimes over-ingeniously—to trace the genealogies of a large number of families among the Ile-de-France nobility,[68] almost all those which it is possible to cite.[69] And even then these studies, valuable though they are, only touch indirectly on the great problems. Is it not possible to extract from the archives and the narrative sources information about the feudal hierarchy in the Ile-de-France, about fiefs and allodial tenures, about the relationships between vassals and their lords, about the constitution of the great lordships, about the origins of the nobility and the handing down in families of the titles of squire and knight? A careful scrutiny of the documents in search of this kind of data would not, I venture to think, draw an absolute blank.

But diplomatic documents and the accounts of the chroniclers will not provide sufficient material for the historian of the feudal system. Coins[70] and seals[71] are two sources of information hitherto neglected in the Ile-de-France; they will furnish details of the names and titles of those who had them struck or used them to authenticate their legal documents. The history of the coinage will have much to tell the historian about the rights, the usurpations and the politics of the chief barons. Above all he will not forget that these barons were the owners of castles, and that the history of the lord's estate is inseparable from that of the fortress which was so often its centre and its source of strength.

In the Middle Ages there were many castles, built by lords or by kings, that cast their shadow—now protectingly and now menacingly—over the Ile-de-France. A large number of them are still standing. Although all of them have suffered in varying degree from the onslaughts of time and human hands, the archaeologist can question these ancient stones and get some answer. Others, however, no doubt more numerous still, have vanished without leaving any trace at all on the ground. Only by reading ancient documents (and sometimes by looking at ancient pictures) can one discover their sites and sometimes form an idea of what they looked like. We have monographs on a few castles, some of them excellent. But there are a great many ruins that have not been explored, and a great many scattered references in documents that have neither been brought together nor interpreted. The fortified towns and boroughs cannot be studied in isolation from the castles; but they likewise have been too frequently neglected by local scholars. To give one example, the village of Boissy l'Aillerie in French Vexin is surrounded by an enclosing wall that has been spared by the years,[72] but as far as I know this enclosure has never been dated.

Moreover the production of monographs, however necessary it may be, is not enough. What is needed is to bring together the information provided by both monuments and documents about the castles and strongholds in the Ile-de-France, and to classify it by periods. Then it will perhaps be possible to arrive at a solution of the problems presented to the archaeologist by the history of military architecture; these are also problems —and serious ones—to the scholar researching into the history of institutions at different periods in the Middle Ages.[73]

At the time of the Norman invasions, *castella* and fortified bridges were built along the waterways of the Ile-de-France. These were only too easily navigated and often carried pagan ships inland. Examples of these bridges are to be found in those built by Charles the Bold at Auvers over the Oise and at Charenton over the Marne.[74] What happened subsequently to these defence works? Is there some link to be discerned between them and the castles of a later age? This is a problem that has never been studied; it may perhaps be an insoluble one. The names of the oldest seigniorial castles in the Ile-de-France—Montlhéry, le Puiset, Yèvres, Montford, Épernon, Gallardon, Illiers, names that were odious to the ecclesiastical chroniclers who transcribed them—seem to make their first appearance in narrative documents dealing with contemporary events in the reign of Robert the Pious. Although these were undoubtedly seigniorial castles, it is as well to wonder whether they had always been so. For one might reasonably conjecture that they had been built by kings and had only passed by a kind of usurped authority into the hands of the feudal dynasties, descended from their original custodians. This hypothesis has been put forward for certain provinces by a variety of scholars,[75] and it is one that should be examined by the historian of feudalism

84

in the Ile-de-France. But would he find that it fits the facts? I do not think so.

It seems certain that from the eleventh century onwards the majority of the castles were built by the barons and for the barons. Not that the kings did not also seek the protection of fortresses. The writings of the eleventh and twelfth centuries are particularly full of names of those fortresses which were built along the Normandy frontier, facing the works by which the English kings sought to protect their overseas duchy.[76] We only know of these early Capetian castles from documentary sources and, being built almost entirely of wood, they were not designed to last. These 'strongholds' consisted ordinarily of a wooden tower of several storeys, surrounded by protective palisades; and the troops of Philip I and Louis VI did not find it easy to scale them. It is probable that the enclosure often embraced a part of the seigniorial village. Moreover the word 'castle' in the language of the Middle Ages was used indifferently for a fortified house or for a complete group of buildings enclosed by walls—the citadel or fortified town. This uncertainty in the use of terms is not the least of the difficulties encountered by the scholar when he is forced to study medieval military architecture with no other guide but written documents.

When did the first stone-built castles make their appearance in the Ile-de-France? In order to answer this question the study of monuments alone will not be enough, for they are often difficult to date without documentary help. The *tour Guinette*, whose broken walls with their four foils look down on Étampes, is undoubtedly one of the oldest dungeons in the region round about Paris. But to what exact epoch does it belong? Archaeologists still do not agree in their answer.[77] Let us therefore see what the documents have to say. In his *Histoire Ecclésiastique*[78] Orderic Vital speaks of the stone fortress,

85

'*lapidea munitio*', which a lord of the locality, a man called Ansoud, the second of that name, erected at Maule, on the borders of Normandy. Now Ansoud died on 24 December 1118. This is I think the oldest stone-built castle whose date is fairly accurately known. In the twelfth and thirteenth centuries the 'stone mantle' of the castles, as well as the churches, covered the Ile-de-France. What share in their construction was contributed by the kings and what by the barons? This would be an interesting subject for research. Philip Augustus, a great builder of fortresses, built or rebuilt Dourdan,[79] Gisors,[80] and the walls of Corbeil and Melun.[81] It is possible that at the end of the thirteenth century and the beginning of the fourteenth, when the Ile-de-France was more peaceful under the rule of more powerful kings, fewer fortified houses were built in its countryside than in the preceding ages. On the other hand many new castles must have arisen during the Hundred Years' War, and old ones must have been repaired or enlarged; and towns and villages that up till then had been unfortified must have been enclosed with walls. In August 1415, for example—the month that witnessed Henry V's landing on the Norman coast—the inhabitants of Rozoy, in the Briard country, asked for authority from the bailiff of Meaux to fortify their borough.[82] This fresh period of the history of fortifications has been even less studied than the preceding ones.

Like all ancient ruins, the remains of medieval castles have inspired popular imagination. People could not fail to be struck by the towers whose menacing outlines rose up on so many of the hillsides and mounds in the Ile-de-France. The memory of the lords or kings who had built them had vanished, and legends arose to take the place of history.

They turned the towers called '*Jour de Gannes*' into castles belonging to the traitor Ganelon. This strange tradition may only be an etymological fiction, for the word *ganne*, in itself rather mysterious, appears originally to have had no connection with the name Ganelon. It would certainly be an interesting matter for study.[83]

The abundant archives left behind by the churches in the Ile-de-France are in striking contrast to the few scattered documents that are all we have left from the lay seigniories. Not that the former have no gaps in them; it is only by comparison that they seem so rich in material. Bishops, deans and abbots appear to have been less careful about preserving documents bearing upon property that they owned in their personal capacity than the canons or the monks were in preserving those which had to do with the estates of chapters or convents. Even the best endowed churches cannot produce many documents from the tenth and eleventh centuries. M. Pourpadin, who has been most assiduous in collecting the 'charters of Saint-Germain-des-Prés', has only succeeded in discovering between the years 900 and 1100 (two centuries) 35 charters, whilst between 1100 and 1200 (only a century) he has found 220, and for subsequent centuries would have found many more. In spite of these reservations—and others which could be made—the number of documents from the Middle Ages handed down by a single religious house often runs into thousands, in the form of originals, copies on loose sheets or written up in the cartularies, rentals, account-books,[84] and deliberations recorded in the capitular registers.[85] How are we to find our way through such a wealth of material? And before plunging in, how are we to get a bird's-eye view of it? For many factors have been at work since the sixteenth century causing the dispersal of ecclesiastical archives. On the other hand there have been numerous publications from the time of the *Ancien Régime* onwards based upon these archives, though of a fragmentary nature. How is one to locate the documents belonging to a particular church in the various repositories of manuscripts among which they have become scattered, and in the series where they have been printed? Excellent working aids come to the rescue in answer to these questions.

M. Stein with laudable accuracy and precision has reckoned up the printed and manuscript cartularies throughout France. Being myself conversant with those of the Ile-de-France, I can testify that I have only come across very few omissions or mistakes in his work. These corrections will be found in a note (with an indication of some collections printed after his *Bibliographie* came out). I hope he will be able to make use of them in a second edition.[86]

A Benedictine, dom Beaunier by name, published in 1724, under the title *Recueil historique des archevêchés, évêchés, abbayes et prieurés de France*, a rather mediocre work put together from a series of notes written on the various ecclesiastical foundations of the kingdom. In our time the Benedictines of Liguge, who carry on the very scholarly traditions of the Congregation of Saint Maurus, have gone back to dom Beaunier's book. They have in fact given us, in what they too modestly call a second edition, an almost completely new and original work. Dom Beaunier's notes have been kept, but they have been greatly filled out. In particular, each of their accounts is now followed by a full and accurate bibliography—an entirely new feature. When this fine undertaking—now only in its early stages—is complete, we shall be able to see at a glance what are the printed and manuscript sources containing the history of every one of the religious houses in the France of former days. This great work will no doubt comprise many volumes. Volume I concerns the Ile-de-France, for it deals with the ecclesiastical province of Paris.[87]

88

Country road through Seine et Marne

The château at Fontainebleau

The chronology of the ecclesiastical dignitaries of the Middle Ages is not easy to fix satisfactorily. But it is absolutely necessary to have this knowledge for anyone to be able to interpret correctly the source-material provided by diplomacy. For many of the legal documents, at least in the early Middle Ages, there is no other means of dating them but by the names of the persons who passed them or gave them authority by signing or witnessing them. MM. Maurice Lecomte and Delaforge have made it their first task to unravel the chronology of the bishops of Meaux,[88] and secondly that of the dignitaries of the abbeys, chapters and priories of the same diocese.[89] At Chartres, the order of succession among the earliest bishops has been studied by M. Lucien Merlet[90] and for the dignitaries of the cathedral chapter by MM. Lucien and René Merlet.[91]

With these working tools, for what kind of work will the historian of the Ile-de-France use the documents which the church archives provide in such generous measure? In fact, an all but complete history of the Middle Ages, at any rate up to the fourteenth century, emerges from these documents and it is completed, though in no way replaced, by the various narrative sources. What would be left of books like M. Luchaire's *Annales de la vie de Louis VI* if the churches, and more especially the churches in the Ile-de-France, had not been in the habit of keeping such documents as might be useful to them?

But we are dealing here only with ecclesiastical history properly so-called. The thought will naturally occur to the scholar who has at his disposal a collection of archives from one religious house: why not write the history of this house, either over its lifetime, or at least for a very long period, such as the whole Middle Ages? This would undoubtedly be an attractive proposition. For the ecclesiastical communities of the Middle Ages were not, as we too often imagine them, peaceful places of refuge, but centres of study and mysticism,[92] convulsed by the strifes which run through all societies that are not dead. They were powerful forces in agriculture, in commerce and in finance; their life during the Middle Ages was active, varied and broad. By their interests and by their habits of thought their leaders were brought to look beyond the narrow confines of their little province, out towards the kingdom or Christendom as a whole. In a feudal society that was always tending towards fragmentation and dissolution, they were a unifying force. Their multifarious activities lie open to the view of the historian. But monasteries and chapters were primarily religious foundations, whose duty it was to procure for all Christians—and especially for those who had enriched them—by means of masses and prayers, the salvation of their souls and sometimes of their bodies as well. The historian must be at pains to recognize the religious impress stamped upon all that they did—even their financial transactions—by the very fact of the Church's religious vocation; and this dimension will impart a deep unity to his studies.[93]

The name of the abbey of Saint-Denis-en-France crops up on every page of the history of the Middle Ages.[94] Its domains extended beyond the kingdom's frontiers. Its relics and its fairs drew merchants and pilgrims from every quarter. Its abbots and monks were the counsellors of the Capetians and the Carolingians. Its basilica, the resting-place of kings, was the first great Gothic church to be built. Some of the most important historical works produced by the Middle Ages came from Saint-Denis. More than one epic legend took its rise from Saint-Denis. M. Luchon had considered the history of this great house a worthy subject for a collective work which he would have liked to have seen carried out by students grouped around him. But all that this undertaking has produced is some good monographs on abbeys, one by M. Dubruel on Fulrad,[95] one by M. Pourpardin on Ebles,[96] and one by M. Cordey on Guillaume de Massouris.[97] Along with these works, mention should be made of the excellent book on abbé Suger, by M. Otto Cartellieri.[98] Among Suger's works, the most interesting ones from the point of view of monastic history —the *Traité sur son administration abbatiale* and the *Petit Traité sur la Consécration de l'Eglise Saint-Denis*—exist only in a rather mediocre edition published by Lecoy de la Marche,[99] and are still awaiting an edition that will be really scientific. M. de Béthune had begun a comprehensive study of the historiography of Saint-Denis, but unfortunately it remains unfinished.[100] M. Bédier has devoted a chapter in the fourth volume of his *Légendes Épiques*[101] to 'the Abbey of Saint-Denis and the *chansons de geste*', and tells us about the work of one of his pupils, M. Jean Acher, on the subject of one of the poems to which the martyr's tomb gave birth, entitled *Le Floovant*. The fairs of Saint-Denis will soon have their historian.[102] As for the archives of the abbey itself, on which many scholars have drawn for several centuries, they have never been used as the basis of an integral piece of work. Will the *Société de l'Histoire de Paris* perhaps give us one of these days a *Recueil des Chartres de Saint-Denis*? The scholar who would undertake this task—if he could establish the rules followed by the Saint-Denis chancery—would make a most valuable contribution to the study of diplomacy.

Historical monographs have been written on several of the ecclesiastical foundations in the Ile-de-France, both in the nineteenth and in the twentieth century. M. Fourrier Bonnard for example has studied Saint-Victor de Paris;[103] M. Giard, Saint-Geneviéve *in monte parisiensi*;[104] M. l'abbé Alliot, Notre-Dame de Gif,[105] and Notre-Dame d'Yerres;[106] M. Torchet[107] and M. Berthault,[108] the abbey of Chelles; MM. Dutilleux and Depoin, Notre-Dame la Royale de Maubuisson.[109] Their works provide a great deal of useful information, but not many interesting historical insights. Moreover, among the above-mentioned abbeys, there are some—Yerres and Gif for example—whose poverty in archives and rather pedestrian history are hardly suitable for making a very stirring story.

The difficulties confronting the historian of a great chapter or a great monastery are of a quite different order. In this case the very abundance of the documents and the almost infinite variety of the questions touched upon by such a history create a risk that the historian will spread his effort too widely and so endanger the outcome. On the other hand documents from a single source, however numerous they may be, are always incomplete and difficult to interpret without external aid. Anyone who has worked on rural history knows that it is impossible to give an accurate description of peasant conditions in a given district by taking evidence from the archives of a single abbey. This procedure leads one to attach too much importance to the eccentricities of monastic administration, and to neglect essential facts whose importance is at first concealed, and only comes out when one sees them cropping up again in a variety of other contexts.[110] I have already given reasons why scholars are attracted to writing historical monographs on the great religious houses. I ought also to have pointed out the dangers of such undertakings. In any case, works of this kind—legitimate and necessary though they are—could not exhaust the material for ecclesiastical history in the Ile-de-France. This history confronts the scholar with problems that cannot be studied by immuring oneself in the over-narrow framework of monographs on particular abbeys. I will point out no more than two of them.

The considerable part played in the monastic development of Merovingian Gaul by an Irish missionary called Saint Columba is well enough known. It seems certain that he passed through the Ile-de-France. His disciples established on the plateau or in the surrounding valleys of Brie several monastic houses: Faremoutiers, Jouarre, Rebais, and Saint Faron de Meaux. The history of the foundation and early days of these monasteries is not at all well known. And it is difficult to unravel because the available sources, such as the lives of saints or diplomatic documents, are often of doubtful authenticity or sincerity.[111] A fair number of scholars have set about elucidating it but their task is far from being finished.[112]

The ecclesiastical reforms of the tenth and eleventh centuries have been studied hitherto much more in their general principles than in their particular applications. Yet it is only local research that can tell us what in practice this great disciplinary and moral movement really was, and show us the results or frustrations in which it ended. In the Ile-de-France, we should like to know what ecclesiastical properties were recovered from lay hands by the clergy, and how this came about. We should like to know who was victorious in the struggle over tithe: the feudal lords, the bishops, the parochial clergy, or the monks. What were the ins and outs of the struggle between the canons regular and the monks? To what abbeys did the monks of Cluny take their rule? These questions, and others like them, would be well worth examining. A historian would have no difficulty in finding in them material for an important book, all the more so as he would have at his disposal not only a fair number of diplomatic documents, but also another literary source of great interest: the collection of letters written or received by a certain Ives de Chartres, who was one of the best soldiers of the reform in these parts. Before using these

93

letters—which only exist in rather indifferent editions[113] —it would no doubt be necessary to establish the correct text by truly scholarly methods, and above all to make an effort to arrange them in a proper chronological sequence, the order up till now having been very uncertain.

Local scholars, whose tastes are perhaps naturally aristocratic, have somewhat neglected the townsmen and peasants in the Ile-de-France. I must be excused for not concerning myself here with the peasants; I would refer the reader to my work on the rural population of the Ile-de-France during the period of serfdom.[114] The communal movement which exercised such a strong influence on the borders of the Ile-de-France did not spare either the towns or the villages of our region. The commune of Meaux, which cannot be separated from the other communes of the county of Champagne and Brie, has been studied by M. Gassies,[115] by M. René Bourgeois[116] and by M. Georges Bourgin.[117] The communes of Vexin and Pinserais, Pontoise, Poissy, Mantes and Meulan have not yet found their historians. The municipal institutions of Chartres have been the subject of a book, which has perhaps not altogether exhausted the available material.[118] Up till now no worker in this field has been at pains to tell us of the life, prosperity and decadence, of the rivalries between the merchants and the artisans, in the towns and boroughs of the Ile-de-France. In many places the crafts established corporations—for example Château-Landon, Étampes, Pontoise, and Chartres. We have particularly abundant and interesting documentary information about the Chartres corporations, enough to illuminate the whole history of corporations in general.[119] It is much to be hoped that work of this kind will soon be set in train.[120]

From the thirteenth century onwards the Ile-de-France, as we have seen, was almost entirely a part of the royal domain. Even the great seigniories, such as the county of

94

Chartres, surviving till the end of the Middle Ages and beyond, were more and more strictly subjected to the royal authority. We should like to know who these royal officials were—the *sergents*, the *prévôts*, the *baillis*, the *commissaires*—each with their own special commissions. Who had risen to such heights, and how did these men use their power? What was their relationship with the clergy, the nobility, the worthy townsmen and dwellers in the plains? What taxes did they raise in the name of the king? We simply do not know. And yet we could know. Our ignorance on these points arises from the negligence of scholars rather than from the paucity of documents. The chancery registers, the Parliamentary archives (though these, it is true, are difficult to consult owing to the lack of catalogues), the remnants of the Exchequer archives, as well as ecclesiastical archives, would all yield up the secrets of the royal administration for anyone willing to submit them to scrutiny. The legal records of the great religious foundations in Paris, studied and published by M. Tanon, give the most lively and valuable information about the struggle between the seigniorial courts and the royal magistrates.[121] The history of the rise of royal sovereignty, that is to say through the slow decline of local authority in face of the king and the king's men, will only be really known to us when scholars have set about the task of writing it up in detail, province by province.

In the history of religious architecture in the Middle Ages, the Ile-de-France played a glorious part. True, this history, as far as we are able to reconstruct it today, hardly begins before the Roman period. Three crypts—at Jouarre (built no doubt in the seventh century),[122] Notre-Dame de Chartres,[123] and Saint-Martin au Val;[124] at Chartres; a few bits of wall at Saint-Denis which the experts have some difficulty in dating:[125] these are about all that remain of pre-Romanesque art in our region.

Excavation may yield some further examples, but it is doubtful whether they will amount to much.

Romanesque art itself has left less numerous and less notable remains in the Ile-de-France than in many other districts. The great churches, whether cathedral or monastic buildings, were nearly all reconstructed in the Gothic period. Consequently it is especially in the country-side that the archaeologist is likely to come across Romanesque buildings or fragments. M. Coquelle has explored Vexin and Pinserais[126] from this point of view, and his example should be followed in other districts of the Ile-de-France.

Is there any evidence for the existence of a Romanesque school of architecture in the Ile-de-France? M. Anthyme Saint-Paul,[127] M. Enlart, and M. de Lasteyrie say yes; M. Lefèvre-Pontalis[128] denies it. May it not be that this scholarly disagreement is simply a matter of words? Even those archaeologists who reserve a place in their classi-fications for such a school, whose limits they extend far beyond the boundaries assigned in common parlance to the Ile-de-France,[129] recognize that it is not distinguish-able by any essential features. But what is the meaning of a school that is not marked by any specific characteristic? The schools of Normandy, Poitou, Burgundy, and the Rhineland all had architectural idiosyncrasies that were peculiar to them. Between the territories where these particular styles prevailed, with practically no rival influences, there stretched during the Romanesque period an enormous region—the whole of northern France, less Normandy—where building went on without any very fixed rules. At one moment the customs of one neigh-bouring district would be adopted, then those of another. More often than not they followed the lead of the Nor-man master-builders.[130] This region, which included the Ile-de-France, was at this time characterized precisely by the fact that no particular architectural school had been formed in it. The schools of the surrounding provinces met in it as though on a no-man's-land. Moreover if Quicheret's famous saying is true, that 'the history of architecture in the Middle Ages is nothing but the story of the architect's struggle against the thrust of the vaults', it must be admitted that those who built churches in the Ile-de-France during the Romanesque period were not brilliantly successful in this struggle, for they did not dare to arch over the naves, and often not even the aisles. How fortunate that their skill failed them in this respect; for it is to this no doubt that we owe the pointed arch and Gothic architecture.

The origins of Gothic architecture are still somewhat veiled in mystery. Not all archaeologists are agreed on this point. This is not the place to enlarge upon this controversy, which is outside the scope of our study. One fact appears certain: wherever it was that saw the first vaulted transept of pointed arches, strong but light, supporting an arched roof, it was very probably not far from Paris, and no doubt on the borders between the region of Paris and Picardy, that the Gothic church type arose and developed.[131] It was there that the masons, who did not dare to throw simple Romanesque arches across a rather wide space, perhaps invented—or at any rate used more methodically than anyone previously—a more skilful device: the ogival vault. This, together with two other architectural contrivances that followed it—the flying buttress and the pointed equilateral arch—are the marks of the new architecture which we call Gothic. Suger, who from about 1125 to 1148 restored and practically rebuilt the basilica of Saint-Denis, which had become too small for the crowds of pilgrims, roofed over the narthex and the chevet that are still there today, and perhaps the nave that disappeared in the following century. The new style spread rapidly through the whole of the Ile-de-France whose solid limestone, which is covered with a resistant skin when it comes out of the quarry, invited the master builders to indulge in great feats of daring. The style made use of all possible forms, even including the flamboyant.

About the same time as Gothic architecture was coming to birth, a great school of sculpture was arising in the Ile-de-France. Statues were beginning to appear at the doors of Notre-Dame de Chartres, Notre-Dame d'Étampes and Notre-Dame de Corbeil, a little stiff as yet, but nevertheless graceful and already full of life. If the west front of Suger's Saint-Denis had not been mutilated by the monks in the eighteenth century, and desecrated in the early nineteenth by François Debret's 'restorations', we should still be able to admire the stone figures of ordinary people that the abbé had grouped round his 'noble portico'. The few fragments that are left *in situ*, intermingled with modern works and the designs carried out in the eighteenth century for Montfaucon, show that our regrets are fully justified.[132] It seems that Saint-Denis was the place where the new school first manifested itself preparatory to spreading over the whole of the Ile-de-France. It appears to us to have flourished very suddenly, perhaps because we have so little knowledge of its origins. Did it come under the influence of the masons' workshops of Burgundy, Provence or Aquitaine? This is an extremely intricate problem, and it is far from being solved. A discussion of it would take us outside the scope of our study, for the debate turns particularly on the date of the works in Burgundy and in the south. The history of medieval sculpture in the Ile-de-France, after such a sudden beginning in the twelfth century, flows smoothly on through the subsequent centuries. Anyone wishing to compare the artists of the twelfth and thirteenth centuries

98

can see the contrast that Chartres offers between its great western door and its two lateral porches. Everyone knows what a marvellous museum of French sculpture for the whole period from the thirteenth to the sixteenth century is provided by the basilica of Saint-Denis. MM. Vitry and Brière have promised us a work on its tombs, which will be very welcome.[133]

Saint-Denis-en-France and Notre-Dame de Chartres: these are the two names with which the history of sculpture in the Gothic period opens in our region; and these are also the names we must repeat, and in the same order, when it comes to considering the art of stained-glass windows. The principal workshops of the glass-makers were situated there before they existed in Paris, and their masterpieces still glow in full splendour in the windows of both these churches, especially the cathedral of Chartres. The archaeologists claim that there should be a catalogue of French stained glass. A series of regional catalogues would be equally useful. Will some scholar be found to undertake this for the Ile-de-France?

Monographs on churches are the necessary foundation, as regards religious architecture, for the work of the archaeologist. Besides the somewhat out-of-date works of M. de Guilhermy, we possess a most valuable little book by MM. Paul Vitry and Gaston Brière,[134] though it is unfortunately too short to do more than touch upon the difficult problems posed by the chequered history of the famous basilica. M. Léon Levillain has given a fresh account of the early days of its history, from the first beginnings up to the partial demolition of Suger's work.[135] Notre-Dame de Chartres has been the subject of many studies which will be found noted down in the bibliographies of the two most useful monographs on this monument—the enormous work by abbé Bulteau, republished by the *Société Archéologique de l'Eure-et-Loir*,[136] and the very level-headed and accurate book by M. René Merlet.[137] We have no good general study on the cathedral of Meaux, in which all the centuries from the twelfth to the sixteenth have had a hand. Many other less important churches have been described and their stories studied. The work of producing monographs goes steadily ahead.[138] Yet there can be no doubt that the archaeologist who explores the small towns and villages of the Ile-de-France would find numerous monuments that are still, so to speak, unpublished. The country churches must not be neglected. Apart from the fact that a close inspection of them often reveals undiscovered beauties, a thorough examination would no doubt give material for solving some of the great problems presented by the development of religious architecture, which the expert has constantly to bear in mind, for they constitute the true interest of his work, and are a justification for the somewhat dry tone of many monographs. These problems include the following: the origins and mutual relationship of architectural styles, particularly the Gothic style in its various forms; and the links between the different architectural types, a study of which will perhaps one day allow a rational system of classification to be set up in accord with the findings of history in general.[139]

The modern and contemporary periods

Dom Toussaint-Duplessis, to whom, as we have already mentioned, we owe a *Histoire de l'Église de Meaux*, has said of this church that it was 'the cradle of heresy'. A chance episcopal nomination did in fact make it one of the oldest centres of the French Reformation. From 1516 to 1534 its bishop was Guillaume Briçonnet, whose vicar-general and official was Lefèvre d'Étaples. The *Commentarii initiatorii in quatuor Evangelia* by Lefèvre is the first book to have been printed at Meaux. In Briçonnet and Lefèvre we have come to recognize the two great pioneers of reform. The history of this little group of *Meldois*, as they were called by their contemporaries, cannot be considered to have been definitely unravelled. It was above all the history of a movement of ideas, in which they found themselves for the moment the most distinguished representatives—a movement in which the spirit of humanism and the spirit of the Reformation were momentarily united before being ranged in mutual combat. But the problems raised are far beyond the limitations of any merely regional study.[140]

How did Protestantism spread through the boroughs and the countryside? Only a series of enquiries pursued by scholars in each of the French provinces will enable us one day to write an accurate account of this spiritual conquest, whose details are often only to be explained by the most minute knowledge of local history. The village of Claye in the Ourcq valley had a Protestant minister as early as 1562; the reason was that its lords belonged to the Anjorrant family, one of the first families in the Parliament of Paris to be won over to reform.[141] In other places the economic habits of the country population explain its religious history. The peasants of Thiérache, at the beginning of the sixteenth century, were in the habit of hiring themselves out to help with the harvest 'in France', that is to say, apparently, in the neighbourhood of Meaux. Here, in this Meldois district which was early reached by the Reformation, some of them became converts to the new teaching, and began to preach it when they returned to their own villages.[142]

There seem to have been representatives among all social classes in the Huguenot groups of the Ile-de-France. Noblemen and churchmen were to be found side by side with small townsmen and labourers. What was the relative size of each class? This is a very intricate problem, deserving the attention of research workers; and it is by no means certain that the documents provide the necessary material for solving it. The sixteenth-century persecutions forced some of the Protestants in the Ile-de-France to leave their native country;[143] some of their names are to be read in the registers at Geneva—for example, the name of Didier Rousseau, merchant, native of Montlhéry, who in 1549 managed to achieve citizenship of Geneva, and who was the ancestor of Jean-Jacques Rousseau.[144] Others remained at home, upholding the Protestant tradition through troublous times until the Edict of Nantes. When the Edict was revoked there were fairly numerous reformed communities in the Ile-de-France, and the revocation did not succeed in rooting them out entirely. The fortunes of the Huguenots of the Ile-de-France could not fail to arouse the interest of the diligent workers in the *Société de l'Histoire du Protestantisme français*. M. Jacques Pannier has devoted a series of studies to the Reformed Churches of the region extending to the south and east of Paris;[145] M. Henry Lehr has written a large book on the churches of Eure-et-Loir 'from 1523 to 1911';[146] though it is rather astonishing to hear of 'Eure-et-Loir' in 1523.

The questions raised by the history of the Catholic Church in modern times are not always easy to confine within a regional framework. One valley in the Ile-de-France was for many years a most enthusiastic centre of Jansenism; but the history of Jansenism overflows the boundaries of the Ile-de-France. The scholar who is attracted to modern times is less drawn than the medievalist to the study of the religious houses. He is less struck by the wealth of their archives because they are not the only ones at his disposal. The less eventful life and the more restricted influence of these communities, sometimes even lapsing into somnolence, means that their history is not always very sustained in interest, or very lively. Some of the monographs on abbeys quoted in the previous paragraph cover both modern times and the Middle Ages. M. l'abbé Meuret has made a careful collection of useful information about the cathedral chapter of Paris, its composition and its wealth, at a time when the Revolution was about to sweep it out of existence.[147] There are no good works on the bishops' administration, even among the most famous ones such as Bossuet.[148] It is surprising to note that among so many scholars devoted to research there has so far been no one to study the recruitment, education, material conditions, and moral life of the clergy in the dioceses of the Ile-de-France, under the *Ancien Régime*; no one to examine to what extent and by what channels the great movements of thought such as Jansenism and philosophy penetrated into the country parishes, the monasteries and the priories. Several of the journals that the country clergy often kept have been found and sometimes published; they should provide some interesting information for Church history. It is not difficult to see what light would be shed on the Revolution by a careful enquiry into the lives of the country clergy in the eighteenth century; for they played a considerable part at all times and in a variety of ways in the history of the Revolution. Again, the economic history of the Catholic Church, up till now[149] hardly touched upon, well deserves the attention of workers in this field.

Scholars undertaking more methodical and continuous research than any so far carried out into the monuments built in modern times on the soil of the region we are studying should not expect them to testify to any kind of regional art. Because it was open to every influence and near to Paris and the court, neither the Ile-de-France nor any of the districts that go to make it up have been able since the Middle Ages to give rise to any architectural style that was truly its own. But it would be a good idea to examine how technical modifications and changes in taste gradually made themselves felt in these parts, in the towns and even in the villages. M. Louis Regnier has written a useful book on the Renaissance in Vexin and a part of Parisis.[150] It is a pity that he has not so far found anyone to follow his example.

The Ile-de-France, at the very gates of Paris, offered the sportsman plenty of forests well stocked with game. The garden-lover found plenty of smiling valleys and streams and what might be called natural gardens; and ornamental châteaux arose in large numbers from the Renaissance up to the end of the eighteenth century. There were palaces built for kings, such as Saint-Germain-en-Laye, Montreaux-en-Brie,[151] Fontainebleau, Versailles with Marly and the two Trianons; there were houses for great men—magistrates or financiers such as Écouen,[152] Dampierre,[153] Saint-Maur,[154] Rambouillet,[155] Meudon,[156] Maisons-sur-Seine,[157] Vaux-le Vicomte,[158] Conflans,[159] Sceaux,[160] Louveciennes, Ermenonville.[161] The 'country houses' were once upon a time to be found in plenty in this attractive landscape; and the traveller in our day can still, in spite of the destruction that has taken place, often recognize them as he goes past by their high slate roofs or attics, their turrets and their pediments, and sometimes by their seigniorial dovecotes. Examined together, one would see unfolding before one's eyes the sequence of variations in art and fashion that occurred over three centuries; above all, these expressions in stone would bring home to one the changes in the habits of life of the wealthy classes that took place during this period. The most famous palaces have not been the most adequately studied. Saint-Germain-en-Laye has had its historian,[162] but Fon-

Chartres: la Cathédral des Blés Verts
seen across the cornfields of Beauce

Chartres cathedral: *the west front*
and the rose window in the south transept

tainebleau is still waiting for one. Not that there have not already been a good many articles and even books about this immense and complicated building on which so many kings have left their impress one after the other, and which carries, alongside its striking beauties, the marks of so much clumsy patching. But none of these works is of a definitive character. The best of them is certainly the little volume in the collection of the *Villes d'Art* in which M. Louis Dimier has dealt with Fontainebleau.[163] The history of Versailles is encumbered with errors and legends; but to be content with an imperfect knowledge of it is to resign ourselves to ignorance about half the history of the French monarchy and French art over more than a century. Fortunately, M. de Nolhac has undertaken the task of reconstituting it with an equal display of scholarship and good taste.[164]

At the end of the eighteenth century, the districts that we have subsumed under the title 'Ile-de-France' were divided between the three military *gouvernements* of the Ile-de-France, Champagne, and the Orléanais, and between the two *généralités* of Paris and Orléans.[165] As far as judicial institutions are concerned, it was divided into numerous bailiwicks, all coming under the authority of the *Parlement de Paris*. The district adjacent to Orléans, by virtue of its status as an *apanage*, was in a rather special situation. The scholars who have attempted to disentangle the administrative geography of the *Ancien Régime* have almost all chosen to describe it as it was in 1789, being less concerned to explain how the administrative districts had gradually grown up than to give a detailed account of the convocation of the Estates General. This was the essential purpose of M. Armand Brette's great works which have rendered such good service to regional history.[166] The same intention has been at the back of M. Coüard's researches into the bailiwicks that covered the territory later to become the Seine-et-Oise,[167] and M. Camille Bloch's *Géographie judiciaire de l'ancienne circonscription territoriale qui a formé le département du Loiret.*[168] M. Longnon, however, in an article already referred to more than once in the early pages of our study, has sketched the topographical history of the military *gouvernement* of the Ile-de-France.[169] M. de Boislisle and M. de Beaucorps have provided some information about the formation of the *généralités* of Paris[170] and Orléans.[171] M. Fourgeron has turned his attention to the *apanage* of Orléans.[172]

If we were to mark on the map of the Ile-de-France the boundaries of the various military, judicial, financial and strictly administrative districts covering this region in the last three centuries of the monarchy, or, more simply, up to a certain date—1789 for example—the pattern thus presented would take a great deal of deciphering. The criss-crossing of the lines and the strange courses followed by them would mirror pretty accurately the essential characteristics of administration under the *Ancien Régime*, which was singularly lacking in clarity and system. The institutions varied according to the particular locality. The rules laid down by the central power often remained without validity in the provinces, and sometimes were not even intended to be applied to them. Practice carried more weight than the theory of public law; it would indeed be a strange history of taxation that was modelled only upon royal decrees. To depict in such terms the administration under the absolute monarchy is another way of saying that only a series of regional studies can give us a faithful picture of this vast structure raised by so many generations of officials, with no general plan. Indeed, it is something much too complex and disparate for a general conspectus to be easily attainable. In no sphere is it more necessary and justifiable to limit one's research to a restricted territorial framework. And there is no point on which local output has been so unsatisfactory.

M. de Boislisle had formed a plan to publish, in the collection of *Documents inédits*, the *Mémoires des Intendants sur l'état des généralités, dressés pour l'instruction du duc de Bourgogne.* The *Mémoire de la généralité de Paris* is the only one so far to have appeared.[173] M. de Boislisle has prefaced the text with a useful introduction, containing, along with information on the geography of the *généralité*, a list of the *intendants*.[174] But no one has studied the work of these *intendants*. On the administration of three successive *intendants* from 1686 to 1713—MM. de Creil, Jubert de Bouville and de la Bourdonnaye—M. Charles de Beaucorps has written a conscientious and substantial memoir.[175] These *intendants*, who were really royal factotums, were called on to deal one after another with an infinite variety of subjects. Their actions extended over an almost unlimited field, and the scholar who would seek to follow their every footstep and to describe minutely their multifarious duties would merely be distracted and lose his way in a maze of detail. It would be better to concentrate on one regional study of an institution rather than the history of a particular administrator. The organization of public assistance in the *généralités* of Paris and Orléans and their neighbours has formed the subject-matter of an important book by M. Camille Bloch, throwing a new light not only on the administrative history of the *Ancien Régime*, but even on that of the Revolution. It shows once again that we shall only understand the Revolution when we have obtained accurate knowledge of eighteenth-century institutions.[176] No research has so far been carried out on seigniorial justice and its decline, or on the organization of the royal courts. M. Lucien Merlet and M. Arsène Defresne have collected some documents on the societies formed by inhabitants in the boroughs and villages of le Dunois[177] and the district round Versailles.[178] The municipal records of Pontoise from 1608 to 1683 have been published by M. Ernest Mallet.[179] But there is no good study of municipal life.

All this obviously does not amount to very much. Where are we to look for the causes of such a deplorable dearth of literary effort? It cannot be the state of the documents, for they are there in abundance. Perhaps we should seek them in the apparently arid nature of work on administrative history, though its high value must be apparent to anyone who is attempting to understand the formation of the French State. But these causes lie perhaps above all in the intolerable difficulties created by the absence of any convenient work of reference on the institutions of the *Ancien Régime*, difficulties that are constantly felt by all local research-workers. Up till now no scholar has given us a manual on these institutions comparable to the innumerable précis compendia bearing upon classical antiquity, or to M. Luchaire's book on the Middle Ages. As long as this lacuna, without doubt the most serious one in our historical writings, remains unfilled, the regional study of French administration will probably remain more or less unexplored territory. Some general treatment is an essential preliminary for detailed study, though this in its turn will soon render it out of date.

In 1787 the king's government set on foot a kind of national consultation organized, no doubt, in order to make it unnecessary to convoke the Estates General, though it proved in fact to be only a prelude to this step. Parochial, district and provincial assemblies met in the Ile-de-France and throughout the kingdom. It is of importance that we should know how they worked, what they undertook, and what exertions they made. They were a prelude to the Revolution. The parochial assemblies

of the *généralité* of Orleans, the provincial assembly of
Melun (that is to say, the *généralité* of Paris) and the
provincial assembly of Orléans, have all been studied by
MM. Camille Bloch,[180] Auberge,[181] Fernand Bournon[182]
and Henry Fromont.[183]

Next came the great popular consultation of 1789, the
record[184] of which is contained in the '*cahiers de doléances*'.
Some of the *cahiers* of the Ile-de-France have been lost;
others still in existence remain unpublished; others again,
though printed, have only been partially reprinted—such
as the lists from the *prévôté* and *vicomté* of Paris-outside-
the-walls, most of which can only be read in volumes IV
and V of the *Archives Parlementaires*, a collection that has
justly acquired a poor reputation.[185] On the other hand
we possess excellent editions of the *cahiers* from the
bailliages of Versailles, Meudon,[186] Étampes,[187] Montford-
l'Amaury,[188] Orléans[189] and Pontoise.[190] But printing
the *cahiers* is not the end of the matter: before they can be
used they need some critical background, some attempt
to determine the circumstances in which they were drawn
up and to examine their connections. M. Adalbert Wahl
has examined the parochial *cahiers* of Paris-outside-the-
walls from this point of view. But his memoir, though
giving some useful information, is marred by the violently
anti-revolutionary tone which runs through all his
works.[191] The observations put together by MM.
Legrand and Marquis and M. Camille Bloch in the intro-
ductions to their editions of the *cahiers* of Étampes and
Orléans are extremely accurate.

The Constituent Assembly broke up the administrative
framework of the *Ancien Régime* and created the *départements*. How, on what principles, and after what compro-
mises were these new districts fixed? How were their
capitals and the district capitals chosen? It is not without
interest to seek the answers to such questions, even if the

detailed history of the constitution of *départements* often becomes confused with the not very important history of local rivalries. M. Fernand Bournon has studied the formation of the *département* of Paris, which in 1795 became the *département* of the Seine;[192] and M. Lhuillier has studied the formation of Seine-et-Marne.[193]

The most striking scenes of the revolutionary drama were enacted in Paris. But we shall not understand the Revolution and the course that it took, strange though it may sometimes appear, until we come to know with extreme accuracy how opinion moved in the *départements*, and how Paris reacted on the provinces and the provinces on Paris. There have been a few monographs of rather restricted scope to prepare the material for the historian who will undertake the tracing of the political vicissitudes of the Ile-de-France in the revolutionary period. Some of the municipal records have been published, or analysed.[194] The Melun[195] and Fontainebleau[196] clubs, and the watch-committee of Melun[197] have provided the theme for useful works. Histories of Versailles,[198] Meulan,[199] Longjumeau[200] and Villiers-le-Bel[201] during the revolutionary period have already been written. M. Tambour has studied the departmental administration of the Seine-et-Oise[202] and M. Lhuiller (in a book of indifferent quality) the work done by the members of the Convention who were sent on a mission to the Seine-et-Marne.[203] The risings provoked by the feudal question and by the dearness of food have been the subject of some articles.[204] On the insecurity of conditions in the countryside, there is a small book by M. Coudray-Maunier—to be consulted with some caution—about the appalling exploits of the highwaymen of Orgères.[205] Neither the elections, nor the plebiscites, nor the religious struggle, have been the subject of any serious research. In short, not a single one of the great problems raised by the history of the Revolution in the provinces has been tackled directly in the Ile-de-France, or treated at all fully. The outstanding events of the revolutionary period, such as the taking of the Bastille, the flight of the king, the uprising of 10 August, the September massacres, the king's trial, the tragedies of the Convention's rule, the *coup d'état* of the Directory, the eighteenth Brumaire—what did these mean to the country-side and the little towns? How did they receive them? What were the feelings of the Ile-de-France about the widespread fear, the mass risings, the attack on Christianity, the Terror, the Thermidorian reaction? What share did the various social classes have in the work of Revolution, and in its different phases, or in the counter-Revolution? These are questions to which the scholars engaged on the story of the Ile-de-France under the Revolution will one day find an answer, provided they do not confine their efforts too narrowly to a single town or a single village, but give their studies a certain breadth and consider the episodes in revolutionary history not so much in terms of their anecdotal or purely local interest, but rather for their national significance.

The political history of the nineteenth century has been neglected by scholars in the Ile-de-France. Some books on the administrative work of the *conseils généraux* of the Seine[206] and the Seine-et-Marne,[207] an article on *Les Élections à la Constituante de 1848, dans le Loiret*,[208] are about all that are worth referring to on this point. No one has made a study of the local press. In short, we know nothing of the lines along which public opinion moved in our region from the First Empire onwards.

We are poorly informed about the Ile-de-France's intellectual history in modern and contemporary times. A few research-workers have turned their attention to the printing-presses at Meaux,[209] Melun,[210] Étampes[211] and Châteaudun.[212] Scholars have shown little interest in societies of the intelligentsia who undoubtedly held their meetings in our towns, or in the local theatres, or in local literary fashions. There are few notable studies on education.[213] There is an amusing book from the pen of M. J. M. Garnier on popular imagery and songs,[214] and on the subject of country tales, a work by M. Chapiseau dealing with the folklore of Beauce.[215]

The economic habits of the agricultural population vary from place to place. Differences of soil and climate bring about differences of make-up in the social grouping. Peasants, who in a general way are not fond of new customs or foreign ways (and the word 'foreign' describes things that are only a short distance from one's own parish), are in many respects governed—and used to be governed still more—by traditional custom, peculiar to each region or even to each village. Our ancient documents often spoke of the 'custom of the country', *consuetudo patrie*, as the Latin charters phrase it. The '*pays*' as understood by these texts often means the village. The history of the countryside, inextricably bound up with the changing soils of our regions and with peasant society, which was subdivided into a whole number of very individual societies, stands to gain more from local studies than any other branch of history; and the truth is that it can only make progress by drawing upon their assistance.

When we attempt to compare the economic conditions of two agrarian groups before the time when the metric system was introduced into the country (and even today it can hardly be said to be the master system) we meet with an obstacle, and sometimes an insurmountable one, at the very outset. Each district and often each village had its own agrarian measures—its *arpent*, its *journal*, its *sétérée*; and the measures applicable to crops varied in the same manner. Add to this the fact that both of these no doubt became modified in the course of time, so that it is extremely difficult to compare the state of property in one and the same village at two different periods. When the native system was introduced most of the *départements* drew up tables showing the equivalence between the ancient local measures and the new national ones.[216] It will be of advantage to historians to consult them, and likewise the similar tables ordinarily included in the collections of local customs compiled in the nineteenth century. More valuable still will be the researches conducted in a strictly scholarly spirit by M. Thoison on the ancient measures of Gâtinais,[217] and by M. Leroy on those of Brie.[218] These works on measures, many more of which are needed, are like dictionaries—absolutely indispensable for anyone who wishes to decipher the language of rural history. Seeing the state of the documents, we must resign ourselves to having imperfect dictionaries, and recognize the inevitable uncertainty of agrarian statistics dealing with a somewhat remote past.

The importance of the forests in the rural geography of the Ile-de-France is a salient fact; and the history of assarting and of the chase has something picturesque about it which seems to attract research-workers. Most of our forests[219] have been subject of special study: the forest of Orléans;[220] the forest of Fontainebleau;[221] the bois de Rouvray, which later became the bois de Boulogne;[222] the forest of Artie in Vexin;[223] and the wooded *massifs* which border on the French plateau to the north[224] and to the east;[225] and that forest of 'Maant', which used in former times to stretch with its huge thickets from the Marne to the Grand Morin.[226] Much reduced today by clearance, it has even lost its true name, which the rather too fanciful cartographers employed by the Army Geographical Service have changed into the *forêt de Mans*. The forest of Iveline has not so far had its historian.

Solid research into the techniques of agriculture is the

necessary basis for any study of the rural economy. There is some useful information on the seventeenth and eighteenth centuries in 'Recherches historiques sur l'agriculture dans le département de Seine-et-Marne', by M. Leroy,[227] and in *Lectures sur l'histoire de l'agriculture dans le département de Seine-et-Marne*, by abbé Denis.[228] But the great revolution that came about from the eighteenth century onwards in agricultural techniques through the introduction of industrial crops, the growing of fodder-crops, and the suppression of bare fallows, has not received the attention it deserves. Since men first began to work the land, there has certainly been no greater change in the exploitation of the soil, for in the regions usually practising a three-course system (as the Ile-de-France did) it liberated a third of the cultivated area every year from the traditional obligation of lying fallow. This appears to be a fairly slow change. The *Traité des prairies artificielles dans la Généralité de Paris*, by Gilbert, which appeared in 1789,[229] shows that in the region round Paris the bare fallow had begun to disappear at the end of the eighteenth century. But there is other evidence, particularly in the most ancient *Usages locaux*, that goes to prove the survival of the old ways far into the nineteenth century.[230] These *Usages locaux*, originally private collections, but now almost all official, are a first-class source for local history. It is well known that in the absence of any stipulation to the contrary they were of binding force between the parties for the interpretation of farming contracts; moreover they contain information about the local farming rules, such as the form of vineyard leases, rights of common grazing, etc. A search through the different editions will show the changes that have taken place in the economic life of the countryside. It is important that a list of these should be drawn up, but this is a difficult task, which has not so far been taken in hand. The reader will find in a note an attempt at a bibliography on the *Usages locaux* of the Ile-de-France; its imperfections will I think be excused by anyone who has tried to collect information about studies of this kind.[231] The state of agriculture in our region since the second half of the nineteenth century has been the subject of some useful memoirs: the 'Culture de la Beauce' by M. Boutet,[232] the *Étude sur l'économie rurale du département de Seine-et-Marne* by M. Rayer,[233] the *Monographie agricole du département d'Eure-et-Loir* by M. Roussille.[234] The review *Pages Libres* has devoted a number to the description of a Briard village, Voulangis, in the Grand Morin valley.[235] It will be found full of valuable information. But all these essays are much too brief to exhaust the available material. One of the curious features of Beauceron agriculture at the end of the nineteenth century was the survival of common grazing, which had been abolished by this time over the greater part of France.[236] The majority of communes in Beauce, taking advantage of the freedom given them in this matter by the laws of 9 July 1889 and 22 June 1890, maintained this right in their territory. What were the reasons for their action? Have they upheld this decision to the present day? Thorough research on these points would make an interesting contribution to our knowledge of the Beauceron economy.

To whom did the soil of the Ile-de-France belong in the last centuries under the monarchy? And in what proportions was it divided between the various social classes? What kind of cultivation prevailed—large-scale, small-scale, or medium? These questions are difficult even to formulate and difficult to answer; and no one has so far examined them. How are we to distinguish the different social classes and the different scales on which cultivation was carried out? And as for the word 'property', it leads to many confusions when applied to a period in which the feudal system still survived. An exclusively statistical method would not yield sufficiently clear results on this particular point. But by adding to the data from the tax-registers[237] information drawn from the collections of archives—a very rich source left to us by the ecclesiastical and even lay lords—and by extending research beyond the period immediately before 1789, and including a period long enough to allow us to trace a whole line of development, it ought to be possible to write an important book on the state of rural property under the *Ancien Régime* in the country round about Paris.

As long as such a book does not exist we shall not be able to make an accurate assessment of the economic upheaval caused by the Revolution in our region through the sale of national property and the enclosure of the common land. M. Boris Minres[238] has written a small book on the sale of national property in the Seine-et-Oise. This is a useful and conscientious piece of work, and one of the oldest devoted to this kind of question. It should be carried on and completed so as to take in the other *départements* in the Ile-de-France. The enclosure of the common land seems to have been particularly ruthless in our *départements*, for it almost completely disappeared.[239] There are a few detailed works on this subject, but no inclusive study of the whole.[240] As for the régime of private property in the nineteenth and twentieth centuries and the transformation of the Parisian suburbs by the extension of private property belonging to city-dwellers and by market gardening, and the slow extension of capitalist methods over the cultivation of the land, no one seems to have been attracted to going into these questions.

How could they make sure of being able to feed the hundreds of thousands, and then the millions who were crowding within the walls of Paris and into its suburbs? Here was a problem that haunted governments under the *Ancien Régime*, in the Revolution and in later days. The cornlands of the Ile-de-France were some of the first to be pressed into service. A thorough study of the feeding of Paris would therefore certainly throw new light upon the economic history of the Ile-de-France. The scholar undertaking it will find material collected in some articles on the trade in grain and the legislation governing it in our region under the *Ancien Régime* and during the Revolutionary period.[241] It will be to his advantage to consult the only too scanty works we possess on the roads and waterways—*Les routes de Seine-et-Marne avant 1789* by M. Hugues,[242] the *Recherches* of M. Bourgeois *sur le port d'Étampes*,[243] and M. Paul Pinson's work on the navigation of the Huine and the Essonne;[244] also the book in which M. Guilmoto has enumerated the tolls on the Seine downstream from Paris.[245]

As for the history of industry in the region that concerns us, practically nothing has so far been written about it. Apart from two articles on the paper works of Essonnes,[246] I can find nothing worth referring to on the formation, organization and development of those groups of factories whose tall chimneys often constituted a new feature in the nineteenth-century landscape of the Ile-de-France. The popularity of economic history as a subject of study, which is so noticeable among certain historians, has hardly influenced those among whom the majority of students of local history are recruited. It is strange that these studies have practically no place in the periodicals published by the learned societies in our *départements*. This neglect is all the more tiresome because economic, and more especially industrial, history would provide local researchers with a large number of interesting subjects which would not suffer at all from being treated in a restricted territorial framework. Such people, moreover, would probably find it easier than researchers coming from outside to gain access to private records of industrial firms where so many treasures lie hidden. A history of some of the large factories, if handled by a writer conversant with the concepts of economic history and sociology, and used to their methods of classification, would be a most valuable contribution to our knowledge of French capitalism.

A Benedictine whose name I have mentioned several times, dom Charles Toussaint-Duplessis, devoted the preface of his *Histoire de la Ville et des Seigneurs de Coucy*[1] to a defence under three heads of *les histoires particulières*,[2] that is to say, historical monographs, especially on local history. Though it was no doubt useful at the time when it was written, this plea seems unnecessary today. 'Local histories' have long ago won their case, and I shall not rise up to defend them. But from the long examination of local history that we have undertaken, certain lessons would seem to stand out.

Dom Toussaint-Duplessis wrote: 'A general history might be defined as a genuine summary of all histories' (that is to say, all 'local' histories). This is an exaggeration. To put together a number of summaries of specialized monographs would never produce a synthesis. The examination of a problem in all its aspects produces a quite different result from that achieved by cutting it up into a series of little local problems. Not until we are in possession of a succession of studies on feudalism covering all regions of France, or better still the whole of western Europe, shall we be in a position to know what the feudal system really was; but even then our knowledge will not be complete. We shall still have to co-ordinate and compare the results of these enquiries, recognize the likenesses, explain and reject the anomalies, and discern the essential facts among the infinite number of regional varieties. And this will be no small task. Local history does not make the study of larger subjects so easy that it is thereby rendered almost unnecessary; on the contrary, it alone makes the study of more general problems possible, and that is saying a great deal. Scholars who are giving their time to it are preparing material for a work which transcends their own contributions. If they do not want their efforts to be wasted, if they wish for the stones they contribute to find their proper place in the building to which they belong, they must have this building in mind from the start. They will do well when choosing their subject and defining its limits to ask themselves: how can I make the most effective contribution to general history? In short, a good local history may be defined as follows: it is a question of general scope put to documents of a particular region.[3] The question will be provided by general history; or at any rate it will produce a provisional question which will not fail to undergo some modification as it comes face to face with the documentary evidence. But how are the territorial boundaries to be determined? This business of laying down limits is always extremely delicate, and in the case of the Ile-de-France it is fraught with peculiar difficulties.

Specialist articles have been published on the past history of the Ile-de-France, political, economic and artistic. But it is very significant that no history of the Ile-de-France has ever been written.[4] One may well hope that none ever will be. The composition of a provincial history is only a legitimate undertaking if the province in question has formed down the ages a coherent social entity, distinct from and even hostile to its neighbours, enclosed within more or less stable frontiers, and conscious in some fashion of its unity. Such is the case for certain regions that once used to be almost independent states. When they subsequently became French, they still kept traces of their former autonomy in their political organization as well as in their customs. Such were Franche-Comté, Lorraine, Brittany, or even Normandy. The Ile-de-France on the other hand emerged from a state of feudal fragmentation only to be swallowed up in the unity of France. The streets of Nancy and Besançon have often re-echoed with shouts of 'Long live Lorraine', or 'Long live Burgundy!', but who ever shouted 'Long live the Ile-de-France!'? The name 'Ile-de-France' is comparatively recent. As we have seen, it was first applied to the small area between the Seine, the Marne and the Oise and only came to be applied to the region round Paris as a whole by a piece of administrative misinterpretation. The old name 'France' was a vague designation for the region to the north of the Loire; and its domain was either extended or restricted according to the changes and chances of politics. It is often convenient—as we have found here—to group the regions round Paris under the name Ile-de-France. But the Ile-de-France has no real regional unity; it does not offer any precise boundaries which the historian has to treat seriously.

Some of the regions that go to make up the Ile-de-France—Beauce or Brie for example—have a decided individuality of their own. But alongside them there are fairly extensive territories—such as the area extending to the south of the Seine as far as Beauce—which have no specific characteristics, and have no names distinguishing them from the adjoining regions. And then our *pays*, even the most distinctive of them, owe their original character entirely to their soil and to the conditions that it imposes on their economic, or rather on their agrarian, life. One can imagine a history of the agriculture of Beauce being written but one can hardly imagine a religious or political history of Beauce. It should also be added that Beauce has specialized in a form of agriculture which does not enable it to feed its own inhabitants; its economic life is dependent on the surrounding areas, so that it would be difficult to study it in isolation. In short, the *pays* hardly ever offers a convenient framework for historical research.

The frontiers of administrative and religious divisions are usually fairly clear-cut. This is no doubt why historians have often chosen them as the boundaries of their work. A collection has been made of documents on the Knights Templar in the Eure-et-Loir. The conjunction of the two terms makes us smile. But after all this is an innocent enough oddity for we are only dealing with a collection of texts. Someone has written on the agriculture of Seine-et-Marne, before and after 1789. Here, the mistake is more serious, even as regards the post-revolutionary period. For the Seine-et-Marne comprises very varied agricultural districts, none of which falls completely within the *département*. The *généralités*, the *départements* and the dioceses were all fixed in too arbitrary a manner for them to afford a convenient frame of reference for historians in general.

We noticed at the outset of this study that each discipline uses the word 'Ile-de-France' in a different sense. For the linguist the Ile-de-France is not the same as for the archaeologist, nor is it the same as that described in geological textbooks. At first sight this diversity of usage is surprising. But a little reflection will show that it is both legitimate and necessary. The bounds of any field of observation must needs vary with the object that the scholar is observing. Why should one expect the jurist who is interested in feudalism, the economist who is studying the evolution of property in the countryside in modern times, and the philologist who is working on popular dialects, all to stop at precisely identical frontiers?

There is no one regional framework ready-made to suit all historians, whatever their branch of study. According to the nature of their subject all scholars must be prepared to carve out their own regions, and they will in every case be different.

Notes

chapter one

1 *Les Régions de la France*, IX, *L'Ile-de-France*, '*Bibliothèque de Synthèse historique*', Paris, 1913, 136 pp.

2 For the history of the names, France and Ile-de-France, the essential works are the three following memoirs: Benjamin Guérard, 'Du nom de France et des différents pays auxquels il fut appliqué' in *Annuaire de la Soc. de l'Hist. de France pour 1849*, pp. 152–68; A. Longnon, 'L'Ile-de-France, son origine, ses limites, ses gouverneurs', in *Mém. de la Soc. de l'Hist. de Paris*, vol. I, 1875, pp. 1–43, with map; Lucien Gallon, 'Une region naturelle française, Le Pays de France', in *Atti Cong. Intern di Scienze Storiche*, vol. X, Rome, 1904, pp. 19–24, an article reprinted in the same author's book—*Régions naturelles et Noms de Pays. Étude sur la région parisienne*, 8vo, Paris, 1908, pp. 180–92, ch. IX: 'La France, le Parisis'. Equally well worth consulting are A. de Valesio, *Notitia Galliarum*, folio, Paris, 1675, pp. 200–208; Félix Bourquelot, 'Sens des mots France et Neustrie sous le régime mérovingien', in *Bibl. de l'Éc. des Chartres*, 6th series, vol. I, 26th year, 1865, pp. 566–74; A. Longnon, *Géographie de la Gaule au VIe siècle*, 8vo, Paris, 1878, pp. 192–3, and *Atlas historique de la France, Texte explicatif*, large 8vo, Paris, 1907, p. 48; Pauly-Wissowa, *Real-Encyclopädie der classischen Altertumswissenschaft*, on the word 'Franci' (vol. VII, pp. 82–7); Louis Halphen,'La royauté française au XIe siècle d'après un ouvrage récent', *in Revue histor.*, vol. LXXXV, May–August 1904, pp. 275–87; *Œuvres de Froissart*, ed. Kervyn de Lettenhove, *Chroniques*, vol. XXIV, 8vo, Brussels, 1877, p. 319. Also to be consulted are the works relating to the problem of the 'Duchy of France', referred to below, Chapter One, note 6. I am greatly indebted for my study on *Le nom de l'Ile-de-France* to the memoirs of M. Longnon and M. Gallois, to which the reader is referred whenever he does not find a specific indication at the foot of the page. All the same I have felt bound to differ from them on several points. An essential task, for anyone seeking to find a definitive solution to this difficult problem of the history of the name 'France', would be to discover and above all to classify the medieval texts in which this name appears. The *Table des noms propres de toute nature compris dans les Chansons de Geste imprimées* drawn up by M. Ernest Langlois (8vo, Paris, 1904) would be of very great service to anyone willing to undertake this work.

3 *Monachi Sangallensis de gestis Karoli imperatoris libri duo*, Pertz, *Scriptor*, II, p. 735, 11: 'Franciam vero interdum cum nominavero omnes cisalpinas provincias significo'.

4 *In gloria confessorum*, c. 40, ed. Arndt, *Mon. Germ. histor. Script. rev. germ.*, vol. I, p. 773.

5 *Hist. Francor.* Book IV, c. 14, ed. Arndt, p. 151.

6 Some have imagined that France (in the restricted sense) formed at one moment in the tenth century a territorial duchy, analogous to the duchies of Burgundy and Aquitaine and to the German duchies; and two members of the Robertian family, Hugh the Great and Hugh Capet, are said to have been invested with the duchy of France. Among modern historians, the chief author to uphold this thesis is Pfister in his *Études sur le règne de Robert le Pieux*, 8vo, Paris, 1885, Book II, ch. 11, 'Le duché de Francia'. But several historians give a different explanation of the title *dux Francorum* attributed in certain texts to Hugh the Great and to Hugh Capet; they take it to be the expression of a kind of vice-regal authority over the kingdom as a whole. This opinion has been upheld in particular by A. de Barthélemy, 'Les origines de la maison de France', in *Rev. des quest. histor.*, vol. XIII, 1873, pp. 108–44; by Luchaire, *Histoire des institutions monarchiques de la France sous les premiers Capétiens*, 2nd ed., 8vo, Paris, 1881, vol. I, p. 13, and by M. F. Lot, *Les Derniers Carolingians*, 8vo, Paris, 1891, p. 173, note 4. The thesis developed by M. J. Flach in vol. III of his *Origines de l'Ancienne France*, 8vo, Paris, 1904, is too complex to be summarized here; it has been attacked by M. Halphen in the article quoted in Chapter One, note 2.

7 *Liber de illatione S. Benedicti, Aurelianis Floriacum, Hist. de France*, vol. IX, p. 143.

8 Ed. de Certain (*Public. de la Soc. de l'Hist. de France*), 8vo, Paris, 1858, p. 148.

9 *Recueil des Actes de Philippe Ier* (*Hist. de France*, new series), p. 410.

10 *La vie de saint Thomas le Martyr, archevêque de Canterbury*, ed. by C. Hippeau, 8vo, 1859 (*Collection des poètes français du Moyen Age*, I), p. 205, line 5820.

11 *Hist. de France*, vol. XXII, pp. 623–73. Cf. Borrelli de Serres, *Recherches sur divers services publics*, 8vo, Paris, 1895, pp. 26–9.

12 Of course it does sometimes happen that the term '*coutume de France*' refers to the legal customs of the kingdom as a whole. The context makes it clear whether it is to be understood in the wide or the restricted sense.

13 Ed. Salmon, vol. II (*Collect. de textes pour servir à l'enseignement de l'histoire*), 8vo, Paris, 1900, § 1780, p. 403.

14 See the *Table alphabétique des lieux régis par la coutume de Paris*, in *Le Nouveau Coutumier Général* of Bourdot de Richebourg, vol. III, folio, Paris, 1724, pp. 88–92.

15 I have not been able to procure the work by Servais *La Neustrie sous les Merovingiens*, Turin, 1889.

16 For these words *Hérupe* and *Hurepoix* see (besides the memoir by M. Longnon quoted in Chapter One, note 2, and the *Table des noms propres* by M. E. Langlois) L. Gallois, *Régions naturelles et Noms de Pays*, ch. 4, pp. 83–100, and Otto Rohnström, *Étude sur Jean Bodel* (Fac. Lettres Uppsala), 8vo, Uppsala, 1900, pp. 111ff.

17 Doublet, *Histoire de l'abbaye de Saint-Denys-en-France*, 4to, Paris, 1625, p. 901 (cf. d'Arbois de Jubainville, *Histoire des ducs et comtes de Champagne*, vol. V, 8vo, Paris, 1863, p. 230, no. 1711). I must warn the reader that my search was confined to the printed texts, and is consequently very incomplete.

18 Doublet, p. 560.

19 Doublet, p. 907. Cf. Jean Cordey, 'Guillaume de Massouris, abbé de Saint-Denis', in *Troisièmes mélanges d'histoire du Moyen age publiés sous la direction de M. Luchaire*, 8vo, Paris, 1904, p. 237, no. 120. The expression only appears on the abbots' seals from the time of Matthieu de Vendôme, in 1275 (*Archives de l'Empire*, a collection of seals by Douët d'Arcq, vol. III, 4to, Paris, 1868, p. 126, no. 9022).

20 The first opinion is that of the editor of the poem; ed. Koschwitz, *Karls des Grossen Reise nach Jerusalem und Constantinopel*, 3rd ed., 12mo, Leipzig, 1895; and it was shared by G. Paris, *La Poésie du Moyen Age*, first series, 6th ed., 16mo, Paris, 1906, pp. 119ff. and p. 257; and *Romania*, vol. IX (1880), p. 50. The second theory has been supported by M. J. Coulet, *Étude sur l'ancien poème français du voyage de Charlemagne en orient* (thèse Fac. Lettres Paris, 8vo, Montpellier, 1907).

21 Line 86, p. 6, 'Saint-Dynis de France' is likewise used for the name of the abbey in a little poem known as *La Destruction de Rome*, which was added towards the end of the twelfth century as a prologue to the longer poem of *Fierabras* (ed. Groeber, *Romania*, vol. XXX, pp. 161–75). It will be noticed that the *Fierabras*, like the *Voyage de Charlemagne* (of which the *Destruction de Rome* is, after all, only a part) is a poem in praise of the relics possessed by the abbey.

22 There are numerous examples in the *Table des noms propres* by E. Langlois.

23 Langlois' *Table des noms propres* only calls attention to the expression 'Saint-Denis en France' in *Les Enfances Ogier*, a poem from the end of the thirteenth century (ed. A. Scheller, 8vo, Brussels, 1874, p. 2, 40) and in a sort of preamble in a manuscript of the fifteenth century to the poem *Doon de Mayence* (ed. A. Pey, in the collection *Les Anciens Poètes de la France*, 16mo, Paris, 1859, p. 348). The expression 'Saint-Denis *en* France' is met with in the following texts, which are older: *Fierabras*, a poem put together about 1170, probably inspired by the monks of Saint-Denis, ed. A. Kroeber and G. Servois (*Les anciens poètes de la France*), 12mo, Paris, 1860, p. 1, line 4 (a quotation which Langlois has omitted from his *Table des noms propres*); *les Enfances Guillaume*, an unpublished poem, which, in its

present known form, seems to go back to the beginning of the thirteenth century; a line quoted by Léon Gautier, *Les Épopées françaises*, 2nd ed., vol. IV, p. 201, 1, and p. 276, 1; *Renaud de Montauban*, the version contained in an Oxford MS., Douce 121, dating from the first half of the thirteenth century; a line quoted by J. Bédier, *Les légendes épiques*, vol. IV, p. 167, note 2; *Jehan de Lanson*, an unpublished poem composed in the thirteenth century; a line quoted by L. Gautier, *op. cit.*, vol. IV, p. 276, note 1. On the other hand Philippe Mousques in his *Chronique rimée*, composed in the first half of the thirteenth century and known in a manuscript belonging to the same century, writes (lines 9 and 10) 'Saint-Denise *de* France': Pertz, *Scriptor*, vol. XXVI, p. 721. Furthermore, is it possible to determine for certain which of these two expressions, 'Saint-Denis *de* France' or 'Saint-Denis *en* France', was used in the first place? I fear that the answer is in the negative. It is not enough to rely upon the age of these epic poems; we also have to consider the age of the manuscripts in which texts have been handed down. The fact that we read '*en* France' in a certain manuscript must not lead us to conclude that this was the original version, for the copyist may very well have changed *de* into *en*, either quite inadvertently, or because—consciously or not—he was substituting for an outmoded form the form that was normally used in his own day. The opposite error may equally well have crept in. We should only have a right to affirm the priority of the expression '*de* France' over '*en* France' if the former had come down to us in the most ancient poems and in the most ancient manuscripts. But this is far from being the case. The oldest manuscript of the *Voyage de Charlemagne* (which has *de* France) does not go back earlier than the end of the thirteenth century, whilst the Oxford manuscript of *Renaud de Montauban*, where the form *en* France occurs, dates from the beginning of the same century; moreover it is quite certain that the version of *Renaud* contained in this manuscript was drawn up well after the *Voyage de Charlemagne*. In the present state of our knowledge the small problem of nomenclature presented by the expressions 'Saint-Denis *de* France' and 'Saint Denis *en* France' remains insoluble. The word 'France' was still sometimes applied in the sixteenth century to the left bank of the Seine, as is shown by the text referring to Montlhéry quoted below in Chapter Four, note 144.

24 Examples quoted by Longnon, *L'Ile-de-France*, p. 16.

25 '*Τὴν καλουμένην νῆσον*', Polybius, III, 49, 5–7. Cf. Livy, XXI, 31, 4. This 'island' has sometimes been identified with the promontory that separates the Rhone from the Saône, above their point of confluence. On the theories arising out of these texts from Polybius and Livy, cf. Jullian, *Histoire de la Gaule*, vol. 1, 8vo, Paris, 1908, p. 474, note 3. Wherever one locates the territory 'called an island', it seems certain that it was what we should nowadays call a peninsula.

26 Ed. Kervyn de Lettenhove, vol. XII, 8vo, Brussels, 1871, p. 67.

27 Quoted by Monstrelet, ed. Douët d'Arcq (*Soc. de l'histoire de France*),

vol. IV, 8vo, Paris, 1860, p. 342. Cf. a letter of the Duke of Guyenne's in 1411, analysed by Monstrelet, vol. II, 1858, p. 171.

28 Quoted by Longnon, *L'Ile-de-France*, p. 30.

29 On the *gouvernement* of the Ile-de-France, consult Longnon, *L'Ile-de-France* and Armand Brette, *Recueil de documents relatifs à la convocation des États généraux de 1789*, (*Collect. des Doc. inédits*), vol. I, 4to, Paris, 1894, pp. 378–81.

30 In the memoir quoted above.

31 For the boundaries of Picardy and the characteristics of this region, cf.—besides Longnon, *L'Ile de France*—Vidal de la Blache, *Tableau de la géographie de la France* (Lavisse, *Hist. de France*, I, 1), pp. 98–9, and A. Demangeon, *La Plaine Picarde* (thèse Fac. Lettres Paris), 8vo, Paris, 1905, 496 pp. The dioceses of Beauvais, Noyon and Laon (not indeed Senlis) were included in what was called the Picard 'nation' at the University of Paris. It will be observed that in the twelfth century Garnier de Pont-Sainte-Maxence, who was born to the north of Senlis, nevertheless considered himself as having been born in 'France'. In the absence of any serious study on the linguistic geography of Picardy and the Ile-de-France, this anomaly must remain unresolved.

32 Longnon, *L'Ile-de-France*, p. 19, note 3.

33 P. 447.

34 And to that of le Boulonnais, which formed a *gouvernement* by itself.

35 *Bullet. Soc. hist. Paris*, vol. I, 1874, p. 36.

36 Paris has often had a governor distinct from that of the Ile-de-France; but it has always been the capital of the Ile-de-France.

37 Cf. *Cahier du Tiers-État d'Auxerre*, quoted by Armand Brette, *Atlas des bailliages ou jurisdictions assimilées ayant formé unité électorale en 1789 . . .* folio, 1904 (*Doc. inédits*), Introd., p. xvi.

38 Cf. the two volumes entitled: *Procès-verbal des séances de l'assemblée provinciale de l'Isle-de-France tenue à Melun dans le mois d'août 1787*, 4to, Paris, Imprimerie Royale, 1787, 67 pp.; and *Procès verbal des séances de l'assemblée provinciale de l'Isle-de-France tenues à Melun en novembre et décembre 1787*, 4to, Sens and Paris, 1788, LXXXIV, 452 pp. The volume referred to in the second place contains, at the same time as the reports of proceedings at the November and December sessions, the reports of proceedings for the August sessions, which are contained on their own in the volume first referred to above. The '*Règlement fait par le roi*' (8 July 1787) will be found on p. XIII of the volume published in 1787. For the use of the word 'province' in the sense of '*généralité*', consult: Jacques Soyer, 'Le mot "province" employé comme synonyme de généralité au XVIIIe siècle', in *Bull. soc. arch. de l'Orléanais*, vol. XV (1908), pp. 98–100.

39 *Procès-verbal des séances*, edit. of 1787, p. 12.

40 In the popular usage of the Middle Ages, the word Ile-de-France must sometimes have carried a linguistic connotation. It was customary,

no doubt, to contrast under the name of 'France' the countries using the 'French' language with those using Picard or Norman. A study of the dialect of the Ile-de-France has not yet been undertaken (cf. Chapter One, note 31).

41 The most important work today on the geology of the Ile-de-France is the one by M. Paul Lemoine, *Géologie du bassin de Paris*, 8vo, Paris, 1911, 11 + 408 pp. It is unfortunately a collection of material rather than a real synthesis. It contains an abundant bibliography with almost 800 entries (pp. 349–77). See also St Meunier, *Géologie des environs de Paris*, 8vo, Paris, 1912, 540 pp. The work by Gallois, *Régions naturelles et Noms de Pays*, quoted in Chapter One, note 2, is the essential book to be consulted by anyone interested in the geography of the region round Paris. May I be allowed to say at this point how much I owe to Gallois, both to his book and to his teaching. Reference should also be made to the pages devoted by Vidal de la Blache to the Ile-de-France in his *Tableau de la Géographie de la France* (pp. 124–49). The book by A. de Lapparent, *La géologie en chemin-de-fer. Description géologique du Bassin Parisien et des régions adjacentes*, 18mo, although rather out-of-date, contains descriptions that are still worth reading. Cf. also Ardouin-Dumazet, *Voyage en France*, vols. XLII, XLIII, XLIV, XLV, XLVI, XLVII, 12mo, Paris, 1905–7.

On the whole, the Ile-de-France and the different districts included in it have up till now attracted very few geographers. The historian and the geographer would often do well to consult the ancient maps of the region on which they are working. In Gallois' book they will find a most valuable study of the *Progrès de la cartographie de la région parisienne jusqu'à la carte Cassini* (pp. 244–348; with illustrations). Cf. Léon Vallée, Bibliothèque Nationale, *Catalogue des plans de Paris et des cartes de l'Ile-de-France, de la généralité, de l'élection, de l'archevêché, de la vicomté, de l'université, du grenier à sel et de la cour des aides de Paris conservés à la section des cartes et plans*, and the following short accounts: L. Pannier, *Note sur les cartes et plans de Paris et de l'Ile-de-France exposés au Palais des Tuileries à l'occasion du congrès international des sciences géographiques de 1875, ibid.*, pp. 141–57; C. Constant, 'Souvenir du Congrès des sciences géographiques de Paris en 1875. Simple note sur les cartes et plans concernant l'arrondissement de Fontainebleau', *Bullet. soc. archeol. Seine-et-Marne*, vol. VIII (1875–7), pp. 105–9; E. Mareuse, *Bibliographie des Cartes et documents cartographiques, [du dép. de Seine-et-Oise], Confér. des Soc. sav. de Seine-et-Oise, Prem. réunion* (1902), 8vo, Versailles, 1903, pp. 105–18; G. Marcel, 'Un bénédictin géographe, Dom Guillaume Coutans', *Bullet. géogr. hist. et descript.*, 1888, pp. 27–36 and 330–1.

42 It goes without saying that I have no intention of ignoring the influence of tectonic phenomena on the region round Paris. Cf. Lemoine, *op. cit.*, pp. 32–49.

43 On the hydrography of Beauce, consult G. F. Dolfus, 'L'Eau en Beauce', *Bullet. des services de la carte géolog. de France*, vol. XVI (1904–5), no. 107, 46 pp., and Ernest Cord, 'L'Hydrologie en Beauce', *Confér. des*

Soc. sav. de Seine-et-Oise, Quatrième réunion (1908), 8vo, Étampes, 1909, pp. 192–5. The water table in Beauce appears to be subject to variation.

44 The presence of the limestone below the *limon* has a double advantage. In the first place, the limestone, being very permeable, drains the *limon* to some extent. In the second place, it provides on the spot a means of marling the *limon* and so improving its quality.

45 '*Belsia graniparis*', says a contemporary of Philip Augustus, Guillaume le Breton, in his *Philippide*, verse VI; see 330, p. 164 of vol. II of the Delaborde edition ('Oenores de Rigord et Guill. le Breton', *Public. de la Soc. de l'Hist. de France*), 8vo, Paris, 1885.

46 *Gargantua*, ch. XVI.

47 Cf. J. Devaux, 'Essai sur les premiers seigneurs de Pithiviers', *Annales Soc. histor. Gâtinais*, vol. III (1885), pp. 254–6, and F. Lot, 'Héloïse de Peviers, soeur de Garin le Lorrain', *Romania*, vol. XXVIII (1899), pp. 273–9.

48   *Belsia triste solum, cui desant bis tria solum :*
        Fontes, prata, nemus, lapides, arbusta, racemus.
The *Dictionnaire Joanne* attributes these two lines to Fortunat. There is no doubt that this is a confusion easily explained by the fact that Fortunat is the oldest writer in whose works the word Beauce occurs (*Vita S. Germani, c.* XLIX, ed. B. Krusch, *Mon. Germ. histor. Auctor, antiquissimi*, vol. IV, 2, 4to, Berlin, 1885, p. 22). The ancient form of the name Beauce appears to have been Belsa, not Balsia.

49 A. Holder, *Altceltischer Sprachsatz*, vol. I, 4to, Leipzig, 1896, p. 396. Cf. Gallois, *op. cit.*, p. 82, and Vidal de la Blache, *Séances et travaux de l'Acadèm. des Sciences Morales*, 1910, I, p. 113, note 1. Herm. Groehler, 'Über Ursprung und Bedeutung der französischen Ortsnamen' (*Samml. romanischen Elementar und Handbücher*, vol. I, 12mo, Heidelberg, 1913, p. 167), refuses to accept the etymology of *belsa*—'a grass plain'—given by the Gallo-Roman grammarian Virgile (cf. Holder, *loc. cit.*); he thinks that the word *belsa* originally meant not a region, but an inhabited place. But I cannot find any substantial proofs to support his opinion.

50 G. Fagniez, *Études sur l'industrie de la classe industrielle à Paris au XIIIᵉ siècle et au XIVᵉ siècle, Bibl. Éc. des Hautes Études*, section 33, 8vo, Paris, 1877, p. 154.

51 Abbé Bordas, in his *Histoire du Dunois*, written in the eighteenth century, speaks of 'the part of Dunois which is said to be situated in Perche *because of the fields surrounded by hedges*, or rather because of the forest of that name which stretched as far as this part' (édit. de la Soc. Dunoise, vol. I, 8vo, Châteaudun, 1884, p. 2). I should like to express my warm thanks to my friend René Musset for so kindly sending me a manuscript memoir on Perche.

52 On the meaning to be ascribed to this word 'forest', used in this sense by ancient texts to denote a country rich in trees, see below, pp. 24–5, for what is said about Brie.

53 I use the word Gâtinais here in the sense it has come to have in popular usage, that is to say, I apply it only to the plateaux on the left bank of the Loing. Its historical and political connotation was much wider. Cf. Gallois, *op. cit.*, p. 107. There is a useful description of Gâtinais in an article by J. Devaux, 'Introduction à l'histoire du Pithiverais', *Annales histor. Gâtinais*, vol. XXIII (1905), pp. 1–12.

54 Maxime Beauvilliers, 'Le Safran en Gâtinais', *Bullet. Soc. archéolog. Seine-et-Marne*, vol. VII (1873–4), pp. 303–32.

55 E. Thoison, 'La viticulture en Gâtinais', *Étude historique statistique*, *Bullet. Soc. agricult. arrond. Fontainebleau*, vol. XIII (1890), vol. XIV (1900).

56 On the left bank of the Seine the point where the limestone of Brie meets that of Beauce, which lies above it, is marked by a small escarpment whose slopes, facing east, are in their upper layers made of Beauce limestone, and in their lower layers made of sand or Fontainebleau gravel. This escarpment continues from la Ferté-Alais to the immediate outskirts of Paris. There is an isolated gravelly mound jutting out in front of it, above the valley of the Orge, on which the tower of Montlhéry is situated.

57 For these references, see Gallois, *op. cit.*, pp. 130–1. The name Brie appears in the seventh century, about the same time as the name Beauce. Cf. Holder, *Altceltischer Sprachschatz*, vol. I, p. 531.

58 Gallois, *op. cit.*, p. 129.

59 Some of the Brie forests—the forest of Senart among others—are on the beds of gravel brought down and deposited on the edges of the plateau by the rivers in early times.

60 H. d'Arbois de Jubainville, *Histoire des ducs et des comtes de Champagne*, vol. IV, 2nd part, 8vo, Paris, 1865, p. 864.

61 See above, pp. 9–11.

62 The bishopric of Meaux—the boundaries of which are perhaps in their broad lines identical with those of the Gallic 'city' of the *Meldi*—used to extend on both sides of this line of wooded hills.

63 In Chapter Four of this study I shall explain how, as a result of the Treaty of Saint-Clair-sur-Epte, the Vexin came to be divided into French Vexin and Norman Vexin.

64 Cf. Jules Sion, *Les Paysans de la Normandie Orientale* (thèse Fac. des Lettres de Paris), 8vo, Paris, 1908, p. 18.

65 I have borrowed this expression from the description given by Boileau of the small village of Haute-Ile (between Mantes and la Roche-Guyon) in his *Sixth Epistle*, line 5.

66 For the Ile-de-France rivers, the essential works are still the fine books by Belgrand, *Le Bassin parisien, La Seine aux âges anté-historiques* (*Collection de l'Histoire génér. de Paris*), CVI + 288 + 25 pp. and plans, and atlas, 4to, Paris, 1869, and *La Seine, Études hydrologiques*, 8vo, Paris, 1872, XI—623 pp. and atlas—where some interesting information will be found not only about hydrography, but also in a general way about the geography of the region round Paris. Cf. also A. de Préaudean, *Manuel hydrologique du*

Bassin de la Seine, 4to, Paris, 1884, 124 pp., maps and plans; Edm. Maillet, *Supplément au manuel hydrologique du Bassin de la Seine*, 4to, Paris, 1909, XIII + 56 pp. and plans; Lemoine, 'État actuel de nos connaissances sur l'Hydrometrie du bassin de la Seine', *Annales de Géogr.*, vol. II, 1911, pp. 26–45; L. Gallois, 'Sur la crue de la Seine de Janvier', 1910, *Annales de Géogr.*, vol. XX (1911), pp. 112–21. For a general view of the very extensive literature on the floods of 1910, I must refer the reader to the *Bibliographies Annuelles* of the *Annales de Géogr.*, 1910, no. 341, and 1911, no. 283B.

The history of the development of the hydrographic system for the Paris region is not yet at all clear. It is remarkable that the Beauceron rivers that flow towards the Seine flow against the general slope of the plateau. An episode from this history has been sketched in an all too brief note by G. Ramond and Paul Combes fils, 'Un intéressant phénomène de capture aux environs de Paris, la Bièvre, l'Yvette et l'Orge', *Assoc. franç. pour l'avancement des sciences, 35e session*, Lyons, 1906, *Notes et documents*, pp. 1204–6.

67 When one has oneself neither the time nor the necessary competence to make use of the documents provided by meteorological statistics, it is impossible to make anything but vague and general remarks about the climate of the Ile-de-France. For no monograph has been written on this climate. The work of J. Jaubert, *Climatologie de la région de Paris*, 8vo, Paris, 1898, only deals with Paris and its suburbs. The most useful information about the climate is still to be found in the works on hydrology quoted in the previous note.

68 This phrase is taken from the famous description of Lutetia by the Emperor Julian, *Misopogon*, 341B.

chapter two

1 Bonneval, Eure-et-Loir, *arrondissement* of Châteaudun.

2 The first part of the *Chronique de Bonneval* was published with a useful introduction by M. René Merlet, *Petite chronique de l'abbaye de Bonneval de 857 à 1050 environ*, 8vo, Chartres, 1890, 30 pp. For the second part, put together about the middle of the twelfth century, one must refer to the edition given in the *Histoire abrégée de l'abbaye de Saint-Florentin de Bonneval* des RR. PP. dom Jean Thiroux et dom Lambert, ed. V. Bigot, 8vo, Châteaudun, 1875, pp. LXVII–LXVIII.

3 Morigny, commune of Morigny—Champigny, Seine-et-Oise, canton of Étampes. The chronicle will be found in the Léon Mirot edition (*Collect. de textes pour servir à l'étude et à l'enseignement de l'histoire*), 8vo, Paris, 1909, XIX + 98 pp. For the editorial history of the chronicle, see the introduction there.

4 p. 1.

5 p. 64

6 Rouen, 1587, 56 sheets. The work was republished. *Les Antiquitez et Singularitez de la ville de Pontoise, réimpression de l'ouvrage de Noël Taillepied, édition revue et annotée sur les manuscrits des Archives de Pontoise, et collationnée sur l'imprimé de 1587*, by A. François, preceded by *Notice Biographique et Bibliographique sur l'Auteur*, by Henri Le Charpentier, 8vo, Paris and Pointoise, 1876, IV + 141 pp. This new impression is based upon somewhat shaky philological principles. On Taillepied—who wrote some other works —one can consult the articles by M. Depoin, 'Les pionniers de l'histoire du Vexin', *Mém. Soc. histor. Pontoise*, vol. I (1879), pp. 12–18, and 'Étude sur les historiens du Vexin', *Bullet. Soc. histor. Pontoise*, vol. VII (1885), pp. 77–80. These two articles refer to certain ancient works bearing upon the history of Pontoise or Vexin of which I cannot give details here. The ecclesiastical history of Vexin (which was part of the diocese of Rouen) is very closely connected with that of Normandy, for which the reader should refer to Prentout's book, *Les Régions de la France, La Normandie*, 8vo, Paris, 1910 (*Publication de la Rev. de Synthèse histor.*).

7 4to, Paris, 1628, 759 pp.

8 p. 8.

9 As is testified by the sonnet addressed to Rouillard by a certain Florent de Crouayne, which may be read on sheet 6 *r* of the first part of the *Parthenie* (see below, p. 37).

10 A certain number of works from the land of Séb. Rouillard will be found enumerated in *L'Intermédiaire des Chercheurs et des Curieux*, vol. LII, 1905, part 2, col. 503, 706, 927.

11 *Les Antiquitez de la ville, comté et chatelenie de Corbeil, de la recherche de Me Jean de la Barre, cy-devant prévost de Corbeil*, 4to, Paris, 1647, 280 pp. For la Barre, consult A. Dufour, 'Un mot sur Jehan de la Barre, prévost et historien de la ville de Corbeil', *Bull. Soc. hist. Corbeil*, vol. XIII (1907), pp. 140–3, and 'Notes sur Jehan de la Barre, prévôt de Corbeil (1607–1624)', *Confér. des Soc. sav. de Seine-et-Oise, Quatrième Réunion*, Paris, 1909, pp. 94–7. The Bibliothèque Nationale under no. 4618 of the French section contains a MS. of the *Antiquités de Corbeil* which differs in certain points from the printed text.

12 4to, Paris, 1683, 618 pp. Dom Fleureau had left behind him in manuscript a *Briefve histoire de l'abbaie Nostre-Dame la Royale de Villiers proche la Ville de la Ferté-Aales* which was printed in 1893 in vol. XI of the *Annales de la Soc. histor. du Gâtinais*, pp. 1–125, with a preface by M. Pinson and supporting documents collected by the same scholar. For dom Fleureau consult: A. Boulé, 'Dom Fleureau historien d'Étampes', *Bullet. Soc. histor. Corbeil*, vol. VII (1901), pp. 134–41, and Ch. Fonteau, 'L'Acte de baptème de dom Basile Fleureau', *ibid.*, pp. 141–5. One can also consult on dom Fleureau: E. Dramard, 'Dom Basile Fleureau et ses Antiquités d'Étampes, Étude biographique et bibliographique', *Le Cabinet hist.*, vol. XIX, 1st part (1873), pp. 305–23.

13 4to, Paris, 1630. For dom Morin, there are both *Dom Morin, sa vie et ses œuvres*, in vol. III of Laurent's edition (see next note), pp. 1–52, by M. l'abbé, Th. Cochard, and a work by the abbé E. Jarossay, *Histoire d'une abbaye à travers les siècles, Ferrières-en-Gâtinais*, 8vo, Orléans, 1901, pp. 347–60. The historian of the Ile-de-France would do well to consult the histories of the Orléanais. First and foremost of these is *L'Histoire du païs orléannois*, by Canon Hubert (1620–94); this work, which has not been printed, forms MS. no. 560 in the Orléans city library. Cf. Loiseleur, 'Manuscrits du chanoine Hubert acquis par la Bibliothèque d'Orléans. Note sur Hubert et ses écrits', *Bull. Soc. archéolog. Orléanais*, vol. III (1862), pp. 73–80. *L'Histoire de l'Orléanais depuis l'an 703 de la Fondation de Rome jusqú'à nos jours*, by the Marquis de Luchet (4to, Amsterdam and Paris, xvi + 419 + 106 pp.), appears to be a work of rather mediocre merit.

14 Three vols, 4to, Pithiviers, Chartres, Paris, 1883–9, [18] + 460; 477 (numbered from 461 to 838) + [18]; viii + 424 pp., plans and maps. Vols. I and II include a reprint of dom Morin's text. Vol. III contains the *Notice* by abbé Cochard quoted on p. 329, note 1, of the 'Notes', an *Armorial de l'Histoire du Gastinois* and a Table, by contributors, chief of whom was M. Paul Quesvers.

15 Adrien Dupont, 'Curiosité bibliographique sur Dom Morin', *Annales Soc. histor. Gâtinais*, vol. I (1883), pp. 249–52. See vol. I of Laurent's edition, p. 303. It goes without saying that the responsibility for this strange lapse must rest on the editors of 1630 as much as dom Morin himself.

16 8vo, Paris, 1609, 250 + 291 sheets. *Le Petit Traité, composé par Estienne Prévost, Official de Chartres, touchant la fondation et érection de l'Église nostre Dame et cité de Chartres*, published at Chartres in 1558 (8vo, 32 pp.), is only a work of pious edification. The book of 'Radulphus Botereius', *Urbis gentisque Carnutum historia*, 8vo, Paris, 1624, 83 pp., has some historical value, but is too short and is no longer useful today. The history of the Chartres Dominicans was written in the seventeenth century, with much care and accuracy, by Brother Nicolas Le Febvre: *Praedicator Carnuteus, sine Instituto Conventus Carnutensis Ordinis Fratrum Praedicatorum*, 8vo, Chartres, 1637, 286 pp. A monk originally from Chartres, Guillaume Laisné, was prior of Mondonville, and died in 1635. He compiled a collection of documents and memoirs relating to the country around Chartres. The fourteen volumes contained in this collection (the last but one consists of tables) have passed from the Gaignières collection to the manuscript department of the Bibliothèque Nationale, where they may be found today under the classification 24124–24136 *bis* in the French section. M. de l'Épinois has analysed the first four volumes in the *Mémoires de la Soc. archéolog. d'Eure-et-Loir*, and an extract from the fifth (*Mém. Soc. arc. Eure-et-Loir*, vol. I, pp. 90–112, and 258–81; III, pp. 209–64; IV, pp. 151–79; VI, pp. 89–100.

17 J. B. Souchet, *Histoire du diocèse et de la ville de Chartres (Publications*

de la Soc. archéolog. d'Eure-et-Loir), 4 vols., 8vo, Chartres, 1866–73, XLVII + 570, 624, 602, 483 + 70 pp. This edition is preceded by a good biographical note by M. Lecoq. The churches and dioceses of Sens and Orléans also had their historians in the seventeenth century. The works to which the historian of the Ile-de-France should refer are: Jacques Taveau, *Sensonensium archiepiscoporum vitae actusque*, 4to, Sens, 1608, vii, 146 pp. (a mediocre and not very useful work); *Annales Ecclesiae Aurelianensis saeculis et libris sexdecim . . . auctore Carolo Saussego*, 4to, Paris, 1615, [26] + 842 pp.

18 F. Jacques Doublet, *Histoire de l'abbaye de S. Denys en France, contenant les Antiquitez d'icelle, les Fondations, Prérogatives et Privilèges, Ensemble les Tombeaux et Épitaphes des Rois, Reynes, Enfans de France et autres signalez Personnages qui s'y Trouvent jusqu'à présent*, 2 vols., 4to, Paris, Nicolas Buon, 1–649, 651–1377 pp., and Jean de Heuqueville, 1 vol., same date, same pagination. Gregory of Tours, who is the only historian through whom we have some fairly definite information about Saint-Denis, Bishop of Paris and patron of the abbey of Saint-Denis-en-France, relates that this confessor of the faith 'was put to death by the sword' in the time of the Emperor Decius, that is to say in the second half of the third century (247–251) (*Histor. Francor.*, I, c. 30, ed. Arndt, p. 48). In spite of this testimony, Saint-Denis, Bishop of Paris, has often been identified with the judge of the Areopagus named Denis, who, as the Acts of the Apostles say (Acts XVIII, 34), was converted by St Paul. This identification has been accepted and defended by some and contested by others; it has provided material for a lively controversy and an abundant literature from the ninth to the nineteenth century. The history of this will be found in a book by a priest experienced in scholarly criticism, abbé Eugène Bernard, *Les origines de l'église de Paris, Établissement du christianisme dans les Gaules, Saint Denys de Paris*, 8vo, Paris, 1870, VII + 557 pp. Jacques Doublet entered the lists, not only in his *Histoire de l'abbaye de Saint-Denis*, where he came down in favour of the identification of the two saints, but also in a special work published on this subject: *Histoire chronologique pour la vérité de S. Denys Areopagite, apostre de France et premier évesque de Paris*, 4to, Paris, 1636, 633 pp. Cf. below, Chapter Four, pp. 75–6.

19 A manuscript chronicle of Saint-Germain-des-Prés, in Latin. There are eight copies of it in the Bibliothèque Nationale, Latin section, nos. 12837–12844. Cf. J.-B. Vanel, *Les Bénédictins de Saint-Maur à Saint-Germain-des-Prés*, 4to, Paris, 1896, p. VII, n. 1. The reader will find other works by dom du Breul also bearing upon Saint-Germain-des-Prés in Chapter Two, note 23. On du Breul, see Le Roux de Lincy and Bruel, 'Notice historique et critique sur dom Jacques du Breul, prieur de Saint-Germain-des-Prés', *Bibl. Éc. Chartres*, vol. XXIX (1868), pp. 56–72 and 479–512.

20 D. Marrier published two works on Saint-Martin-des-Champs: (*a*) a collection of texts: *Martiniana, id est litterae, tituli, cariae, privilegia et documenta . . .*, 8vo, 1606, 183 sheets; (*b*) a *Monasterii regalis S. Martini de Campis paris. ordinis Cluniacensis historia*, 4to, Paris, 1636, 576 pp. For dom

Marrier, see Douët d'Arcq, 'Documents bibliographiques sur dom Marrier', *Bibl. Éc. Chartes*, vol. XVI (1855), pp. 322–58; cf. *ibid.*, p. 581. Certain copies of the *Monasterii regalis S. Martini . . . historia* are dated 1637.

21 Jean de Thoulouse was prior of Saint-Victor from 1636 to 1641 and died in 1659. He played a major part in the abbey's history during this period, which was a time of great unrest. Cf. Fournier-Bonnard, *Histoire de l'abbaye et de l'ordre des chanoines réguliers de Saint-Victor de Paris*, vol. II, 8vo, no date [1907], ch. VII. He published in 1640 an *Abrégé de la fondation de l'abbaye de Saint-Victor lez Paris, succession des abbez, privileges et singularity d'icelle*, 4to, Paris, 78 pp., which proclaims itself as a 'reveüe', that is to say a revised and corrected edition of the notice on Saint-Victor in du Breul's *Théâtre des Antiquitez* (cf. Chapter Two, note 23), the work of R. P. Jean Picard. Besides this, Jean de Thoulouse left important manuscripts concerning the history of the abbey; the reader will find these enumerated in Fournier-Bonnard, *Saint-Victor de Paris*, vol. I [1904], pp. XXVI–XXVII.

22 In the second book of his work entitled *La Vie et les Éminentes Vertus de Saint-Maur, abbé*, 8vo, Paris, 1640, pp. 291–474. Father Ignatius of Jésus-Maria (whose real name was Jacques Sanson) belonged to the family of the Sansons of Abbeville, the famous geographers. For information about him, see *Bibliotheca Carmelitana*, vol. I, folio, Paris, 1752, col. 707, and dom Ansart, in his *Histoire de Saint-Maur-des-Fossés*, B.N. MS. Fr. 18925, folio 198.

23 The reader should also consult the notes on the monasteries of Paris, and the chief monasteries in the diocese inserted by dom Jacques du Breul in his *Théâtre des Antiquitez de Paris*, 4to, Paris, 1612, 2nd ed. 1639, Book IV. Cf. also for Saint-Germain-des-Prés and Saint-Maur-des-Fossés the *Supplementum Antiquitatum urbis Parisiacae quoad Sanctorum Germani a Pratis et Mauri Fossatensis Coenobia*, by the same du Breul, 4to, Paris, 1614, 205 pp.

24 2 vols., 4to, Paris, 1690 and 1710, XLVII + 824 + XII + 684 + XLVIII pp. Volume II is posthumous.

25 On A. Duchesne, see M. René Pourpardin's introduction to his *Catalogue des manuscrits des collections Duchesne et Bréquigny* (Bibliothèque Nationale), 8vo, Paris, 1905, p. Iff. M. Pourpardin (p. I, n. I) gives some indication of the work that had been done on the subject before his own.

26 *Histoire généalogique de la maison de Montmorency et de Laval*, folio, Paris, 1624, 696 + 419 pp. For the modern period, A. Duchesne's work can be filled out with the help of Désormeau's, *Histoire de la maison de Montmorenci*, 2nd ed., 5 vols., 12mo, Paris, 1768.

27 *Histoire de la maison de Chastillon-sur-Marne*, folio, Paris, 1621, 726 + 286 pp.

28 *Histoire généalogique de la maison royale de Dreux et quelques autres familles illustres qui en sont descendues par femmes*, folio, Paris, 1631. The first part of the volume (338 pp.) is devoted to the house of Dreux.

29 The *Histoire généalogique de la maison de Broyes et de Chasteauvillain*

forms the sixth part of the volume referred to in the previous note (80 + 67 pp.).

30 The *Généalogies Orléanoises* of Canon Hubert may be of service to the historian of the Ile-de-France. For canon Hubert, see above, Chapter Two, note 13. The *Généalogies* are in eight manuscript volumes now kept in the Orléans city library, nos. 608–15. Vassal published a list of them under the title *Généalogies des principales familles de l'Orléanais. Table analytique des manuscrits d'Hubert*, 8vo, Orléans, 1862, 452 pp.

31 *Histoire littéraire de la Congrégation de Saint-Maur*, 4to, Paris, 1770, xxi pp.

32 *Annales Ordinis Sancti Benedicti dd. annum MCLVII*, 6 vols., Paris, 1703–39.

33 The volumes of the *Gallia* bearing on the Ile-de-France are especially vol. VII, folio, Paris, 1744 (diocese of Paris) and vol. VIII (the suffragan bishoprics of Paris), 1744; vol. VII was the work of dom Étienne Brice and dom Félix Hodin; vol. VIII is by the same monks and (for the dioceses of Meaux and Chartres) dom Toussaint-Duplessis, vol. XI (the province of Rouen), which came out in 1759, and vol. XII (the province of Sens), which came out in 1770, bear upon certain parts of the Ile-de-France.

34 For this work and its different editions, see A. Giry, *Manuel de Diplomatique*, p. 80.

35 The plates of the *Monasticon Gallicanum* were published in the nineteenth century by Peigné Delacourt, 2 vols., 4to, Paris, 1871, L + 16 pp. + 76 plates and 94 plates. The preface of this edition, written by Léopold Delisle, contains a list of historical notices on the monasteries, drawn up by dom Germain or his collaborators. See also L. Courajod, *Le Monasticon Gallicanum*, folio, Paris, 1869, 28 pp.

36 *Ouvrages posthumes de D. Jean Mabillon et de D. Thierri Ruinart*, vol. II, 4to, Paris, 1724, pp. 91–5.

37 p. VII.

38 By dom Racine, Bibl. Mazarine, MS. 3380. *La France Monastique*, by dom Beaunier, new ed., vol. I, 8vo, Paris, 1905, refers on p. 70 to an *Abrégé de l'histoire de l'abbaye royale de Chelles*, by dom Porcheron, in three manuscript volumes kept in the Bibl. du Séminaire de Maux. In spite of inquiries I have not been able to find out where this manuscript is at the present time.

39 By dom Estiennot, 1671, Bibl. de la ville de Pontoise, MSS. 22 and 25. For dom Estiennot and his historical work, consult J. Depoin, 'Un historien du Vexin: Dom Claude Estiennot', *Mém. Soc. histor. Pontoise*, vol. XXVIII (1907), pp. 183–90, and A. Vidire, *Un ami de Mabillon, dom Claude Estiennot, Mélanges et Docum. publiés à l'occasion du 2e Centenaire de la mort de Mabillon*, 8vo, Ligugé and Paris, 1908, pp. 281–312.

40 By dom Estiennot, Bibl. de la ville de Pontoise, MSS. 16, 17 and 18, and by dom Racine, Bibl. Mazarine, MS. 3368.

41 By dom Victor Cotron, Archives de Seine-et-Oise, series H.

42 The history of Bonneval was written first of all by dom Thiroux, then continued by dom Lambert. The work of the two Benedictines was printed in the nineteenth century, with additions taken from other manuscript memoirs on the abbey: *Histoire abrégée de Saint-Florentin de Bonneval des RR. PP. Dom Jean Thiroux et Dom Lambert, continuée par l'abbé Beaupère et M. Lejeune, publiée sons les auspices de la Société Dunoise*, by Dr V. Bigot, 8vo, Châteaudun, 1875, 258 pp. To the histories of monasteries written by Benedictines mentioned in the text, add the following works, classified under monasteries: *Bonneval*, by dom Jean Élie, a copy in the Bibl. de Chartres, MS. 112; *Saint-père de Chartres*, by dom F.-Ch. Dujardin, *ibid.*, MS. 1515, and a copy in the Bibliothèque Nationale, MS. franç. 22474; *Josaphat-les-Chartres*, by dom Fabien Buttreux, Bibl. de Chartres, MS. 1163; *Saint-Pierre-de Lagny*, by dom J.-Ch. de Changy, two copies in the Bibl. de Lagny, MSS. 1 and 3; *Saint-Maur-les-Fossés*, MSS. franç., 18924 and 18925; this last work—very mediocre in quality—is anonymous; it should probably be attributed to dom André-Joseph Ansart (cf. *B.N. Catal. Gén. des ms franç, Anc. Saint-Germain franç.*, vol. III, p. 124, and *Nouveau supplément à l'hist. littér. de la Congrég. de Saint-Maur, Notes de Henry Wilhelm, publiées et complétées par dom Ursmer Berlière*, vol. I, 8vo, Paris, 1908, pp. 14–16); it contains a life of Saint Maurus and a history of the abbey; it was meant to be printed (cf. MS. franç. 18924, fol. 3r⁰–5vo and dom Tassin, p. 752, note 1); Quérard, *La France littéraire*, vol. I, p. 68, in the article on dom Ansart, refers, as though it had been published, to a *Histoire de Saint-Maur, abbé de Glanfeuil*, but this is not in the possession of the department of printed books of the Bibliothèque Nationale. As regards the history of Saint-Martin de Pontoise written by dom Estiennot, it is important to note that the documents transcribed and analysed by dom Estiennot are reproduced by M. Depoin in his *Cartulaire* and his *Chartrier de Saint-Martin de Pontoise* referred to below, Chapter Four, note 86.

43 Dom Jacques Bouillard, *Histoire de l'abbaye royale de Saint-Germain-des-Prés*, folio, Paris, 1724, 328 pp., plates, illus.

44 Dom Michel Félibien, *Histoire de l'abbaye royale de Saint-Denys en France*, folio, Paris, 1716, 592 + ccxxxiii pp. plates, illus.

45 2 vols., 4to, Paris, 1731, 782 + 669 pp. Dom Duplessis had made use of some manuscript works on the history of the diocese of Meaux referred to by him in the preface. As we have already seen (Chapter Two, note 33), he was responsible for drawing up the part relating to the diocese of Meaux in the *Gallia Christiana*.

46 One can consult on this prelate J.-G. Gossel, 'Henry de Thiard, cardinal de Bissy, un essai d'action commune de l'épiscopat français en 1735', *Rev. de l'Hist. de l'Église de France*, vol. II (1911), pp. 539–53 and 679–701.

47 See—besides dom Tassin, p. 756—Fernand Labour, 'Dom Toussaint Duplessis et MM. du Chapitre de l'Église de Meaux', *Rev. de*

Champagne et de Brie, vol. XIV (1883, 2nd term), pp. 125–30, and Maurice Lecomte, 'Observations sur l'histoire de Meaux de dom Toussaint Duplessis', *Almanach histor. de Seine-et-Marne,* 1906, pp. 97–115. Cf. also Lhuillier, *Bibliographie de Seine-et-Marne* (referred to below, Chapter Three, note 31). Dom Duplessis also engaged in polemics with a member of the *Académie des Inscriptions,* Lancelot by name, about a passage in the *Histoire de l'Eglise de Meaux,* in which, says dom Tassin, he laid it down 'as a more or less definite and indubitable principle that the art of falsifying to suit one's own interests was an almost universal vice round about the eleventh century'.

48 For abbé Lebeuf, consult the introduction to the Cocheris edition (cf. below, Chapter Two, note 52).

49 *Réflexions sur les trois premiers tomes de l'histoire de la Ville et de tout le Diocèse de Paris, par M. l'abbé Lebeuf, de l'Académie Royale des Inscriptions et Belles-Lettres; pour servir d'éclaircissement et de supplément aux Nouvelles Annales de Paris, par dom Toussaint Duplessis, Religieux Bénédictin de la Congrégation de Saint-Maur, Mercure de France,* June (pp. 99–108), July, I (pp. 124–36), July, II (pp. 107–21), September (pp. 103–23), 1756. The editors of the *Mercure* shortened dom Duplessis's articles (August, p. 164). A friend of Lebeuf's replied (September, pp. 123–34).

50 4to, Paris, 1753, IV + 350 pp.

51 See the memorandum entitled *Projet d'une histoire de la ville de Paris sur un plan nouveau,* 4to, Harlem, 1739, 49 pp., composed after the appearance, in the *Mercure de France* of December 1739, vol. II (pp. 3106–10), of Lebeuf's programme, entitled *Projet d'une description des Paroisses de la Campagne, voisines de Paris, situées dans le Diocèse de cette Capitale.* From 1739 to 1743 Lebeuf likewise brought out his *Dissertations sur l'Histoire ecclésiastique et civile de Paris, suivies de plusieurs éclaircissements sur l'Histoire de France,* 3 vols., 12mo, Paris. Some of the dissertations collected in this volume are of interest to the historian of the Ile-de-France. A table of contents for the three volumes will be found in the Cocheris edition, vol. I, pp. 90–2.

52 The original edition came out in 15 vols. in Paris, from 1754 to 1758, published by Prault *père.* There were two reprints during the nineteenth century. The first, by M. Cocheris (4 vols., 8vo, Paris, 1863–70), is only of interest to us for its preface, for it stopped before getting beyond the part of Lebeuf's work relating to Paris and its immediate suburbs. The second reprint, which is complete, was undertaken by M. Augier. It comprises 7 vols, of III + XXII + 664, 666, 5999, 651, 453, IX + 540, 548 pp., 8vo, Paris, 1883–93. Vol. VII contains the tables of contents; vol. VI the *Rectifications et Additions* (by Fern. Bournon) which do not relate to the city of Paris.

53 See the *Projet* referred to above, Chapter Two, note 51.

54 Published by the Soc. Dunoise, 2 vols, 8vo, Châteaudun, 1884, LXIII + 406 + 372 pp. A shortened edition had appeared in 18–10. 5The

preface added by M. Brossier-Géray to the edition of 1884 contains some information on Dunois historiography.
55 Vol. I, p. 220.
56 2 vols., Chartres and Paris, xxxviii + [14] + 431 + 522 pp.
57 Vol. II, pp. 358–9.

chapter three

1 See *Revue de Synthèse historique*, vol. XXV, p. 209 and above, p. 1.
2 Some information on the work of local history in the Seine-et-Marne during the nineteenth century will be found in an article by M. Maurice Lecomte, 'De l'Histoire locale en Seine-et-Marne', which appeared in the *Revue Brie et Gâtinais*, vol. I (1909), pp. 4–9. The volume entitled *Conférence des sociétés savantes de Seine-et-Oise. Première réunion (1902)*, 8vo, Paris, 1903, pp. 4–28, contains a series of notes on the various local societies in the *département*. The historian of the Ile-de-France will constantly need to refer to the publications of the Orléannais learned societies: *la Société Archéologique et Historique de l'Orléanais, l'Académie de Sainte-Croix d'Orléans, l'Académie de Sainte-Croix d'Orléans, la Société d'Agriculture, Sciences, Belles-Lettres et Arts d'Orléans*. On the history of these societies, consult the works of J. Loiseleur, 'Les Archives de l'Académie d'Orléans', in *Mém. Soc. Sciences Orléans*, vol. XIV of the 2nd series (1872: vol. XLV of the complete collection), pp. 39–82 (cf. *ibid.*, vol. XV, 1873, pp. 27ff.); Guerrier, 'Histoire de la Société d'Agriculture, Sciences, Belles-Lettres et Arts d'Orléans et de ses travaux', in *Mém. Soc. agricult. Orléans*, 4th series, vol. XXXVII (68th vol. of the Collection), pp. 1–248; and Fauchon, 'La Société d'agriculture, sciences, belles lettres et arts d'Orléans, de 1809 à 1909', in *Mém. Soc. agricult. Orléans*, 5th series, vol. IX (1909), pp. 255–88. I would remind readers of the fact that information about the publications of the learned societies is obtainable in the *Bibliothèque Générale des travaux historiques et archéologiques publiés par les Sociétés savantes de la France*, compiled by M. R. de Lasteyrie and his collaborators. The great work comprises: (*a*) 4 vols. 4to giving a survey up to the end of the year 1885; (*b*) a *Supplement*, covering the years 1886–1900; a single vol. has appeared with a list of all the publication of the societies in all the *départements*, from the Ain to the Haute-Savoie (in alphabetical order of *départements*); (*c*) annual *Bibliographies*: 9 sections, covering the period 1901 to 1909, the last having come out in 1911.
3 From 1837 to 1847 the Society simply published some isolated instalments with reports of its sessions. Besides its *Mémoires*, it has also published since 1894 a *Bulletin* and since 1899 a three-monthly review entitled *Revue de l'Histoire de Versailles et Seine-et-Oise*.
4 For the activities of this society when first formed, see a letter by M. Moutié, inserted in vol. X (1844) of the *Bulletin Monumental*, p. 304.

140

Cf. A. de Dion, 'Auguste Moutié et la Société Archéologique de Rambouillet', in *Mém. Soc. archéol. Rambouillet*, vol. III (1887–8), pp. 5–15.

5 The *Société Archéologique de Rambouillet* has published since 1870 some *Mémoires et Documents*; it has also subsidized various publications.

6 *Procès-verbaux de la Soc. archéol. Eure-et-Loir*, vol. I, p. 10. Cf. abbé Sainsot, 'Histoire de la Société Archéologique d'Eure-et-Loir', in *Mém. Soc. archéol. Eure-et-Loir*, vol. XII (1901), pp. 294–302.

7 The *Société archéol. d'Eure-et-Loir*: (*a*) has since 1858 published *Mémoires*; (*b*) since 1861 *Procès-verbaux* (reports of proceedings); (*c*) subsidized various works.

8 The *Société de l'Histoire de Paris* publishes: (*a*) a *Bulletin*; (*b*) *Mémoires*; (*c*) *Documents*. Three decennial tables of contents of the Society's publications have been produced, in 1885 (1874–83), 1894 (1884–93), 1909 (1894–1903).

9 This society publishes *Mémoires* (decennial tables of contents for the years 1879–90) and *Documents*; and it has subsidized various publications. Among the learned societies in the Ile-de-France, this is perhaps the one which best appreciates the duty of local societies to publish hitherto unpublished documents. Unfortunately, its publications are not altogether beyond criticism; how can the leading scholars who run it have forgotten that the publication of incomplete texts is not really of very much assistance to historians?

10 The aim of this society is 'the study of the monuments, customs, and history of the Gâtinais district, including l'Étampois, le Giennois and la Puisaye'. It publishes *Annales*, which give an excellent review of local history (general table of contents, for the first fifteeen volumes, 1885–97, in vol. XV, 1897, pp. 293–351—the work of M. H. Stein). It has also subsidized various publications.

11 It publishes a *Bulletin, Mémoires* and *Documents*. This society has also founded a museum at Corbeil (the Musée Saint-Jean). One might also mention the *Société d'Histoire et d'Archéologie de Brie-Comte-Robert, Mormant, Tournan, et la Vallée de l'Yères*, founded in 1898; it publishes a *Bulletin*. There was founded at Meaux in 1893 a *Société Littéraire et Historique de la Brie*, which seems to have been only moderately active. The review *Brie et Gâtinais*, which has been published at Meaux since 1909, is useful to refer to, and provides the archaeologist with some excellent photographs.

12 Tables of contents for the first ten volumes (by E. Perrier, 1891) and for vols. XI to XXI (by J. Depoin, 1905).

13 The papers read at each of the conferences are printed and bound up together in a single volume.

14 Along with the publications of the learned societies one must mention the semi-official material available in annual departmental publications. They often contain articles on local history, which are sometimes of first quality; but they are not of much use to historians because they most of them lack adequate tables of contents. The best of these depart-

mental year-books referred to here, *l'Almanach Historique de Seine-et-Marne* (which has been published since 1861) is particularly blameworthy for it entirely lacks a table of contents. *L'Annuaire du Département de Seine-et-Oise* has been published ever since Year Ten (1801–2) but publication has been interrupted several times. The year-book for 1883 contains (on p. LI) some *Tables générales des Annuaires de Seine-et-Oise* drawn up by L. Thomas. The *Annuaire du Département d'Eure-et-Loir* has been published since 1839; the volumes for 1906 and 1907 contain a *Table générale de la partie historique de l'Annuaire d'Eure-et-Loir* (1839–1905), the work of M. G. Téton. *L'Annuaire du Département du Loiret* has been published since 1806. One can read an account of the vicissitudes through which this publication has passed in a note entitled *L'Annuaire du Loiret*, which appeared in the issue for 1899, on p. 28. The year-book for 1912 contains (p. 25) a list of the *Notices historiques ou statistiques contenues dans nos précédents annuaires du Département.*

15 Large 4to, Fontainebleau, 1883, v + 335 pp. The articles entitled 'Inventaire des titres et pièces du Trésor des Chartes, pour servir à l'histoire de l'Ile-de-France et du pays de Paris en particulier', which came out in the *Cabinet Historique*, vol. III, 2nd part, pp. 199–215, 245–59, vol. IV, 2nd part, pp. 42–8, vol. V, 2nd part, pp. 208–19 and 245–52, are simply an abstract of the parts relating to the Ile-de-France from the *Inventaire du Trésor de Charles* compiled in the seventeenth century by Dupuy. Some useful information about the archives relating to the communes in the *département* of the Seine will be found in M. Mentienne's work, *Memorandum ou guide nécessaire à ceux qui voudront écrire les monographies des communes du département de la Seine*, small 8vo, Paris, 1899, 142 pp. For source-material bearing upon the part of the Ile-de-France which is included today in the Seine-et-Oise *département*, it is useful to consult the two following notes, both published in the volumes entitled *Conférence des Sociétés savantes de Seine-et-Oise*, *Première réunion* (1902), 8vo, Versailles, 1903: A. Coüard, 'Les Sources et instruments de travail applicables aux études historiques' (pp. 74–83), and J. Depoin, 'Cartulaires et Inventaires civils ou ecclésiastiques du département de Seine-et-Oise', pp. 83–104.

16 The Seine archives contain little material for the historian of the Ile-de-France. Cf. Marrius Barroux, 'Les archives de la Seine en 1900 et leur histoire', in *Bullet. du bibliophile* (1900), pp. 217–26, 291–304, 340–56, 405–10, and the article entitled 'Les Archives départementales de la Seine et les archives communales de Paris', in *Révol. franç.*, vol. XLVII (1904, II), pp. 183–6.

17 The *Collection du Vexin* has been listed by M. Ph. Lauer, *Collections Manuscrites sur l'histoire des provinces de France*, vol. II, 8vo, Paris, 1911, pp. 319–64. For the origins of the collections, cf. the introduction to vol. I (Paris, 1905), p. XXXI. As regards Brie, it might be worth referring to the collection of documents bearing upon Champagne formed in the eighteenth century by the Benedictines, and now in the keeping of the Bibliothèque

Nationale. It has been listed by M. Lauer in vol. I of the *Collections manuscrites sur l'histoire des provinces de France*, Paris 1905, pp, 61–108.

18 *Inscriptions chrétiennes de la Gaule antérieures au VIIIe siècle*, vol. I, 4to, Paris, 1856, and *Nouveau Recueil des Inscriptions chrétiennes de la Gaule antérieures au VIIIe siècle*, 4to, Paris, 1892 (*Doc. inédits*).

19 F. de Guilhermy and R. de Lasteyrie, *Inscriptions de la France du Ve siècle au XVIIe, Ancien Diocèse de Paris*, 5 vols., 4to, Paris, 1873–83 (*Doc. inédits*).

20 Paul Quesvers and Henri Stein, *Inscriptions de l'ancien diocèse de Sens publiées d'après les estampes d'Edmond Michel, Vol. IV. Inscriptions des doyennés de Milly et du Gâtinais*, 4to, Paris, 1904, 762 pp.

21 M. Loisel, 'Épigraphie du Canton de Montfort-l'Amaury (Seine-et-Oise)', in *Mém. Soc. archéol. Rambouillet*, vol. VII (1882–3), pp. 1–112; A. de Dion, Supplément à l'Épigraphie du canton de l'Amaury, *ibid.*, pp. 203–306.

22 I shall not refer here to the archaeological collections relating to monuments of single periods. Some information on the history of archaeology in the Ile-de-France, and in particular on the museums set up by local societies, will be found in the following two articles: Desnoyers, 'État des études archéologiques dans le département du Loiret', in *Congrès archéol.*, vol. LIX (1892), pp. 139–53; abbé Sainsot, 'Les Études archéologiques dans le département d'Eure-et-Loir depuis cinquante ans', *ibid.*, vol. LXVII (1900), pp. 85–95.

23 8vo, Chartres, 1911, 95 pp. (*Publicat. de la Soc. archéol. d'Eure-et-Loir*). For the Seine-et-Oise, classified domestic objects have been dealt with in a similar work. *Liste des objets mobiliers classés de Seine-et-Oise à la date du 30 juin 1909*, 8vo, Versailles, 1909 (*Publicat. de la Commis. des Antiqu. et des Arts*); cf. 'Album des objets mobiliers de Seine-et-Oise', in *Mém. Soc. hist. Corbeil*, vol. X (1910).

24 *Statistique monumentale du canton de Chaumont-en-Vexin*, eight sections, 8vo, came out between 1891 and 1906. The ninth (Chaumont continued, Boissy-l'Aillerie, Saint-Brice) is missing.

25 *Commission des Antiqu. et Arts de Seine-et-Oise*, 3rd series, 1883, pp. 91–103.

26 *Les monuments de Seine-et-Marne, description historique et archéologique, et réproduction des édifices religieux, militaires et civils du département*, folio, Paris, 1858, 208 pp.

27 *Monuments religieux, civils et militaires du Gâtinais (Dép. du Loiret et de Seine-et-Marne) depuis le XIe jusqu'au XVIIIe siècle*, 4to, Lyons, Orléans and Paris, 358 pp. and an atlas of CVII plates. In the *Collection des Richesses d'Art*, Edm. Michel is also the author of a note on 'Les Églises du Département du Loiret', which was included in vol. I of *L'Inventaire général des richesses d'art de la France. Province. Monuments religieux*, pp. 183–359, and of the volume: *Inventaire des richesses d'art de la France: arrondissements de Gien et de Montargis*, Paris, 1885. For the religious monuments of the diocese of

Chartres, consult *Églises et chapelles du diocèse de Chartres publiées par l'abbé Ch. Métais, Archives du diocèse de Chartres*, vols. II, IV and IX, 8vo, Chartres.

28 4to, Paris, 1719, xxxvi + 364 pp. By *'ancien diocèse de Chartres'* dom Liron means the diocese as it existed before the establishment of a bishopric at Blois, whose territory was made up of a portion of the former diocese of Chartres. There exists in the Orléans city library (MS. no. 631) a manuscript copy, in the author's hand, of dom Liron's work; it seems that this manuscript was intended for the publication of a new edition, which never came out; cf. also Bibliothèque Nationale, fonds franç., MSS. 17005 and 17006. The *Bibliothèque chartraine* was subjected to some fairly lively criticism. See the *Lettre d'un conseiller de Blois à un chanoine de Chartres sur la Bibliothèque Chartraine* . . . . 16mo, no place of publication, 1719, 20 pp.; if one is to believe a manuscript note in the Bibliothèque Nationale copy, the author of this brochure was a certain Perdoux de la Perrière. The Société des Bibliophiles Bretons began in 1897 to publish dom Liron's *Bibliothèque d'Anjou*, 4to, Nantes.

29 Cf. L. Jarry, 'Dom Gérou, Sa vie et ses travaux littéraires, d'après sa correspondance inédite', in *Academ. de Sainte-Croix d'Orléans, Lect. et Mém.*, vol. VI (1880), pp. 137–88. Dom Gérou's work forms MSS. nos. 633–4 in the Orléans city library. Cf. MSS. nos. 632, 635, 636, 637, 638, which are complementary to those of Gérou.

30 *Mém. Soc. archéol. de l'Orléanais*, vol. XIX (1883), pp. 1–446. Let us here mention two other Chartrain biographies: one forms ch. VII in the Doyen's *Histoire de Chartres* mentioned above, and is called: 'Notice des auteurs et autres personnes nés au pays chartrain ou qui s'y sont distingués sans y avoir pris naissance, dont les noms out mérité de passer à la postérité, à peu près par ordre chronologique' (vol. II, pp. 380–482); the other, which is not in the shape of a bio-bibliography, is contained in vol. II of the *Histoire Générale, civile et religieuse de la cité de Carnutes et du pays chartrain, vulgairement appelé la Beauce*, published at Chartres in 1836, by M. J.-E. Ozeray (8vo); it is entitled: 'Notice de divers ouvrages manuscrits et imprimés relatifs à l'Histoire de Chartres, au pays chartrain et aux villes et pays environnants' (pp. 442–62).

31 T. Lhuillier, *Seine-et-Marne : essai de bibliographie départementale*, 18mo, Meaux, 1857, iv + 117 pp. The most useful paragraph in Lhuiller's work is undoubtedly the one devoted to newspapers. The Librarie Champion, has published the catalogue of M. Lhuillier's private library, *Catalogue d'une bibliothèque spéciale sur le département de Seine-et-Marne, formée par M. Lhuillier, de Melun*, 8vo, Paris, 1905, 60 pp. The historian interested in Brie should consult A. Denis' books, *Recherches bibliographiques en forme de dictionnaire sur les auteurs morts et vivants qui ont écrit sur l'ancienne province de Champagne ou Essai d'un Manuel du Bibliophile champenois*, 8vo, Châlons-sur-Marne et Paris, 1870, viii + 190 pp., and a work by L. Techener, *Bibliothèque champenoise*, 8vo, Paris, 1886, xvii + 580 pp.

32 Léon Thomas, *Bibliographie de la ville et du canton de Pontoise, Publicat. Soc. histor. et archéolog. de l'arr. de Pontoise*, 8vo, Pontoise, 1883, VIII + 206 pp.

33 Alfred Potiquet, *Bibliographie du canton de Magny-en-Vexin*, 2nd ed., 8vo, Magny-en-Vexin, 1878, 67 pp. A supplement came out in 1881, 8vo, 58 pp.

34 Paul Pinson, *Bibliographie d'Étampes et de l'arrondissement, ou catalogue par ordre alphabétique des noms d'auteurs et d'anonymes, des documents imprimés, cartes et plans relatifs aux villes, bourgs, villages, hameaux, abbayes, châteaux, rivières, hommes remarquables, avec des notes bibliographiques et littéraires,* Étampes and Paris, 1910, VI + 155 pp. A committee is engaged in drawing up a bibliography for the *département* of Seine-et-Oise on the same plan. I have not been able to see F. Chéron's *Catalogue des livres relatifs à l'histoire de la partie sud du département de Seine-et-Oise*, Étampes, 1903. The historian of Versailles will do well to consult J.-A. Le Roi, *Ville de Versailles; catalogue des livres relatifs à l'histoire de la ville*, 8vo, Versailles, 1875; and the historian of Melun, G. Leroy's 'Recherches sur l'introduction de l'imprimerie à Melun', in *Bullet. Soc. archéol. Melun*, vol. VIII (1875-7), pp. 51-69.

35 We must call attention here to two most valuable bibliographies on the history of Paris, in which there are naturally a large number of works bearing upon the Ile-de-France as a whole. Both of them come from the pen of M. Marius Barroux, *Essai de Bibliographie critique des généralites de l'histoire de Paris*, 8vo, Paris, 1908, VI + 155 pp., and *Le département de la Seine et la ville de Paris. Notions générales et bibliographiques pour en étudier l'histoire*, 8vo, Paris, 1910, XI + 444 pp. Cf. also the work by Mentienne referred to above, Chapter Three, note 15.

36 Vol. XII (1800), vol. XIII (1890), vol. XVIII (1896), vol. XXI, (1899). Vols. XII, XIII, XIX (1897) and XXI contain in addition a bibliography of the rare autographs and pamphlets relating to le Vexin and the Seine-et-Oise, the work of M. Depoin.

37 Vols. XXV (1898), XXVI (1899), XXVII (1900), XXVIII (1901), XXIX (1902), XXX (1903), XXXI (1904), XXXII (1905), XXXIV (1907). The first of these bibliographies contained inventories of works that appeared in 1876 concerning the region corresponding to the former military *gouvernement* of the Ile-de-France. The bibliography of 1879 (which appeared along with the one for 1896 in vol. XXV) and all the subsequent ones are wider in scope, covering the whole region comprising the five *départements* of Seine, Seine-et-Oise, Seine-et-Marne, Oise and Aisne. A good up-to-date bibliography of ecclesiastical history will be found in the *Revue Mabillon*. This review, which has been published since 1904, publishes a *Chronique Bibliographique* where works bearing upon local ecclesiastical history are classified by (ecclesiastical) provinces. See the heading: *Provinces de Paris et de Sens*, and (for French Vexin) the heading: *Province de Rouen*. It may also be useful to consult the abstract of local publications by local societies produced under the title of *Bulletins*

régionaux by the *Revue d'Histoire de l'Église de France* (*Analecta Gallicana*), founded in 1910.

chapter four

1 Or, much more rarely, of a rather larger area—a canton for example. As for the history of the Ile-de-France as a whole, it has never been seriously tackled. The work by Denis Lagarde, *Résumé de l'histoire de l'Ile-de-France, de l'Orléanais et du Pays Chartrain*, 18mo, Paris, 1826, 416 pp., is of no value. I only mention it here to save the reader the trouble—which I had to take—of consulting it.

2 I can only give a few bibliographical indications on the subject of these removals of towns—and ordinary villages, which I have not mentioned here—from one site to another in the high Middle Ages. I hope to take up this study more fully on another occasion, with full reference to the authorities. For Pithiviers, consult J. Devaux, 'Essai sur les premiers seigneurs de Pithiviers', in *Ann. Soc. Hist. Gâtinais*, vol. III (1885), pp. 168–78, 250–65, 290–321; and for the history of the relics of Saint Salomon: dom Plaine, *Saint Salomon, roi de Bretagne et martyr*, 8vo, Vannes, 1895, p. 57ff. For Corbeil, the work by La Barre quoted above in ch. 2; and for the history of the holy relics, see on the one hand F. Lot, 'Date de l'exode des corps saints hors de Bretagne', in *Ann. de Bretagne*, vol. XV (1899–1900), pp. 60–76 (where there are references to earlier works on the subject) and on the other hand J. Lair, 'Études sur les origines de l'évêché de Bayeux, II', *Bibliothèque de l'École des Chartes*, XXIV (1863), pp. 280–323, and *Acta Sanctorum Augusti*, I, pp. 53–4. For Étampes, apart from dom Fleureau's book quoted above in Chapter Two and the works referred to below in Chapter Four, note 8, see E. Dramard, *Notice historique sur l'origine de la ville d'Étampes*, 8vo, 1855, 61 pp.

3 This is only a hypothesis, but an extremely probable one. M. L.-E. Lefebvre put it forward in a piece of work called 'La Façade Occidentale: portails et fortifications de l'église Notre-Dame d'Étampes', in *Bullet. Soc. hist. Corbeil*, vol. XIII (1907), pp. 17–30. M. E. Lefèvre-Pontalis' research work on Notre-Dame d'Étampes has moreover confirmed it. This archaeologist connects the construction of the west front of the church, and the embattled circular passage-way crowning this west front and continuing along the south side and the chevet, with a building plan that was carried out 'about 1210'—or as we should probably say (less accurately but more cautiously)—at the beginning of the thirteenth century: ('Les Campagnes de construction de Notre-Dame d'Étampes', in *Bullet. monument.*, vol. LXXIII (1909), pp. 7–31, and *Confér. des soc. savantes de Seine-et-Oise, Quatrième réunion*, Paris, 1909, pp. 208–36). Now it was between 1 November 1199 and 1 April 1200 that Philip Augustus 'broke up' the commune of Étampes and made the concession 'to the churches

and to the knights that in future there should be no commune of Étampes'. Cf. L. Delisle, *Catal. des actes de Phil. Auguste*, 8vo, Paris, 1856.

4 2 vols., Chartres 1854 and 1858, IV + 568 + 664 pp., no. 571. For the contemporary period, add A. Bethouart, *Histoire de Chartres* (1789–1900), 2 vols., 8vo, Chartres, 1903, IV + 435 + 366 pp.

5 *Histoire de Meaux et du pays meldois*, 8vo, Meaux and Paris, 1865, 564 pp.

6 *Histoire de Melun, depuis les temps les plus reculés, jusqu'à nos jours*, large 8vo, Melun, 1887, 517 pp. Cf. by the same author, *Le vieux Melun, supplément à l'histoire de la même ville*, 8vo, Melun, 1904, XVI + 553 pp. and Maurice Lecomte, *Histoire de Melun*, 8vo, Melun, 1910.

7 *Histoire de la ville de Corbeil depuis l'origine de la ville jusqu'au 21 septembre 1792*, 2 vols., 8vo, Lagny, 1901 and 1902, 542 + 557 pp.

8 Cf. especially Léon Marquis, *Les rues d'Étampes et ses monuments*, 8vo, Paris, 1881, VII + 434 pp., and L.-E. Lefebvre, 'Étampes et ses monuments au XIe et XIIe siècles. Mémoire pour servir à l'étude archéologique des plus anciens monuments étampois', in *Ann. Soc. histor. Gâtinais*, vol. XXV (1907), pp. 145–248 and 289–436. This is an article which, although it only bears a modest title, is an inclusive work on the history of Étampes during the two centuries under review. Cf. also Maxime Legrand, *Étampes pittoresque, guide du promeneur dans la ville et l'arrondissement*, 3 vols., 8vo, 1897, 1906 and 1907.

9 F. Bournon's work, *Histoire de la ville et du canton de Saint-Denis*, 12mo, Paris, 1892, 167 pp., and the historical notice devoted by the same scholar to Saint-Denis in *L'État des Communes* in the Seine *département*, are both very inadequate.

10 These notices, by M. Ed. Lefèvre, dealt with the communes in the cantons of Nogent-le-Roi, Anneau, Courville and Janville. Though they appeared separately, they form a series of twelve volumes entitled *Documents historiques et statistiques sur les cantons de . . .*, 2 vols. per canton, published at Chartres between 1866 and 1874.

11 Since 1862. In the exhibition of 1900 there were manuscript monographs from about 600 communes in the Seine-et-Oise; they are now kept at Versailles, in the offices of the *Inspection Académique*. In the *Bulletin de la conférence d'histoire du dioc. de Meaux* (July 1894, pp. 8–12), abbé F.-A. Denis drew up a *Programme et questionnaire pour l'étude d'une monographie communale et paroissiale* which does not seem likely to be of any great service. Historians wishing to write a village monograph of a purely geographical kind would do well to consult an article by C.-M. Jourdan, 'Les Monographies de village', which came out in the *Congrès nationale des soc. franç. de Géogr.*, *XXIVe (1903)*. *Comptes rendus publiés par le bureau de la Soc. Normande de Géogr.*, 8vo, Rouen, 1904, pp. 198–209. All the same one must reproach M. Jourdan with not having attached enough importance within the framework of his plan to the manner in which property was divided and to the form of the fields.

147

12 Cf. L. Serbat, 'Excursion à Larchant', in *Bullet. monum.*, vol. LXXV (1911), pp. 285–91.

13 Chelles, Seine-et-Marne, Canton de Lagny. For the deposits at Chelles, cf. J. Déchelette, 'Manuel d'archéologie préhistorique de la Beauce', in *Congrès préhistor. de France*, vol. I, 8vo, Paris, 1908, pp. 65–7, where some bibliographical information will be found.

14 Cf. G. Courty, 'Sur les habitations préhistoriques de la Beauce', in *Congrès préhistor. de France, 3ᵉ session, 1907*, 8vo, Paris, 1908, pp. 256–7.

15 It goes without saying that I am not here intending to draw up a bibliography—which should be a critical one, if it is to be of any use—of studies dealing with the prehistory of the Ile-de-France. I will simply refer to certain works which give a provisional synthesis for a particular district in the Ile-de-France. Some of these works are of interest not only for the study of prehistory strictly speaking, but also for Celtic or even Gallo-Roman antiquities. Some general information will be found in the book by L. Belgrand, *Le Bassin parisien. La Seine, aux âges ante-historiques*, quoted in the notes to Chapter One, pp. 131–2, note 66. For the Seine-et-Oise, consult especially the three following studies: P. Guégan and A. Dutilleux, 'Tableau et carte des monuments et objets de l'âge de la pierre dans le département de Seine-et-Oise', in *Annuaire du départ. de Seine-et-Oise pour 1878*, pp. 483–90, and separately, 8vo, Versailles, 1878, 22 pp.; P. Guégan, 'Étude retrospective sur l'habitat de l'homme le long des rives de la Seine et de l'Oise, depuis les temps géologiques jusques et y compris la période Franque-Mérovingienne', in *Commiss. des antiqu. et arts du départ de Seine-et-Oise*, vol. XI (1891), pp. 115–30 (with map); E. Delessard, 'Le préhistorique en Seine-et-Oise', in *Bullet. Soc. hist. Corbeil*, vol. IV (1898), pp. 55–74. For the Seine-et-Marne: Emmanuel Paty, 'Mémoire sur les antiquités galliques et gallo-romaines de Seine-et-Marne', in *Bullet. monumental*, vol. XIV (1848), pp. 373–400. For Eure-et-Loir, the excellent *Statistique archéologique d'Eure-et-Loir* by M. Boisvillette, 8vo, Chartres, 1864, xxxii + cxi + 303 pp., unfortunately brought to an end by the author's death (in the second part of the volume dealing with *La Gaule romaine* the section '*Monuments meubles*' is missing); the article by abbé Marquès, 'Monuments celtiques du département d'Eure-et-Loir', in *Procès-verb. de la Soc. archéol. d'Eure-et-Loir*, vol. VI (1876–9), pp. 190–6, is a good deal inferior to Boisvillette's work. Cf. also A. Peschot, 'L'âge de la pierre dans l'ancien Dunois, d'après les collections du musée historique de l'Orléanais', in *Bullet. Soc. dunoise*, vol. XI (1905–8), pp. 123–7, and the not very useful article by Desnoyers, 'Le Préhistorique dans l'Orléanais', in *Congrès archéol.*, vol. IX (1892), pp. 166–76.

16 For the dioceses of the Ile-de-France, the oldest complete lists are dated as follows: Paris, about 1205; Rouen, about 1240; Chartres, about 1272; Sens, about 1350; Meaux, about 1353; Orléans, 1369. The dioceses of Orléans and Sens both possess such a list, but a very fragmentary one, dating from the eleventh century. It is well known that these documents

have been brought together and studied in the collection of registers of benefices forming part of the new series (4to) of the *Recueil des Historiens de la France*. For the Ile-de-France, cf. *Pouillés de la province de France*, published by Aug. Longnon, 4to, Paris, 1904, LXXXV + 790 pp., and also *Pouillés de la province de Rouen*, by the same editor, 4to, Paris, 1903.

17 Aug. Longnon, *Introduction aux pouillés de la province de Sens*, p. XXXVII.

18 Aug. Longnon, *ibid.*, p. LIV, and *Atlas Historique*, text, pp. 107–9.

19 Maurice Lecomte, 'L'extension Sud-Est du "Pagus Meldensis", ou "Civita Meldorum", au VIIe siecle', in *Le Moyen Age*, vol. VIII, 1895, pp. 1–5.

20 Cf. the very ingenious article by M. Camille Jullian, 'Notes gallo-romaines, LII. Les Gaulois au confluent de l'Oise', in *Rev. des Ét. anciennes*, vol. XIII (1911), pp. 424–5, and map —but bear in mind the remarks above on the hypothetical nature of the proposition identifying diocesan frontiers with those of the Gallic peoples.

21 Caesar, *De bello gallico*, II, 4.

22 For the name *Aureliani* cf. Jacques Soyer, 'La légende de la fondation d'Orléans par l'empereur Aurélien', in *Mém. Soc. agricult. Orléans*, 5th series, vol. X (1910), pp. 74–88.

23 Cf. in Adrien Blanchet's book, *Les enceintes romaines de la Gaule*, 8vo, Paris, 1907, pp. 67–8 on Chartres, pp. 82–5 on Melun and Meaux. For Chartres, cf. the following note.

24 'Ce que nous savons sur Chartres gallo-romain', in *Rév des. Ét. anc.*, vol. XV (1913), pp. 60–71.

25 *Paris à l'époque gallo-romaine, Étude faite à l'aide des papiers et des plans de Th. Vacquer (Collect. de l'Histoire générale de Paris)*, 4to, Paris, 1912, XLII + 192 pp. plates and maps. (Cf. C. Jullian, 'Les origines de Paris capitale', in *Rev. de Paris*, vol. VI (1912), pp. 549–69.)

26 Thèse de la Fac. des Lettres de Bordeaux, 8vo, Paris, 1902, 199 pp. and map; M. Dubuc, understanding by the 'city' of the Suessiones the territory of the tribe of Suessiones as it was before the Roman conquest, has included in his study the 'city' of the Meldi. Cf. C. Jullian, 'A propos des "Suessiones" ', in *Rev. des Ét. anc.*, vol. V (1903), pp. 28–36.

27 I mention by way of reminder two essential general works: Nicholas Bergier, *Histoire des grands chemins de l'Empire romain*; the first edition, 4to, 856 pp., came out in Paris in 1632; the latest at Brussels, 2 vols., 4to; Alexis Bertrand, 'Les voies romaines en Gaule, résumé du travail de la Commission de topographie des Gaules', in *Rev. archéol.*, I (1863), pp. 406–12, II (1863), pp. 62–70, 148–73, 342–50, and separately (with the sub-title, giving a clearer indication of the restricted scope of the work, *Voies des itinéraires*), 8vo, Paris, 1864, 61 pp. One should also consult ch. II (pp. 21–34) of M. Pachtère's book, quoted in Chapter Four, note 25, the chapter entitled 'Lutèce et ses relations routières à l'époque romaine'; also the books by Boisvillette and Dubuc quoted above, Chapter Four, notes 15 and

26. For a certain number of references to Roman roads in the Eure-et-Loir, see the *Table générale* in the *Annuaire du département d'Eure-et-Loir, Annuaire pour 1907*, p. 75 in the *Table*. For information on the Roman roads of particular parts of the Ile-de-France, see A. Melaye, 'Carte des voies romaines dans les départements de Seine-et-Marne, Oise et les départements limitrophes', in *Bulletin de la Soc. littér. et histor. de la Brie*, vol. III, Section 2, 8vo, 32 pp., and map (does not give its sources); A. Hugues, *Les routes de Seine-et-Marne avant 1789*, 8vo, Melun, 88 pp., and map; (Graves), *Notice archéologique sur le département de l'Oise*, 2nd ed. *Annuaire du département de l'Oise pour 1856*, and separately, 8vo; Beauvais, 1856, pp. 198–21 (for the Roman roads to the north of Paris, even outside the *département* of the Oise): A. Dutilleux, *Recherches sur les routes anciennes dans le département de Seine-et-Oise* dans *Annuaire du département de Seine-et-Oise pour 1881*, pp. 493–557, and separately, 8vo, Versailles, VII + 94 pp. (makes use particularly of the reports of the road-surveyors); P. le Roy, 'Notes sur la topographie du Gastinois aux époques celtique et gallo-romaine, en ce qui concerne plus particulièrement l'arrondissement de Montargis', in *Ann. Soc. histor. Gâtinais*, vol. I (1883), pp. 65–78; A. de Dion, 'Les anciens chemins de l'Iveline et du comté de Montfort', in *Mém. Soc. archéol. Rambouillet*, vol. I (1870–2), pp. 217–28, and *Mém. Soc. archéol. Eure-et-Loir*, vol. V (1872), pp. 269–77. The following works deal, not with the Roman roads in a particular region, but each with a specific Roman road. For the Paris-Orléans and Chartres-Orléans roads see Carolus Molinaeus (Charles du Moulin), *Commentarii in Consuetudines Parisienses*, section I, gloss 3, 30, ed. of 1526, vol. I, folio, Paris, p. 41; de Caylus, *Recueil d'antiquités*, vol. IV, 4to, Paris, 1761, pp. 378–81 and pl. CXIV; de Torquat, 'Notice historique et archéologique sur la baronnie de Chevilly' (Loiret), in *Mém. Soc. archéol. Orléannais*, vol. XI (1868), p. 362; de Tourquat, 'Découvertes, faites au chemin dit de César, entre la Croix-Briquet et Artenay', in *Bullet. Soc. archéol. Orléanais*, vol. XI (1868–73), pp. 310–14. For the le Mans-Sens road, Vergnaud: 'Romagnési, Mémoire sur des monnaies gauloises trouvées près d'Artenay (Loiret)', in *Rev. numismatique*, vol. I (1836), p. 384. For the Paris-Rouen road via Pontoise: abbé Belley, 'Mémoire sur une voie romaine qui conduisait de l'embouchure de la Seine à Paris', in *Rev. Acad. Inscriptions*, vol. XIX (1753), pp. 648–71; C. Magne, 'Note sur les fouilles de l'église d'Ermont', in *Bullet. archéol. du Com. des trav. histor.* (1886), pp. 414–19; J. Depoin, 'La chaussée dite de Jules César et sa véritable origine', in *Commiss. des antiquit. et arts de Seine-et-Oise*, vol. XXIX (1909), pp. 100–20, which rather oddly attributes the construction of this road to the Emperor Julian. For the links between Paris and the north: abbé Caudel, 'Étude sur les principales voies romaines et gallo-romaines partant de Senlis', in *Congrès archéol.*, vol. XLIV (1877), pp. 396–432; A. Longnon, 'Note sur les voies romaines de Paris à Reims', in *Rev. archéol.*, new series, vol. XXXIX (1880), pp. 301–4 and *Bullet. Soc. hist. Paris*, vol. VIII (1881), pp. 52–5, with map. For the roads.

leaving Meaux: abbé Caudel, 'Voie romaine de Senlis à Meaux', in *Congrès archéol.*, vol. XLIV (1877), pp. 474–81; A. Héron de Villefosse, 'Le chemin-paré de Troyes à Meaux', in *Almanach histor. de Seine-et-Marne*, 1905, pp. 193–206.

28 On the '*Tombe Isoré*', consult J. Bédier, *Les légendes épiques*, vol. I, 8vo, Paris, 1908, pp. 348–53 (with bibliographical information), and de Pachtère, *op. cit.*, p. 94.

29 Joachim Lelewel, *Géographie du Moyen Age, Épilogue*, 8vo, Brussels, 1857, p. 293. Cf. M. Karl's Study of 'Un Itinéraire de la France et de l'Italie imprimé à la fin du XVᵉ siècle', in *Rev. des langues romanes*, vol. LI (vol. I of the 4th series, 1908), p. 551.

30 Suger, *De rebus in administratione sua gestis, Œuvres*, edit. Lecoy de la Marche (*Public. de la soc. de l'histoire de France*), 8vo, Paris, 1867, p. 171.

31 Boisvillette, *Statistique archéologique*, p. 188, and Dutilleux, *Ann. du dép. de Seine-et-Oise*, 1881, pp. 519–23.

32 4to, Paris, XXIV + 254 pp.

33 *Dictionnaire des anciens noms des communes du département de Seine-et-Oise, précédé d'une notice sur l'origine des noms de lieux de l'arrondissement de Corbeil*, 8vo, Versailles, 1874, 56 pp.

34 *Dictionnaire historique, archéologique et commercial des communes et des hameaux . . . du département du Loiret*, 8vo, Orléans, no date, 112 + VIII pp.

35 For the registers of benefices cf. above, Chapter Four, note 16. The *Obituaires de la province de Sens* form 4 vols., 8vo, Paris, 1902, 1906, 1909, CIX + 632 and 633 to 1380, XXVII + 675, XXVII + 641 pp. Among the publications that may be most useful for the identification and study of place-names, mention should be made of: the *Dictionnaires géographiques* put in as an appendix by B. Guérard to his editions of the *Cartulaires de Notre-Dame de Paris*, vol. IV (*Doc. inédits*), 4to, Paris, 1840, and the *Cartulaire de Sainte-Croix d'Orléans*, Thillier et Jarry, *Mém. soc. archéol. Orléanais*, vol. XXX, in the Introduction, entitled: 'Les possessions de l'Église d'Orléans. Leur situation, identification des noms de lieux', pp. XXVII–CIX. Also to be consulted are: A. Longnon, *Examen géographique du tome Iᵉʳ des Diplomata imperii* (*Monumenta Germaniae Histor.*), a collection of articles published in the *Revue Critique*, II (1873), pp. 74, 89, 107, 121, collected into one vol., large 8vo, Paris, 1873; and with some caution A. Jacobs, 'Géographie des diplômes mérovingiens. Diplômes de l'abbaye de Saint-Denys', in *Rév. des soc. savantes*, 2nd series, vol. VII (1862, I), pp. 52–67, 162–8, 232–51. For the Seine-et-Marne, while waiting for the topographical dictionary, use can be made of the 'Recherches sur la topographie gâtinaise', brought out by M. H. Stein in the *Annales de la soc. archéol. du Gâtinais depuis 1890*. The work by Frédéric Chéron, *Noms de lieux du canton de la Ferté-Alais*, 8vo, Paris, 1898, 16 pp., gives—in spite of some fanciful etymologies—a useful account of the ancient forms. M. Alphonse Boulé has studied two changes of place-name in the *Bullet. de la Soc. de l'hist. de Paris*: 'Comment Lieux est devenu Vauréal', vol. XX (1893), pp. 25–70; 'Châtres sous Montlhéry . . .

devenant Arpajon', vol. XXIV (1897) pp. 185–90. For the change of the name 'Tour' into 'Saint-Prix', cf. two articles in the *Bullet. Soc. hist. Paris* by M. Aug. Rey, vol. XXIX (1902), pp. 42–8, and *Mém. Soc. histor. Pontoise*, vol. XXIV (1902), pp. 55–65. Cf. also the following note 36.

36 *Bullet. du Com. des trav. histor. Géogr. histor.*, 1912, pp. 56–74. M. Soyer designates by the word 'Orléanais' the territory of the former diocese of Orléans. Cf. also J. Vendryes, 'Le nom de la ville de Melun', in *Mém. Soc. linguistique de Paris*, vol. XIII (1903–5), pp. 225–30; E. Drouin, 'Notices philologiques sur quelques noms de lieux de la Brie', in *Bullet. soc. archéol. Seine-et-Marne*, vol. VII (1873–4), pp. 133–43; J.-A. Leriche, 'Origine du nom de Versailles', in *Rev. d'hist. de Versailles*, vol. II (1906), pp. 150–7. I have not been able to obtain the following work: Alb. Melaye, *Monographie étymologique: principaux lieux-dits de l'Ile-de-France, Parisis, Bie, Goële, Picardie, Valois, Senlisien, Champagne, etc.*, 8vo, Dammartin, 26 pp.

37 As far as I am aware, this peculiar feature of Beauceron toponomy has not been pointed out by anyone except the fanciful author of a work whose comment on this point is the only one worth recording: *Étymologie géographique de Seine-et-Oise . . . par G . . .*, 8vo, Paris, 1876, 56 pp., p. 54.

38 'Savinianum et Potentianum, sanctumque eorum imitatorem, Altinum', *Vie de S. Savinien, seconde rédaction*; edit. Fliche (see following note), p. 76.

39 For the ecclesiastical origins of the Ile-de-France, consult in the first place the excellent work of Mgr Duchesne, *Fastes épiscopaux de l'ancienne Gaule*, 2nd ed., vol. I, 8vo, Paris, 1907, pp. 11–12, and especially vol. II, 1910, pp. 395–430 and 457–79. Cf. Ad. Harnack, *Die Mission und Ausbreitung des Christentums in den ersten drei Jahrhunderten*, 2nd ed., vol. II, 8vo, Leipzig, 1906, pp. 227–8. For the would-be mission of Saints Savinien, Potentian, Altin and Edoald, there is an excellent work by M. Aug. Fliche, *Les vies de Saint Savinien, premier évêque de Sens. Étude critique suivie d'une édition de la plus ancienne Vita* (thèse Fac. Lettres, Paris), 8vo, Paris, 1912, 11 + 106 pp. For the Church in Paris, cf. abbé Eug. Bernard's book referred to above, vol. XXV, p. 351, note 3, and Pachtère's book, *Paris à l'époque gallo-romaine*, ch. VI and apps. III and IV. The story of the controversy about the apostolicity of the churches of Chartres and Orléans, in the nineteenth century, has been told by A. Houtin, *La controverse de l'apostolicité des églises de France au XIX* siècle, 2nd ed., 8vo, Paris and Laval, 1901, pp. 87ff. For Rouen, cf. H. Prentout, *La Normandie*, p. 33.

40 The *actes de Saint Sanctin*, the most ancient text in which this doubtful saint is mentioned, was offered to Charles the Bald in 876 by Hincmar, archbishop of Reims, who had composed it. Cf. H. Schroers, *Hincmar, Erzbischof von Reims*, 8vo, Fribourg-in-Br., 1884, pp. 454–5. Cf. *Acta Sanctor octobr.*, V, pp. 585–603 and Ch. Cuissard, 'Les premiers évéques d'Orléans', in *Mém. Soc. archéol. Orléanais*, vol. XX (1886), pp. 22–4.

41 Cf. Aug. Longnon, *Géographie de la Gaule au VI* siècle, pp. 5–6.

Duchesne, *Fastes épiscopaux*, vol. II, pp. 394–5; E. Lesne, 'La Hiérarchie épiscopale, en Gaule et Germanie (742–882)', in *Mém. et travaux publiés par les professeurs des Facultés Catholiques de Lille*, vol. I, 8vo, Lille and Paris, 1905, p.9.

42 For the *pagi* in the Ile-de-France, see, in addition to Aug. Longnon's *Atlas historique de la France. Texte explicatif*, pp. 98, 99 and 107–13, H. Guérard, *Polyptyque de l'abbé Irminon*, vol. I, 4to, Paris, 1844, pp. 50–104.

43 Cf. Ch. Cuissard, 'Théodulfe, évêque d'Orléans', in *Mém. Soc. archéol. Orléanais*, vol. XXIV (1892), ch. 1: 'Topographie du diocèse d'Orléans', pp. 7–40, and Et. Fourgeron, *Condition juridique de l'Orléanais dans l'Ancien Droit* (thèse Fac. Droit, Paris), 8vo, Paris, 1912, pp. 6–15.

44 Mérey, Eure, canton of Pacy-sur-Eure; this is the hypothesis put forward by M. Longnon.

45 Méré, Seine-et-Oise, canton of Montfort-l'Amaury; this is the hypothesis put forward by Guérard. On the *pagus Madriacensis* cf. also the following articles: A. de Dion, 'Le Comté de Madrie', in *Mém. Soc. archéol. Rambouillet*, vol. I (1870–2), pp. 1–11 (which does not reach a firm conclusion), and J. Béranger, 'Le Pagus Madriacensis. Son origine, son histoire, ses comtes', in *Rev. cathol. de Normandie*, vol. XVI (1906), pp. 89–107 (which, without pronouncing on the etymology of the word *Madriacensis*, gives the Eure as the western boundary of the *pagus*, thus rejecting even M. Longnon's theory).

46 Cf. *Vie de Bouchard le Vénérable, par Eudes de Saint-Maur*, ed. de la Roncière (*Collect. de textes pour servir à l'ét. de l'hist.*), 8vo, Paris, 1892, particularly p. XIII, and Maurice Prou, 'Les monnaies de Bouchard, comte de Paris', in *Annuaire Soc. numismatique*, vol. XX (1896), pp. 279–86.

47 The title of comte d'Étampes was revived in 1327 in favour of Charles d'Évreaux, who already possessed as an *appanage* the lordship over the town, but without the title of count; cf. dom Fleureau, *Histoire d'Étampes*, p. 151. I have not been able to obtain the book by L. Marquis, *Les seigneurs d'Étampes; chronologie des barons, comtes et ducs d'Étampes*, 8vo, Étampes, 1901, IV + 35 pp. Cf. on this work a review (pointing out two omissions) by Henri Stein, *Annales Soc. histor. Gâtinais*, vol. XXI (1903), p. 254.

48 E. Mourin, *Les comtes de Paris, histoire de l'avènement de la troisième race*, 2nd edit., 8vo, Paris, 1872, XXIII + 528 pp.

49 By Gabriel Monod, *Revue crit.*, 1874, part 2, pp. 163–70.

50 Cf. especially A. de Barthélemy, 'Les origines de la maison de France', in *Rev. des quest. hist.*, vol. XIII (1873), pp. 139–40. (Cf. *Rev. crit.*, 1873, part 2, pp. 97–101.)

51 *Mém. Soc. histor. Pontoise*, vol. XXXI (1912), pp. 83–117.

52 J. Devaux, *Étude chronologique sur les comtes du Gâtinais*, vol. III, 1885, pp. 55–83; C. Ballu, 'De la suzeraineté des comtes d'Anjou sur le Gâtinais,' *ibid.*, vol. VIII (1890), pp. 157–82; J. Devaux, 'Origines gâtinaises', *ibid.*, vol. X, (1892), pp. 241–60 and vol. XIV (1896), pp. 292–331; E. Thoison,

'Lettre à M. Jules Devaux', *ibid.*, vol. XI (1893), pp. 126–8; P. Quesvers, 'Gastins en Gâtinais?' *ibid.*, vol. XII (1894), pp. 1–26; G. d'Espinay, 'Les comtes du Gâtinais', in *Mém. Soc. agricult. d'Angers*, vol. I, of the 5th series (1898), pp. 25–42; M. Prou, 'L'acquisition du Gâtinais par Philippe Ier', in *Ann. Soc. histor. Gâtinais*, vol. XVI (1898), pp. 177–90; H. Stein, 'Note sur un diplôme du roi Raoul', in *Le Moyen Age*, 1902, pp. 326–32; L. Halphen, *Le comté d'Anjou au XIe siècle* (thèse Fac. Lettres, Paris), 8vo, Paris, 1906, p. 133 note 2 and 150; Aug. Fliche, *Le règne de Philippe Ier roi de France* (thèse Fac. Lettres, Paris), 8vo. Paris, 1912, pp. 139–43.

53 It goes without saying that the works devoted to county towns— Chartres, Melun, Meaux, Corbeil, etc.—noted in the bibliography for the *monographies locales* or for *l'histoire locale avant le XIXe siècle*, contain information about the counts. There is no need to refer to them again here. For the counts of Chartres, consult R. Merlet, 'Les comtes de Chartres, de Châteaudun et de Blois au IXe et Xe siècles', in *Mém. Soc. archéol. Eure-et-Loir*, vol. XII (1901), pp. 1–34. Cf. A. Dupré, 'Les comtesses de Chartres et de Blois. Étude histor.', in *Mém. Soc. archéol. Eure-et-Loir*, vol. V (1872), pp. 198–236, and (because the history of the County of Chartres is intimately bound up with the dynasty of Blois-Champagne) H. d'Arbois de Jubainville, *Histoire des ducs et comtes de Champagne*, 6 vols., 8vo, Paris, 1859–66.

54 Creuzet, 'Notes sur les comtes de Corbeil', in *Bullet. Soc. histor. Corbeil*, Vol. X (1904), pp. 122–35.

55 J. Depoin, 'Le problème de l'origine des comtes du Vexin', in *Rev. des études histor.*, vol. LXXIV (1908), pp. 473–82.

56 A work of this kind has been sketched out for the whole of France and for the Carolingian period by M. René Pourpardin, 'Les grandes familles comtales à l'époque carolingienne', in *Rev. Hist.*, vol. 72 (1900), pp. 72–95.

57 J. Depoin, 'Les vicomtes de Corbeil et les chevaliers d'Étampes au XIe siècle', in *Bullet. Soc. histor. Corbeil*, vol. V (1890), pp. 1–61, and 'Addition à la Notice sur les vicomtes de Corbeil', *ibid.*, pp. 159–65.

58 J. Depoin, 'La Chevalerie Étampoise, III. Les Vicomtes d'Étampes', in *Bullet. Soc. histor. Corbeil*, vol. XV (1909), pp. 83–90. A. Duchalais, 'Charte inédite de l'an 1138 relative à l'histoire des vicomtes de Melun', in *Bibl. Ec. des Chartres*, 2nd series, vol. I (1844), pp. 239–76.

59 J. Devaux, 'Origines Gâtinaises', in *Ann. Soc. histor. Gâtinais*, vol. XII, pp. 292ff.; H. Stein, *ibid.*, vol. XXVIII (1910), pp. 334–5; Em. Richemond, *Recherches sur les seigneurs de Nemours* (below, Chapter Four, note 63), vol. I, pp. 10ff.

60 J. Depoin, *Sur les comtes et Vicomtes de Meulan. Cartul. de l'abbaye de Saint-Martin de Pontoise (public. soc. histor. Pontoise)*, section 3, 4to, Pontoise, 1901, pp. 306–29.

61 For the history of the title 'comte de Montfort', cf. the work by A. Rhein (referred to in Chapter Four, note 62), p. 250, note 10. There

certainly existed in the Ile-de-France cases of usurpation of the titles of count and viscount a good deal earlier than the Montfort usurpation. But these have not been studied.

62 'La seigneurie de Montford-en-Iveline (X^e–XIVe siècles)', in *Mém. Soc. archéol. Rambouillet*, vol. XXI (1910), pp. 1–363. Cf. A. de Dion, 'Les fiefs du comté de Montford-l'Amaury', *ibid.*, vol. I (1870–2), pp. 289–387.

63 *Recherches généalogiques sur les seigneurs de Nemours du XIIe au XIVe siècle*, 2 vols., 8vo, Bourges, 1907 and 1908, VI + 348 + CXXIX + X + 276 + CXXV pp. Cf. for the later period A. de Maricourt, *Essai sur l'histoire du duché de Nemours, de 1404 à 1666*, pp. 1–72 and 257–98, vol. XXIII (1905), pp. 51–87 and 295–364, vol. XXIV (1906), pp. 168–267.

64 G. Estournet, 'Origines des seigneurs de Nemours', in *Ann. Soc. histor. Gâtinais*, vol. XXX (1912), pp. 1–156.

65 'Essai sur les premiers seigneurs de Pithiviers', in *Ann. Soc. histor. Gâtinais*, vol. III (1885), pp. 168–78, 250–65, and vol. IV (1886), pp. 74–129, 290–321.

66 A. de Dion, 'Le Puiset aux XIe et XIIe siècles', in *Mém. Soc. archéol. Eure-et-Loir*, vol. IX (1889), pp. 1–34, 71–85. Cf. Ch. Cuissard, 'Les seigneurs du Puiset (980–1789)', in *Bullet. Soc. dunoise*, vol. III (1875–80), pp. 313–96 and the notes added by J. Depoin in his edition of the *Liber Testamentorum S. Martini de Campis*, 8vo, Paris, 1905.

67 *Chevreuse, Recherches historiques, archéologiques et généalogiques* (*Mém. et Doc. publiés par la Soc. Archéol. de Rambouillet*), vols. II and III, 2 vols. 8vo, Rambouillet, 1874 and 1876, XII + 605 + 572 pp.

68 The articles on these questions by M. J. Depoin are so numerous and so widely scattered that I cannot give a bibliography of them here. I have already had occasion to refer to some of them. Particularly important are the 'Appendices' added by M. Depoin to his edition of the *Cartulaire de l'abbaye de Saint-Martin de Pontoise*, 4to, Pontoise, 1895–1909, Sections 3 and 5—and the article on 'La légende des premiers Bouchards de Montmorency', in *Dép. de Seine-et-Oise. Commiss. des antiqu. et des arts*, vol. XXVII (1907), pp. 132–54.

69 There are also in existence, for various regions of the Ile-de-France, genealogical works which may be useful to the historian: 'Table des fiefs du Vexin français, avec les noms de leurs possesseurs, relevée sur les manuscrits de Pihan de la Forêt', published by Arthur de Marsy, in *Rev. nobiliaire*, vol. II (1864), pp. 287–305; Adrien Maquet and Adolphe de Dion, 'Nobiliaire et armorial du comté de Montford-l'Amaury', in *Mém. Soc. archéol. Rambouillet*, vol. V (1879–80), pp. 49–516; E. Grave, 'Supplément au nobiliaire et armorial du comté de Montford-l'Amaury', in *Mém. Soc. archéol. Rambouillet*, vol. XIX (1906), pp. 1–260.

70 The mint at Chartres has been the only one to receive considerable study, especially by E. Cartier. There is a reference to his works in the *Répertoire des sources imprimées de la numismatique française* by A. Engel and

R. Serrure, 3 vols., 8vo, Paris, 1887–9. Cf. also Lépinois, *Histoire de Chartres*, vol. I, ch. XIII, pp. 405–20.

71 Cf. J. Roman, *Manuel de sigillographie française*, 8vo, Paris, 1912, pp. 321–36 (Ile-de-France), and 337–9 (Orléanais); Léop. Delisle, 'Recherches sur les comtes de Dammartin au XIIIᵉ siècle', in *Mém. Soc. Antiquaires*, 4th series, vol. I (vol. 31 in the collection, 1869), pp. 189–258.

72 This enclosing wall still existed at any rate in 1886, when M. M. Loisel was bringing out his volume entitled *Boissy-l'Aillerie*, 8vo, Pontoise, 112 pp. However I have not been able to visit Boissy-l'Aillerie myself, unfortunately.

73 A. de Dion has given a short but intelligible sketch of the Ile-de-France châteaux in an article entitled 'Notes sur les progrès de l'architecture militaire sous le règne de Philippe-Auguste', in *Mém. Soc. archéol. Rambouillet*, vol. I (1870–2), pp. 157–81, and in a little brochure: *Quelques notes sur l'architecture militaire du Moyen Age à propos du château de Dourdan*, 8vo, no date or place of publication, 7 pp.

74 Cf. F. Lot, 'Le Pont de Pitre', in *Le Moyen Age*, vol. IX of the 2nd series (1905, XVIII in the collection), p. 6.

75 Cf. for Anjou, L. Halphen, *Le Comté d'Anjou au XIᵉ siècle* (thèse Fac. Lettres Paris), 8vo, Paris, 1906, p. 158ff., and for Maine, R. Latouche, *Histoire du Comté du Maine pendant le Xᵉ siècle* (*Biblioth. Ec. Hautes Études*, sect. 183), 8vo, Paris, 1910, p. 58ff. In these provinces it was the counts and not the kings who really mattered.

76 What remains of the Vexin châteaux (that is to say, castles built in stone) has been studied in a general work by A. de Dion, 'Exploration des châteaux du Vexin', in *Bullet. monumental*, vol. XXXIII (1867), pp. 330–66.

77 Cf. Victor Petit, 'Le donjon d'Étampes', in *Bullet. monument*, vol. XII (1846), pp. 488–501; L. Marquis, *Notice historique sur le château d'Étampes*, 16mo, Étampes, 1885, 109 pp; L. Eng. Lefèvre, 'Étampes et ses monuments', in *Ann. Soc. hist. Gâtinais*, vol. XXV (1907), pp. 313ff.

78 Éd. A. Leprevost and L. Delisle (*Soc. de l'hist. de France*), vol. II, 8vo, Paris, 1840, p. 467. Cf. A. Luchaire, *Louis VI le Gros*, 8vo, Paris, 1890, p. 168, no. 366.

79 The castle of Dourdan has been studied several times by M. J. Guyot, *Chronique d'une ancienne ville royale*, Dourdan, 8vo, Paris, 1869, iv + 488 pp.; 'L'église et le château de Dourdan', in *Bullet. monum.*, vol. XXXVIII (1872), pp. 613–33; 'Quelques fouilles récentes opérées au château de Dourdan', in *Confér. des soc. sav. de Seine-et-Oise. Troisième réunion* (1906), pp. 72–7. Cf. a communication by M. de Montaiglon 'Sur un plan du château de Dourdan', in *Bullet. Soc. hist. Paris*, vol. I (1874), pp. 67–8.

80 Cf. R. de Lasteyrie, 'Quelques mots sur le château de Gisors', in *Bullet. monum.*, vol. LXV (1901), pp. 122–37.

81 Cf. the text of the agreements for the construction of fortresses,

published according to the *Registrum Veterius*, of the French Chancery, or cartulary A of Philip Augustus (Vatican, Ottoboni 2796) by A. Tuetey, *Arch. de Missions*, 3rd series, vol. VI, 1880, pp. 349–51.

82 Cf. the information given on this subject by the lieutenant of the bailiwick of Meaux: 7 August 1415 (National Archives, S 371 B). On the ravages caused in the Ile-de-France by the Hundred Years' War, important information will be found in the register of his visitations kept by Jean Mouchard, Visitor for the archdeaconry of Josas from 1458 to 1470, published by abbé J.-M. Alliot, *Visites archidiaconales de Josas*, 8vo, Paris, 1902, xxxix + 450 pp., with a commentary by M. Petit-Duraillis, 'Un nouveau document sur l'Église de France à la fin de la guerre de Cent Ans', in *Rev. Histor.*, vol. 88 (1905), pp. 298–316. For a criticism of this edition cf. a review (also by M. Petit-Dutaillis), *Le Moyen Age*, vol. IX of the 2nd series (XVIII in the collection: 1905), pp. 36–41.

83 For the 'tours de Gannes', cf. dom G. Morin, *Histoire du Gastinois*, ed. Laurent, vol. III, p. 119; (A. Duchalais), *Mémoire archéologique sur la tour de Monthléry*, 8vo, no date or place of publication, p. 4, and especially J. Quicherat, 'La rue et le château Hautefeuille à Paris', in *Mém. soc. antiquaire*, vol. XLII (1881), pp. 17–18.

84 It would be an interesting task to undertake for the rentals and account-books the equivalent of what M. Stein has done for the cartularies. Only too often the inventories of the archives confuse under the label 'rentals', various classes of document. Particularly important are the accounts of Sainte-Geneviève (Bibl. Sainte-Geneviève, MSS. nos. 351 and 579) and of the commandery of Saint-Denis (Arch. Nat., LL1240ff.). The latter have been worked upon by various scholars, notably by M. H. F. Delaborde, 'Note sur Guillaume de Nangis', in *Bibl. Éc. Chartes*, vol. XLIV (1883), pp. 192–201, and by M. Borrelli de Serres, 'Les variations monétaires d'après les comptes de la commanderie de Saint Denis', in *Rev. numismat.*, 4th series, vol. VIII (1904), pp. 430–7. The Seine-et-Oise archives possess two account books of great interest; one, coming from Maubuisson (1236–42), was published in an incomplete and inaccurate form by Henri de l'Épinois, 'Comptes relatifs à la fondation de l'abbaye de Maubuisson', in *Bibl. Éc. Chartes*, vol. XIX (1858), pp. 550–67; the other, from the fourteenth and fifteenth centuries (with additions from later days), comes from Saint-Martin de Pontoise; M. J. Depoin has studied it and published some extracts: *Le Livre de raison de Saint-Martin de Pontoise (XIVe et XVe siècles)* (*Public. Soc. histor. Pontoise*), 8vo, Pontoise, 1900, 240 pp.

85 Specially to be noted is the fine series of chapter registers belonging to the chapter of Notre-Dame de Chartres, which begins in 1208, but unfortunately has some gaps (Biblioth. de Chartres, MSS. nos. 1007–10) and the registers of Notre-Dame de Paris (Arch. Nationales, LL 1240ff.). The latter have been examined by a scholar of the seventeenth century, Claude Sarrasin. Cf. Léon Legrand, 'Claude Sarrasin, intendant des

archives du chapitre de Notre-Dame de Paris et sa collection d'extraits des registres capitulaires de Notre-Dame', in *La Bibliogr. moderne*, vol. IV (1900), pp. 333–71.

86 A. *Cartularies that have been omitted*: (i) Clairefontaine Abbey, diocese of Chartres, sixteenth century, 55 sheets, 1175–1522, Archives Seine-et-Oise, series II; (ii) Grandchamp Abbey, diocese of Chartres, sixteenth century, 18 sheets, May 1216–May 1561, *ibid.*, (iii) Jarcy Abbey, diocese of Paris, sixteenth century, November 1209–September 1511, *ibid.*, (iv) Joyenval Abbey, diocese of Chartres, eighteenth century, 43 sheets, May 1223–June 1718, *ibid.*, (v) Saint-Louis de Poissy Priory, diocese of Chartres —the Seine-et-Oise archives, series H, contain the following from this priory: (*a*) a cartulary from the seventeenth century drawn up by order of the Prioress Jeanne de Gondi (1583–1623), 276 pp.; (*b*) six cartularies of land grants drawn up in the second half of the eighteenth century, one of which concerns the 'ferry', and has been pointed out by M. Stein under the number 3033; the five others concern respectively the lands of 'Carrières', 'Corny', 'Puchay', 'Noyers' and 'Pissefontaine'. The title of *Cartulaire de la léproserie du Grand Beaulieu et du prieuré de N.-D. de la Bourdinière*, formed and annotated by R. Merlet and M. Jusselin (*Cartul. Chartrains*, II, large 4to, Chartres, 1909). Finally, for the cartularies of Chelles Abbey and those of a seigniorial family, the Bouville, I should perhaps refer to the 'Notes sur les sources de l'histoire de l'Ile-de-France au Moyen Age', which appeared in the *Bullet. Soc. hist. Paris*, vol. XL (1913), pp. 145–64, and above, pp. 677–91, seventeenth century, 275 pp., *ibid.*; (vi) Saint-Martin de Pontoise Abbey, diocese of Rouen, a cartulary dealing exclusively with the d'Amblainville (Oise) domain, sixteenth century, 29 July; twelfth century, 7 January 1413 new style, *ibid.* (vii), La Saussaye Priory, diocese of Paris, inventory-cartulary eighteenth century, 305 sheets, 1161–September 1786; Arch. de Seine-et-Oise, series D (Saint-Cyr section). B. *Corrections*: (i) the chapter of Saint-Germain-l'Auxerrois, in Paris, Stein, nos. 2905ff.; read LL 387 instead of LL 386, LL 388 instead of LL 387, LL 389 instead of LL 388; (ii) Stein, nos. 4123 LL 1575, shown as *cartul. des Minimes du Bois de Vincennes*, is really a cartulary of the house of Aulnoye, the Order of Grandmont, diocese of Sens. C. *Cartularies that have been printed since M. Stein's work came out*: R. Merlet, *Cartulaire de Saint-Jean en Vallée de Chartres* (*Cartul. Chartrains*, I), 4to, Chartres, 1906; R. Pourpardin, *Receuil des Chartes de Saint-Germain-des Prés* (*Public. de la Soc. de l' Hist. de Paris*), vol. I, 8vo, Paris, 1909; R. Merlet et M. Jusselin, *Cartulaire de la léproserie du Grande-Beaulieu* (*Cartul. Chartrains*, II), 4to, Chartres, 1909; H. Omont, 'Chartes inédites de rois de France', in *Bullet. Soc. hist. Paris*, vol. XXXVI (1909), pp. 67–74 (extracts from the cartulary of Longpont Priory, Stein no. 2218, now acquired by the Bibliothèque Nationale and numbered: new acquisition lat. 932). J. Depoin, *Chartrier de l'abbaye Saint-Martin pe Pontoise* (*Public. Soc. histor. Pontoise*), 4to, Pontoise, 1911 (the continuation of Stein's *Cartulaire* no. 3067); J. Depoin, *Recueil de Chartes et de documents*

de Saint-Martin-des-Champs, 2 vols. (*Archives de la France monastique*), XIII and XVI, 8vo, Paris, 1912 and 1913.

87 *La France monastique, Recueil historique des Archevêchés, Évêchés, Abbayes et Prieurés de France par Dom Beaunier, Nouvelle édition, revue et complétée par les Bénédictins de Ligué—Chevetogne*, vol. I: *Province ecclésiastique de Paris*, 8vo, Paris, 1905, xxiv + 296 pp., vol. VI (*Province de Sens*); 8vo, Paris, 1913, 177 pp. The typographical lay-out would appear to be less successful than in vol. I.

88 'Chronologie des évêques de Meaux', in *Bullet. hist. et archéol. du dioc. de Meaux*, vol. II, pp. 396–410, 474–87, and *Supplément à la chronologie des évêques de Meaux*, vol. IV (1905), pp. 77–9. The work by M. Aug. Alloud, *Chronique des évêques de Meaux, suivi d'un état de l'ancien diocése et du diocèse actuel*, 8vo, Meaux, 1875, 408 pp., is of mediocre quality.

89 *Diocèse de Meaux. Dignitaires des abbayes, chapitres et prieurés*, 8vo, Melun, 1885, 98 pp. The author's name does not appear on the cover. The boundaries are those of the present diocese.

90 'Catalogue des évêques de Chartres', in *Mém. Soc. Archéol. Eure-et-Loir*, vol. IX (1889), pp. 453–9. Cf. Haye, 'Évêques attribués par erreur et sans preuves au diocèse de Chartres', *ibid.*, pp. 460–2. For the archbishops of Sens, use should be made of the *Chronique des évêques de Sens au Xe siècle*, published by M. Ferd. Lot as the 6th appendix in his 'Derniers Carolingiens' (*Bibl. Éc. Hautes Études*, no. 87), 8vo, Paris, 1891, pp. 335–7.

91 *Dignitaires de l'Église Notre-Dame de Chartres* (*Archives du dioc. de Chartres*, vol. V), 8vo. Paris, 1900, LVIII + 334 pp.

92 For the part played by the religious communities of Chartres as centres of study in the Middle Ages, there is an excellent book by abbé A. Clerval, *Les Écoles de Chartres au Moyen Age, du Ve au XVIés.*, in *Mém. Soc. archéol. Eure-et-Loir*, vol. XI, 1895, xx + 572 pp.

93 Cf. the detailed points put forward by the author of one of the most penetrating monographs on abbeys that we possess, M. R. N. Sauvage, *L'Abbaye de Saint-Martin de Troarn au diocèse de Bayeux des origines au seizième siècle*, 4to, Caen, 1911, especially pp. 135–6 and 282–3.

94 There is not much to be got out of the work by Mlle Félicie d'Ayzac, *Histoire de l'Abbaye de Saint-Denis en France*, 2 vols., 8vo, Paris, 1860, cxxxi + 597 + 573 pp. For the origins of Saint-Denis—which is as much an archaeological as a historical question—cf. below, Chapter Four, note 125.

95 'Fulrad, Archichapelain des premiers rois carolingiens, et abbé de Saint-Denis en France', in *Rev. d'Alsace*, vol. LII (1901), pp. 139–52, 354–373, 517–40 and LIII (1902), pp. 35–6 and 274–309.

96 'Notes sur Ebles, abbé de Saint-Denis au temps du roi Eudes', *Université de Paris, Bibl. Fac. des Lettres*, vol. III (*Mélange d'Histoire du Moyen Age*), pp. 89–98. Cf. L. Levillain, 'L'abbé Ebles, chancelier du roi Eudes', in *Correspond. histor. et archéol.*, vol. IX (1902), pp. 359–71. M. Levillain has succeeded in establishing the succession of the abbots of

Saint-Denis from 980 to 1049 in an article in the *Revue Mabillon* (Archives de la France Monastique), vol. I, 1905, pp. 41–54, 'Notes sur quelques abbés de Saint-Denis'.

97 'Guillaume de Massouris, abbé de Saint-Denis', *Université de Paris, Bibl. Fac. Lettres*, XVIII (*Troisièmes mélanges d'histoire du Moyen Age*), pp. 187–266.

98 'Abt Suger von Saint-Denis, 1081–1151' (*Histor. Studien veröff.* by E. Ebering, vol. XI), 8vo, Berlin, 1898, xv + 192 pp.

99 *Œuvres complètes de Suger* (*Soc. de l'Hist. de France*), 8vo, Paris, 1867. For Suger's manuscripts, consult the important study by M. Luchaire, *Les œuvres de Suger. Univ. de Paris, Bibl. Fac. Lettres*, vol. VIII: 'Études sur quelques manuscrits de Rome et de Paris', pp. 1–5.

100 Baron François de Béthune, 'Les écoles historiques de Saint-Denis et Saint-Germain-des-Prés dans leurs rapports avec la composition des Grandes Chroniques de France', in *Rev. d'hist. écclésiastique* (Univ. Cathol. de Louvain), vol. IV (1903), pp. 24–38. Cf. Paul Mayer, *Romania*, vol. XXXIII (1904), p. 101.

101 8vo, Paris, 1913, pp. 123–75.

102 For the *Lendit* (a large fair held near Paris in June) one can already refer to an article by M. Ernest Roussel, 'La Bénédiction du Lendit au XIVᵉ siècle', an article that is followed by a 'Note additionelle' by M. L. Delisle, *Bullet. Soc. hist. Paris*, vol. XXIX (1897), pp. 68–83; and *la position de thèses* by M. E. Roussel, *École Nat. des Chartes. Position des thèses soutenues par les élèves de la promotion 1884*, pp. 103–7.

103 *Histoire de l'abbaye et de l'ordre des chanoines réguliers de Saint-Victor de Paris*, 2 vols., Paris, no date [1904–7], xxx + 477 and viii + 327 pp.

104 'Étude sur l'histoire de l'abbaye de Sainte-Geneviève de Paris jusqú'à la fin du XIIIᵉ siècle', in *Mém. Soc. hist. Paris*, vol. XXX, 1903, pp. 41–126. The work by abbé Féret, *L'Abbaye de Sainte-Geneviève et la Congrégation de France*, 2 vols., 8vo, Paris, 1883, x + 365 + 419 pp., is distinctly mediocre.

105 *Histoire de l'abbaye et des religieuses bénédictines de N.-D. du Val de Gif*, 8vo, Paris, 1892, 322 pp.

106 *Histoire de l'abbaye et des religieuses bénédictines de Notre-Dame de Yerres*, 8vo, Paris, 1899, x + 313 pp.

107 *Histoire de l'abbaye royale de Notre-Dame de Chelles*, 2 vols., 8vo, Paris, 1889.

108 *L'abbaye de Chelles, résumés chronologiques*, 3 vols., 8vo, Meaux, 1889 to 1894.

109 *L'abbaye de Maubuisson (Notre-Dame la Royale) Histoire et Cartulaire* (*Docum. éd par la Soc. histor. Vexin*), 4to, Pontoise, 1882–5, iv + 318 pp. It goes without saying that I only refer here to the most important of the monographs on abbeys. The majority of the cartularies or collections of printed charters are preceded by notices on the religious establishments

to which they refer. One of the most important among the abbeys in the Ile-de-France, Saint-Père de Chartres, has been the subject of a thesis by M. E. Berger in the *École des Chartres*; cf. *Positions des thèses soutenues par les élèves de la promotion de 1913*, pp. 9–18.

110 The landed fortune of Saint-Germain-des-Près has been studied by dom Anger, *Les dèpendances de l'abbaye de Saint-Germain-des-Prés*, 3 vols. (*Archives de la France monastique*, vols. III, IV and VIII), Paris, 1906 to 1909, VII + 362, VII + 323 and CIII + 363 pp.—a not very reliable work, to be consulted with caution.

111 This is what M. Bonnet-Maury does not seem to have taken into account in his 'Saint-Colomban et la fondation des monastères irlandais en Brie', in *Rev. histor.*, vol. 83 (1903), pp. 277–99.

112 Cf. V. Leblond, *L'Abbaye de Rebais-en-Brie, sommaire chronologique de 635 à 1800*, 8vo, Beauvais, 1898, 120 pp.; V. Leblond and Maurice Lecomte, *Les privilèges de l'abbaye de Rebais-en-Brie*, 8vo, Melun, 1910, 64 pp.; H.-M. Delsart, *Une fondatrice d'abbaye au VIIe siècle. Sainte Fare, sa vie et son culte*, duodecimo, Paris, 1911, 362 pp. (a rather uncritical work); Maurice Lecomte, 'Le privilège de Saint Faron, évêque de Meaux, pour l'abbaye de Faremoutiers', in *Bullet. Confér. hist. diocèse Meaux*, vol. I (1898), pp. 263–87 (important review by L. Levillain, *Moyen Age*, vol. XI, pp. 469–73); Maurice Lecomte, 'Le testament de Sainte Fare, fondatrice et première abbesse de Faremoutiers', *ibid.*, pp. 321–38 (important review by L. Levillain, *Bibl. Éc. Chartes*, vol. LX (1899), pp. 95–100); Gaston Sénéshal, 'La parenté de Saint Faron et de Sainte Fare', in *Bullet. Soc. archéol. Seine-et-Marne*, vol. XI (1905–6), pp. 323–33; and of course the general works on Columba and his Irish monks to be found in the bibliographies of the history of the Merovingian period. The question of the Briard monasteries is to some extent bound up with the problem of the *Cantilène de saint Faron* (a Latin poem inserted into the *Vita S. Faronis*), and so—rather strangely—with that of the origin of the *chansons de geste*. Cf. *Les légendes épiques*, vol. IV, pp. 289–335.

113 Cf. Aug. Molinier, *Les sources de l'histoire de France*, vol. II, p. 192, no. 1878.

114 Some works bearing upon the rural history of the Ile-de-France in general are indicated below in the course of remarks on the rural history of modern times.

115 'Les chartes de la commune de Meaux (1179–1222)', in *Bullet. Soc. Lettres, Brie*, p. III, sect. I (1900).

116 *Du mouvement communal dans le comté de Champagne aux XIIe et XIIIe siècles* (thèse Fac. Droit Paris), 8vo, Paris, 1940, 180 pp.

117 *La commune de Soissons et le groupe communal soissonnais* (*Bibl. Éc. Hautes Études*, sect. 167), 8vo, Paris, 1908. Third part, ch. V: 'Meaux et les communes de Champagne'. I intend to return elsewhere to the study of the history of communes in the Paris region.

118 André Blondel, *Essai sur les institutions municipales de Chartres*,

spécialement du XIIIe au XIVe siècle (thèse Fac. Droit Paris), 8vo, Paris, 1903, 156 pp.

119 See the thesis in the *École des Chartres* by Mlle G. Acloque, *Études sur le commerce et l'industrie à Chartres depuis le XIe siècle jusqú'à la fin du ministère de Colbert*; cf. *Positions des thèses soutenues par les élèves de la promotion de 1910*, pp. 1–12.

120 The history of law is essentially local history during the Middle Ages. I would give some bibliographical details on the subject and point out the chief problems if it were not for the appearance of a *Histiore de la Coutume de Paris* by M. Olivier Martin which bids fair to reopen the question. The work by M. Buche, *Essai sur l'ancienne coutume de Paris aux XIIe et XIVe siècles*, 8vo, Paris, 1886, 136 pp., is quite inadequate. The great difficulty about the study of the legal history of the Ile-de-France (*coutume de Paris* and neighbouring *coutumes*) during the Middle Ages arises from the state of the source-material. This is very widely dispersed and consists of: (*a*) lawsuits, judgments, records of procedure and contracts; all of these are to be found scattered in the various archive repositories; a very small proportion of the archives of the *parlement* of Paris have been published or listed; the legal registers of a certain number of religious communities in Paris have been published (cf. Chapter Four, note 121); (*b*) the books of customs to which must be added the collection of notable judgments; these works, sometimes printed and sometimes in manuscript, raise some very delicate problems, such as the relationship between them, the degrees of mutual influence, and the influence on all of them (though in varying degrees), exercised by Canon Law and Roman Law. Besides the information given in the manuals, there are the articles published by M. André Giffard over several years in the *Nouvelle Revue Historique du Droit*, under the title: 'Études sur les sources du droit coutumier'; (*c*) royal decrees, or decrees emanating in a general way from public authorities; it will be noted that the oldest text in which the feudal customs of *Francia* are set out is a Languedoc text—a decree promulgated on 1 December 1212 by Simon de Montfort, Viscount of Béziers and Carcassonne, Lord of Albi and le Razès, regulating the customs of his southern territory, and in many points following those of *Francia circa Parisius: Histoire du Languedoc*, by dom Claude Devic and dom J. Vaissete, new ed., vol. VIII, 4to, Toulouse, 1879, cols. 625–35.

121 L. Tanon, *Histoire des justices des anciennes églises et communautés de Paris, suivie des registres inédits de Saint-Maur-des-Fossés, Sainte-Geneviève, Saint-Germain-des-Prés et du registre de Saint-Martin-des-Champs*, 8vo, Paris, 1883, 572 pp. Cf. the *registre civil de la seigneurie de Villeneuve-Saint-Georges*, published by the same author in his work entitled *L'ordre du procès civil au XIVe siècle*, 8vo, Paris, 1886, pp. 85–165.

122 Rethoré, *Les cryptes de Jouarre*, 8vo, 1885.

123 Cf. the bibliographical information given below (Ch. Four, n. 138).

124 Paul Durand, 'Rapport sur l'église et la crypte de Saint-Martin-

au-Val', in *Mém. Soc. archéol. Eure-et-Loir*, vol. I (1858), pp. 305–18.

125 There are three rival theories on the origins of the abbey of Saint-Denis: (*a*) the one shared by Mabillon and Félibien, revived by MM. Vitry and Brière (cf. Chapter Four, note 134) and by M. Léon Maître, 'Le culte de Saint-Denis et de ses compagnons', in *Rev. de l'art chrétien*, vol. LVIII (1908), pp. 361–70 and vol. LIX (1909), pp. 80–94 and 174–83: that the basilica has always been on the site it now occupies and which it occupied from the beginning of the Merovingian period; Dagobert rebuilt it on the same site. (*b*) Julien Havet's theory, 'Les origines de Saint-Denis', in *Bibl. Ec. Chartres*, vol. LI (1890), pp. 5–62, and *Œuvres*, vol. I, 8vo, Paris, 1896, pp. 191–246, to the effect that the basilica originally occupied the site later called Saint-Denis-de-l'Étrée, on the Roman road, and Dagobert, when he founded the abbey, transported the relics of Saint-Denis-de-l'Étrée to a new church constructed by him on the site of the present building. (*c*) M. Levillain's theory (in the article referred to in Chapter Four, note 135): the basilica was originally built at Saint-Denis-de-l'Étrée, but the translation did not take place until the reign of Pépin le Bref. According to the first two theories, the oldest architectural remains beneath the present basilica would be of the Merovingian period; according to the third theory, they would represent the remains of a Carolingian church.

126 'Les Églises romanes du Vexin français', in *Confér. Soc. savantes Seine-et-Oise, Deuxième Réunion* (1904), pp. 35–52, and 'Les Églises romanes du Pincerais', *ibid. Troisième réunion* (1906), pp. 53–68. Besides various works earlier than these two studies, M. Coquelle has published since then 'Les portails romans du Vexin français et du Pincerais', in *Mém. Soc. histor. Pontoise*, vol. XXVII (1906), pp. 41–60.

127 *Ile-de-France (École de l')*, *Encyclopédie de l'architecture et de la construction*, by P. Planat, vol. V, 4to, Paris, pp. 181–201.

128 'Les influences normandes au XIe et au XIIe siècle dans le Nord de la France', in *Bullet. monument*, vol. LXX (1906), pp. 3–37.

129 M. Enlart, moreover, calls it *'école du Nord de la France'*.

130 Lefèvre-Pontalis, the article referred to, Chapter Four, note 128. For the influence of the Rhenish school on the religious architecture of northern France, at the beginning of the Gothic period, see Enlast, 'De quelques influences germaniques dans les premiers monuments gothiques du Nord de la France', in *Mélanges Paul Fabre*, 8vo, Paris, 1902, pp. 258–64.

131 L. Saint-John Crèvecoeur has published, in the *Positions de thèses des élèves de l'École des Chartres: promotion de 1896*, pp. 43–7, a summary of a thesis that has remained in MS., entitled *Étude sur l'architecture religieuse au XIe et XIIe siècles dans l'ancien diocèse de Paris*. I refrain from giving any bibliography bearing upon the problem of the origin of Gothic architecture; it will be sufficient to refer the reader to the manuals of archaeology.

132 The essential work on the beginnings of sculpture in the Ile-de-France is the one by M. R. de Lasteyrie, *Étude sur la sculpture française au Moyen Age*, in *Monuments Piot.*, vol. XVIII, 4to, Paris, 1902, chs. 1 and 2,

pp. 1–44. On the date of the sculptures and in a general way the monuments in the Ile-de-France, M. A. Marignan has put forward some opinions that differ from the usually accepted ones, assigning them dates that are later than those generally accorded them. Cf. his two works *La décoration monumentale des églises de la France septentrionale du XIIe au XIIIe siècle*, 16mo, 1911, xix + 334 pp., and *Les méthodes du passé dans l'archéologie française*, 8vo, Paris, 1911, 242 pp.

133 It must be remembered that a certain number of sculptures now in Saint-Denis were only brought there after the Revolution, many of them coming from other churches in the Ile-de-France.

134 *L'église abbatiale de Saint-Denis et ses tombeaux. Notice historique et archéologique*, 12mo, Paris, 1908, xii + 179 pp.

135 'Les plus anciennes églises abbatiales de Saint-Denis', in *Mém. Soc. hist. Paris*, vol. XXXVI (1909), pp. 143–222.

136 *Monographie de la cathédrale de Chartres*, 2nd ed. revised and augmented (*Soc. archéol. Eure-et-Loir*), 3 vols., Chartres, 1891–1901, v + 288, 415 + 350 + lii pp.; vol. III contains a bibliography by abbé Sainsot.

137 René Merlet, *La cathédrale de Chartres* (*Petite monographie des grands édifices de la France*), small 8vo, Paris, no date, 100 pp. While on the subject, I ought to make my apologies to Sébastien Rouillard: I inadvertently said in Chapter Two that his *Parthénie* could no longer be of interest to anyone but the historians of Celtomania. It can nevertheless be of some assistance to the archaeologist; for however imbued with the Renaissance spirit Rouillard may have been, he admired the Gothic cathedral, and gave some useful descriptions of it.

138 It is of course absolutely impossible to give at this point a bibliography of these monographs; but it may be useful to indicate a few more general studies in which the churches of a particular region are grouped together: (*a*) *the district round Paris*: Anthyme Saint-Paul, 'Notices et observations comparatives sur les églises des environs de Paris', in *Bullet. monum.*, vol. XXXIV (1868), pp. 861–79, and XXV (1869), pp. 707–37; (*b*) *the former diocese of Paris*: P. Hérard, *Recherches archéologiques sur les abbayes de l'ancien diocèse de Paris*, 4to, Paris, no date [1902], v + 178 pp. (the brochures brought together in this volume were first published between 1851 and 1857, and contain some interesting information about the ruins which have decayed considerably since then); (*c*) *Seine-et-Marne*: Mgr. Allou, 'Rapport sur les églises de l'arrondissement de Meaux', in *Bullet. comité arts et monuments*, vol. II (1842–3), pp. 40–54; and especially Gassies, 'Coup d'œil sur l'archéologie du Moyen Age d'après les monuments français et en particulier d'après ceux du département de Seine-et-Marne et de la region avoisinante (Brie, Champagne, Soissonnais, Beauvaisis, etc.)', in *Bullet. Soc. littér. Brie*, vol. II (1894–7), pp. 151–316. I have not been able to see E.-W. Rose, *Cathedrals and Cloisters of the Isle-de-France*, 2 vols., 8vo, London, 1911, which is more particularly, I think, an iconographical collection.

139 M. Lefèvre-Pontalis has quite recently attempted to define the characteristics common to all the churches, not of one region, but of one monastic order: 'Les plans des églises romanes bénédictines', in *Bullet. monum.*, vol. LXXVI (1912), pp. 439–85. M. Albert Mayeux's essay, 'Les grands portraits du XII\u00ae siècle et les bénédictins de Tiron', in *Rev. Mabillon*, vol. II (1906), pp. 96–122, which bears directly upon the Ile-de-France, is a less successful piece of work. Cf. *Bullet. monum.*, vol. LXX (1906), pp. 605–9, review by M. Lefèvre-Pontalis.

140 Cf. N. Weiss, 'Notes et documents sur la réforme en Brie (1518–1776)', *Bullet. Soc. hist. protestant français*, vol. XLVI (1897), pp. 631–58.

141 Cf. J. Pannier, 'Le protestantisme à Claye de 1554 à 1700', *Bullet. Soc. hist. protestant français*, vol. LVIII (1909), pp. 192–244, and Eug. and Ém. Haag, *La France protestante*, 2nd ed., vol. I, 8vo, Paris, 1877—the word 'Anjorrant', pp. 266ff.

142 Cf. O. Douen, 'La Réforme en Picardie', *Bullet. Soc. hist. protestant français*, vol. VIII (1859), p. 391. The fact is quoted, but no references are given.

143 For the wars of religion in the Ile-de-France see: H. Lecharpentier, *La ligue à Pontoise et dans le Vexin français*, 8vo, Pontoise, 1878, 246 + cxiii pp., and G. Baguenault de Puchesse, L. Anvray and B. de Lacombe, *Documents sur la religion dans l'Orléanais*, 1st series (1560–5), 8vo, Orléans, 1902, 15 pp.

144 Cf. Eugène Ritter, 'Didier Rousseau, le quartaïeul de Jean-Jacques', *Bullet. Soc. hist. protestant français*, vol. XLII (1893), pp. 281–92; 'Didier Rousseau, quartaïeul de Jean-Jacques Rousseau, nouveaux documents', *ibid.*, vol. XLIV (1895), pp. 635–8, and J. Pannier, 'Didier Rousseau de Montlhéry et autres réfugiés à Genève', *ibid.*, vol. XLVII (1898), pp. 411–13. Notice the expression Montlhéry 'en France' (more exactly 'Montrichery lès Paris en France'; elsewhere, 'Montlechery'). This proves that the name 'France' was still sometimes applied in the sixteenth century to the district south of the Seine.

145 Most of M. Pannier's studies have appeared in the *Bulletin de la Société de l'histoire du protestantisme français*—some of them under the title *Études historiques sur les églises réformées de l'Ile-de-France*. They will be found enumerated in this *Bulletin*, vol. I (1901), p. 169, note 1, and vol. LVIII (1909), p. 193, note 1. To the information given in this second note add the following article: 'Note complémentaire sur Grigny', *ibid.*, vol. LV (1906), p. 95. M. Pannier is also the author of *Études historiques sur la réforme à Corbeil et aux environs, au XVIᵉ siècle* (*Mém. et doc. de la Soc. hist. de Corbeil*, II), 8vo, Paris, 1900, 51 pp. His book on *l'Église réformée de Paris sous Henri IV* (thèse Fac. Lettres Paris), 8vo, Paris, 1911, is naturally of interest at several points to the historian of the Ile-de-France: Cf. also G. Leroy, *Recherches historiques sur le protestantisme dans le Melunais* (1567–1789), small 8vo, Meaux, 1874, 63 pp.

146 *La Réforme et les églises réformées dans le département actuel d'Eure-et-*

Loir (1523–1911), 8vo, Paris, 1912, vi + 595 pp. Cf. Am. Lefèvre-Pontalis, 'Le calvinisme dans le Dunois au XVIᵉ siècle et au XVIIᵉ siècle', *Bullet. Soc. dunoise*, vol. III (1875–80), pp. 275–92.

147 *Le chapitre de Notre-Dame de Paris en 1790*, large 8vo, Paris, 1903, viii + 297 pp.

148 The book by H. Druon, *Bossuet à Meaux*, 12mo, Paris, 1900, is quite inadequate.

149 Cf. the details given by P. Caron and Sagnac, *L'état actuel des études d'histoire moderne en France*, 8vo, Paris, 1902, p. 66.

150 *La Renaissance dans le Vexin et une partie du Parisis, à propos de l'ouvrage de M. Léon Palustre : La Renaissance en France*, large 4to, Pontoise, 1886, 102 pp.

151 Cf. Th. Lhuillier, *L'ancien château royal de Montceaux-en-Brie*, 8vo, Paris, 1885, 40 pp.

152 Cf. Ferd. de Lasteyrie, 'Un grand seigneur du XVIᵉ siècle. Le connétable de Montmorency', *Gaz. des Beaux-Arts*, 2nd period, vol. XIX (1879), pp. 305–20, and vol. XX (1879), pp. 97–114.

153 Cf. Lorin, 'La Société archéologique à Senlis et à Dampierre', *Mém. Soc. archéol. Rambouillet*, 8vo series, vol. XV (1900–1), pp. 1–118.

154 Cf. Em. Galtier, *Histoire de Saint-Maur-des-Fossés depuis les origines jusqu'à nos jours*, 8vo, Paris, 1912, pp. 131–69.

155 Cf. H. Longnon, *Le château de Rambouillet (Petites monographies des grands édifices de la France)*, 12mo, Paris, no date, 108 pp.

156 Cf. vicomte de Grouchy, 'Meudon, Bellevue et Chaville', *Mém. Soc. hist. Paris*, vol. XX (1893), pp. 51–206.

157 Now Maisons-Laffitte. Cf. Henri Nicolle, *Le château de Maisons son histoire et celle des principaux personnages qui l'ont possédé*, 8vo, Paris, 1858, 187 pp., J. E. Engrand, 'Le château de Maisons de 1642 à l'an V de la République', *Rev. de l'hist. de Versailles*, vol. XIV (1912), pp. 305–36, and Léon Deshairs, *Le château de Maisons-Laffitte. Notice historique et descriptive*, folio, Paris, no date. 4 + viii pp. and 41 plates.

158 Cf. Rod. Penor, *Le château de Vaux-le-Vicomte, accompagné d'un texte historique et descriptif par Anatole France*, folio, Paris, 1888, 72 pp. and 20 plates; Fournier-Salovèze, 'Les châteaux de France, Vaux-le-Vicomte', *Rev. de l'art anc. et moderne*, II (1898), pp. 397–410 and 529–40; and especially U.-V. Châtelain, *Le surintendant Nicolas Foucquet, protecteur des lettres, des arts et des sciences* (thèse Fac. Lettres Paris), 8vo, Paris, 1905, pp. 346–415.

159 Cf. P. Hartmann, 'Conflans près Paris', *Mém. Soc. hist. Paris*, vol. XXXV (1908), pp. 1–188.

160 Cf. Victor Advielle, *Histoire de la ville de Sceaux*, 8vo, Sceaux and Paris, 1883, iii + 546 pp.

161 The pleasant little volume by Stanislas-Xavier de Girardin, *Promenade ou itinéraire des jardins d'Ermenonville*, no author's name, 8vo, Paris, 1788, 68 pp., 2nd ed. in 1811.

162 Georges Houdard, *Les châteaux royaux de Saint-Germain-en-Laye* (1124–1789), vol. I, 4to, Paris, 1909–10, xvi + 264 + 47 pp.

163 *Les Archives du Pincerais, Biblioth. histor. de Saint-Germain-en Laye et de sa Région*, 8vo, Paris, 1908, 102 pp. It contains a bibliography. The article by M. P. Herbet should also be noted: 'Les architectes du château de Fontainebleau sous François Ier, Brie et Gâtinais', vol. I (1909), pp. 424–8, and vol. II (1910), pp. 22–7 and 49–54.

164 M. de Nolhac, *Histoire du château de Versailles*. The following are the chief works on which M. de Nolhac's great history is based: *La Création de Versailles*, folio, Versailles, 1901, 250 pp. (included and summarized in *l'Histoire du château*); 'L'art de Versailles. La chambre de Louis XIV', *Rev. de l'art anc. et moderne*, II (1897), pp. 221–30 and 315–26; *Le château de Versailles sous Louis XV*, 8vo, Paris, 1898, VIII + 280 pp.; 'La décoration de Versailles au XVIIIe siècle', *Gaz. des Beaux-Arts*, I (1895), pp. 265–76; II (1895), pp. 217–32; III (1896), pp. 36–50; I (1897), pp. 104–14 and 185–94; I (1898), pp. 63–76 and 143–56; 'Le château de Versailles au temps de Marie-Antoinette (1770–1789)', *Mém. Soc. sc. morales S-e-Oise*, vol. XVI (1889), pp. 19–124. Cf. also P. de Nolhac and A. Pératé, *Le musée national de Versailles, description du château et de ses collections*, 8vo, Paris, no date, 397 pp.; A. Pératé, *Versailles (Les Villes d'Art célèbres)*, 8vo, Paris, 1904, 203 pp. (with bibliography). The book by Dussieux, *Le château de Versailles*, 2 vols., 8vo, Versailles, 1881, is inaccurate. The work by Ph. Gille and M. Lambert, *Versailles et les deux Trianons*, 2 vols., folio, Versailles, 1899 and 1900, xv + 308 + 297 pp., is above all an iconographical collection. On the Trianons: Léon Deshairs, *Le Grand Trianon*, folio, Paris, no date, xv pp. and 60 plates; *Le Petit Trianon*, Paris, no date, x pp. and 100 plates. For the gardens: P. de Nolhac, *Les Jardins de Versailles*, 4to, Paris, 1906, 186 pp.; J. Guiffrey, *André le Nostre (Les Grands Artistes)*, 8vo, Paris, no date, 126 pp. (a rather mediocre work). The book by Louis Corpechot, *Les Jardins de l'intelligence*, 12mo, Paris, 1912, 285 pp., makes pleasant reading, but it will give not so much information about the gardens of Le Nostre as about the strange and misty ideas that certain minds entertain these days about 'classical' art.

165 Some villages of French Vexin belonging to the Rouen *généralité*.

166 *Recueil de documents relatifs à la Convocation des États généraux de 1789*, 3 vols., 4to, Paris, 1894–1904; *Atlas des bailliages ou juridictions assimilées ayant formé unité électorale en 1789* (with an important introduction), folio, Paris, 1904; *Les limites et les divisions territoriales de la France en 1789*, 8vo, Paris, 1907.

167 *Les bailliages royaux en 1789. Villes, bourgs, paroisses et annexes dont les territoires ont formé en 1790 le département de Seine-et-Oise, répartis suivant les bailliages royaux auxquels ces localités ressortissaient à la date de la convocation aux États généraux de 1789 (Essais et notices pour servir à l'histoire du département de Seine-et-Oise, II)*, 4to, Versailles, 1901, 43 pp and map.

168 A form of introduction to vol. III of *l'Invent. sommaire des archives*

départementales (du Loiret) *antérieures à 1790*, Series B, nos. 1536 and 3025; 45 pp. with map. For the geography of the former *bailliage d'Orléans*, see also an edition of the *cahiers* from this *bailliage* drawn up by M. Camille Bloch. Cf. Chapter Four, note 189.

169 *Mém. Soc. hist. Paris*, vol. I, pp. 1–43 (with map).

170 In the Introduction to the work referred in Chapter Four, note 173.

171 In the memoir referred to in Chapter Four, note 175.

172 *La condition juridique de l'Orléanais dans l'ancien droit* (thèse Fac. Droit Paris), 8vo, 1912, xiii + 161 pp.

173 4to, Paris, 1881, xciv + 854 pp. The important documents on the *généralité* are published in an appendix. The memoir on the Orléans *généralité* is unpublished; but it has been extensively used by M. de Beaucorps in his work referred to below in Chapter Four, note 175.

174 Pages lxxi–xc—already published in the *Mém. de la Soc. de l'hist. de Paris*, vol. VII (1880), pp. 291–8. A list of the governors of the Ile-de-France will be found in M. Longnon's memoir referred to in Chapter Four, note 169.

175 'Une Province sous Louis XIV: l'administration des intendants d'Orléans, de Creil, Jubert de Bouville et de la Bourdonnaye (1686–1713)', *Mém. Soc. archéol. Orléanais*, vol. XXXIII (1911), pp. 37–500.

176 *L'Assistance de l'État en France à la veille de la Révolution (Généralités de Paris, Rouen, Alençon, Orléans, Châlons, Soissons, Amiens), 1764–1790* (thèse Fac. Lettres Paris), 8vo, Paris, 1908, lxiv + 504 pp.

177 L. Merlet, *Des assemblés de communautés d'habitants dans l'ancien comté de Dunois (publié sous les auspices de la Soc. Dunoise)*, 12mo, Châteaudun, 1888, 327 pp.

178 *Documents historiques se rattachant à la vie des villages avant 1789 et sous la Révolution*, large 8vo, Versailles, 1908, 174 pp.

179 *Registres des délibérations municipales de la ville de Pontoise (1608–1683)*, 4to, Pontoise (*Doc. édit. par la Soc. histor. du Vexin*).

180 'Assemblées municipales de 1787; leur caractère économique; leur fonctionnement', in *Études sur l'histoire économique de la France*, 8vo, Paris, 1900, pp. 117–56.

181 'Étude sur l'administration provinciale avant 1789; les assemblées provinciales instituées sous Louis XVI et spécialement celle tenue à Melun en 1789', *Bullet. Soc. archéol. Seine-et-Marne*, vol. VIII (1875–7), pp. 123–44.

182 'L'Assemblée provinciale de l'Ile-de-France. Les départements de Saint-Germain et de Corbeil (1787–1790)', *Correspond. histor. et archéol.*, vol. VI (1899), pp. 258–68 and *Bullet. Soc. histor. et archéol. de Corbeil*, vol. VI (1900), pp. 60–78. Cf. also Adalbert Wahl, 'Die Entstehung der Taille in der Provinz Ile-de-France (Généralité von Paris) unter Ludwig XVI', in *Studien zur Vorgeschichte der französischen Revolution*, 8vo, Tübingen and Leipzig, 1901, pp. 69–90.

183 *Essai sur l'Administration de l'Assemblée Provinciale de la Généralité d'Orléans (1787–1790)* (thèse Fac. Droit Paris), 8vo, Paris, 1907, iv + 634

pp. Cf. Camille Bloch, 'Le département de Pithiviers et de Montargis en 1787', *Ann. Soc. histor. Gâtinais*, vol. XVII (1898), pp. 217–26.

184 For a bibliography of the *cahiers*, manuscripts and printed papers, see A. Brette, *Recueil des documents relatifs à la convocation des États généraux de 1789*, vol. III, 4to, Paris, 1907; Coüard, *Les bailliages* (cf. Chapter Four, note 167). Coüard, *Les états généraux de 1789. Cahiers des paroisses et des corporations, Recherche et public. des docum. relatifs à la vie économ. de la Révol.*, Comité départmental de Seine-et-Oise, section 1 (1907), pp. 39–42.

185 Some have been re-edited; for example the one concerned with Saint-Maur-des-Fossés by M. Émile Gautier, *Histoire de Saint-Maur*, 8vo, Paris, 1912, pp. 172–4; the one on Bourg-la-Reine by M. Fernand Bournon, *Département de la Seine. État des communes à la fin du XIXe siècle, Bourg-la-Reine*, 8vo, Paris, 1890. Most of them have been analysed and studied by Ch.-L. Chassin, *Les élections et les cahiers de Paris en 1789 (Collect. de docum. relat. à l'hist. de Paris pendant la Rév. franç.)*, vol. IV, 8vo, Paris, 1889.

186 J.-F. Thénard, *Bailliages de Versailles et de Meudon. Les cahiers des paroisses avec commentaires*, 16mo, Versailles, 1889, xxxvi + 324 pp.

187 Maxime Legrand and Léon Marquis, *1789. Les trois États du bailliage d'Étampes aux États généraux*, 8vo, Étampes, 1892, x + iii + 410 pp., and *1789. Le bailliage d'Étampes aux États généraux, cahier de la ville et des paroisses*, 8vo, Étampes, 1898, xxiv + 588 pp.

188 E. Coüard and F. Lorin, 'Les trois États du bailliage royal de Montfort-l'Amaury aux États généraux, 1789', *Mém. Soc. archéol. Rambouillet*, vol. XVI (1902), pp. 1–301.

189 *Collection de docum. inédits sur l'hist. économ. de la Rév. franç. Département du Loiret. Cahiers de Doléances du bailliage d'Orléans pour les États généraux de 1789*, published by C. Bloch, 2 vols., 8vo, Orleans, 1906 and 1960, lxxiv + 800 and ii + 514 pp. Cf. C. Bloch, *Les cahiers du bailliage d'Orléans au point de vue économique. Études sur l'histoire économ. de la France*, 8vo, Paris, 1900, pp. 157–223.

190 Ernest Mallet, *Les élections du bailliage secondaire de Pontoise en 1789 (Public. Soc. histor. Vexin)*, 8vo, Pontoise, 1909, 421 pp.

191 'Die Cahiers der ländischen Gemeinden von Paris-hors-les-murs', in *Studien zur Vorgesch. der franzős. Rev.*, 8vo, Tübingen and Leipzig, 1901, pp. 1–68. Cf. Ém. Walch in *La Révol. française*, vol. XLI (1901, II), pp. 373–8 and H. Sée, *Rev. histor.*, vol. CIII (1910, I), p. 292.

192 'La création du département de Paris et son étendue, 1789–90', in *Corresp. histor. et archéol.*, vol. IV (1897), pp. 323–9 and 334–68.

193 'La formation du département de Seine-et-Marne en 1790', in *Bullet. Soc. archéol. Seine-et-Marne*, vol. VII (1873–4), pp. 161–82. A small difficulty for the historian of the Revolution arises through the changes that certain place-names underwent at that period. It is important to note that the portion of the *Index des noms révolutionnaires des communes de France* by R. de Figuières, 8vo, Poitiers, 1896, on the Seine, Seine-et-Oise and

Seine-et-Marne has been re-edited, with corrections, under the following title: *Débaptisations révolutionnaires des communes, 1790–1795, Seine, Seine-et-Oise, Seine-et-Marne*, 8vo, Paris, 1896, 12 pp.

194 For example, Lorin, 'Huit années de l'histoire municipale de Rambouillet', in *Études sur la Révolution*, 8vo, Tours, 1898, 268 pp.; C. Forteau, *Méreville pendant la Révolution (1788–1804); extraits des registres municipaux*, 12mo, Étampes, 1899, IV + 108 pp.; E. Tambour, *Les registres municipaux de Rennemoulin, juillet 1789 à floreal an IV*, 12mo, Corbeil, 1903, 263 pp. Cf. J. Doinel, *Documents de la période révolutionnaire : tableau (par arrondissements et cantons) des documents conservés dans les archives des communes du Loiret. Rapport de l'archiviste du dép. du Loiret au préfet*, 1887, pp. 10–24 and the book by Defresne quoted in Chapter Four, note 178.

195 Ern. Noiriel, 'La société des amis de la constitution de Melun', *Rév. franç.*, vol. XLVI (1904, I), pp. 323–45; G. Leroy, 'Le Club des Jacobins de Melun', *ibid.*, vol. XLI (1901, II), pp. 439–46.

196 Charles Constant, *Histoire d'un club Jacobin en province, Fontainebleau pendant la Révolution*, 12mo, Paris, 1875, VIII + 100 pp. The article by Lorin, 'La société populaire de Rambouillet', in *Études* (cf. Chapter Four, note 194), pp. 237–51, contains hardly more than a list of the club members.

197 Edm. Campagnac, 'Le comité de surveillance de Melun', *Annales révolut.*, vol. I (1908), pp. 467–82, and vol. II (1909), pp. 38–54 and 541–66.

198 L.-A. Gatin, *Versailles pendant la Révolution française*, 8vo, Versailles, 1908, 340 pp. Cf. also Laurent-Hanin, *Histoire municipale de Versailles, politique, administration, finances (1787–1789)*, 4 vols., 8vo, Versailles, 1885–9.

199 Raoul Rosières, *La Révolution dans une petite ville*, 12mo, Paris, 1888, 220 pp.

200 H. Bézault, *Histoire municipale de Longjumeau pendant la Révolution*, 8vo, Paris, 1887, 401 pp.

201 Bertaut-Couture, *Histoire de Villiers-le-Bel (Seine-et-Oise) pendant la Révolution (1787–1795)*, 8vo, Villiers-le-Bel, 1891, 141 pp. Cf. also for Meaux, G. George, 'Les débuts de la Révolution à Meaux', *Brie et Gâtinais*, vol. I (1909), pp. 92–4, 115–20, 148–51, and 'Aperçu de l'Histoire de la Révolution à Meaux de 1791 à thermidor an II', *ibid.*, pp. 287–391, and vol. II, pp. 9–15 and 87–8; for Melun, R. Lajoye, *Chronique de Melun et de son district en 1792 et 1793*, Paris, 1883.

202 'L'administration centrale de Seine-et-Oise et le Directoire', *Rev. de l'Hist. de Versailles*, vol. XIII (1911), pp. 194–213, 304–25, and XIV, pp. 45–67 and 127–39.

203 *Recherches sur l'histoire de la Révolution dans la Brie. Les députés à la Convention en mission dans le département de Seine-et-Marne*, 16mo, Meaux, 1876, 188 pp.

204 See especially A. Hugues, 'Le droit de champart en 1790 et la révolte des paysans du Gâtinais', in *Ann. Soc. hist. Gâtinais*, vol. XX (1902), pp. 113–37; A. Hugues, 'Les troubles de Brie-Comte-Robert en

1790–1791', in *Bullet. Soc. archéol. Brie-Comte-Robert*, I (1898–1901), pp. 70–4; Coüard Luys, 'Une émeute populaire à Versailles, le 13 Sept. 1789, d'après des documents inédits', in *Mém. Soc. Sciences mor. S.-et-Oise*, vol. XVI (1889), pp. 152–84; Rabouin, 'Troubles en Beauce à l'occasion de la cherté du blé; novembre et décembre 1792', in *Révol. franç.*, vol. XLII (1902, II), pp. 392–416.

205 *Histoire de la bande d'Orgères*, 12mo, Chartres, 1858, 108 pp.

206 H. Lanfant, *Le Conseil général de la Seine*, 8vo, Paris, 1903, VIII + 446 pp.

207 A. David, *Le Conseil général de Seine-et-Marne, sous le Consulat et l'Empire*, 8vo, Fontainebleau, 1904, 136 pp.; A. Hugues, *Le département de Seine-et-Marne, 1800–1895, d'après les documents officiels, notamment les délibérations du Conseil général, inédites, jusqu'en 1840*, 8vo, Melun, 1895, IV + 566 pp.

208 By F. Dieudonné, *La Révol. de 1848*, vol. II, 1905–6, pp. 281–313, and vol. III, 1906–7, pp. 79–90.

209 Aug. Bernard, 'Simon de Colines', *Bullet. du bouquiniste*, vol. VII (1860, I), pp. 101–5. Cf. Ph. Renouard, *Bibliographie des éditions de Simon de Colines (1520–1546)*, 8vo, Paris, 1894.

210 G. Leroy, 'Recherches sur l'introd. de l'imprimerie à Melun', *Bullet. Soc. archéol. Melun*, vol. VIII (1875–7), pp. 51–69.

211 H. Stein, 'Nouvelles recherches sur l'imprimerie à Étampes', *Ann. Gâtinais*, vol. XV (1897), pp. 92–6.

212 H. Stein, 'Notice sur l'imprimerie à Châteaudun avant la Révolution', *Bullet. Soc. Dunoise*, vol. VI (1888–90), pp. 211–24.

213 Reference can be made to: Th. Lhuillier, *Recherches historiques sur l'enseignement primaire dans la Brie*, 8vo, Meaux, 1884, 130 pp.; the studies by M. Godard on 'l'École Centrale de Seine-et-Oise', in the *Revue de l'histoire de Versailles*, years 1909–11 (vols. XI–XIII), and, in the same review, the studies by Dr Duhaut on 'Le Lycée de Versailles de 1803 à 1860', years 1907–11 (vols. IX–XIII).

214 *Histoire de l'imagerie populaire et des cartes à jouer à Chartres suivie de recherches sur le commerce du colportage des complaintes, canards et chansons des rues*, 12mo, Chartres, 1869, VIII + 450 pp.

215 *Le Folk-Lore de la Beauce et du Perche (Les littératures populaires de toutes les nations)*, 2 vols., small 8vo, Paris, 1902, XIII + 306 + 356 pp. For popular speech in the district round Paris, see Charles Nisard, *Étude sur le langage populaire ou patois de Paris et de sa banlieue*, 8vo, Paris, 1873; Théod. Rosset, *Les origines de la prononciation moderne étudiées au XVIIe siècle d'après les remarques des grammairiens et des textes en patois de la banlieue parisienne*, 8vo, Paris, 1911, 418 pp. (thèse Fac. Lettres Paris), with an Appendix containing patois texts of the seventeenth century, 8vo, Paris, 1911, 84 pp. Cf. also J. Depoin, *Proverbes et locutions du Vexin française*, *Confér. des Soc. sav. de Seine-et-Oise, Deux. réunion* (1904), p. 66, and some indications of a linguistic nature given by Cassan in his *Statistique de l'arrondissement de Mantes*, 8vo, Mantes, 1833, pp. 47ff.

216 See, besides the general work by F. Gattey, *Tableau des rapports des anciennes mesures agraires avec les nouvelles*, 3rd ed., 8vo, Paris, 1812; *Tableau des anciennes mesures du département de Seine-et-Marne comparées aux mesures républicaines, par ordre du Ministre de l'Intérieur*, 4to, Paris, year VIII; F.-A. Delacroix, *Manuel pratique des nouveaux poids et mesures, spécialement destiné aux habitants du Loiret*, 12mo, Orléans, year XI (1802), 74 pp. Cf. also A. Benoit, *Anciennes mesures d'Eure-et-Loir*, small 4to, Chartres, 1843, 70 pp.

217 'Recherches sur les anciennes mesures en usage dans le Gâtinais Seine et Marnais et sur leur valeur en mesures métriques', *Bullet. histor. et philolog.*, vol. XXI (1903), pp. 328–406.

218 'Anciennes mesures agraires de la Brie. Le jugère et le journal', *Bullet. Soc. hist. Brie-Comte-Robert*, vol. II (1801–3), pp. 167–9.

219 One must remember the existence of the rather old-fashioned but still useful book by Alfred Maury, *Les forêts de la Gaule et de l'ancienne France*, 8vo, Paris, 1857, VIII + 501 pp. (a new edition, with an additional memoir, came out in 1860 in vol. IV, 2nd series, of the *Mém. présentés par divers Savants à l'Acad. des Inscriptions*). Some information about the forests of the Ile-de-France will be found in Daubrée, *La crue récente de la Seine dans ses rapports avec la question forestière, Ministère de l'Intérieur. Commission des inondations. Rapports de documents divers*, 4to, Paris, 1910, pp. 501–24.

220 L. de Maulde, *Étude sur la condition forestière de l'Orléanais au Moyen Age et à la Renaissance*, 8vo, Orléans, no date, XI + 532 pp. (cf. for identification of the place-names, Aug. Longnon, *Rev. critique*, II (1873), pp. 264–7); Paul Domet, *Histoire de la forêt d'Orléans*, 12mo, Orléans, 1892.

221 Paul Domet, *Histoire de la forêt de Fontainebleau*, 16mo, Paris, 1873, III + 404 pp.—a very inadequate book; not much is to be had from Félix Herbert, *Dictionnaire historique et artistique de la forêt de Fontainebleau*, 8vo, Fontainebleau, 1903, xx + 522 pp., and from Émile Michel's *La forêt de Fontainebleau dans l'histoire, dans la littérature et dans l'art*, 8vo, Paris, 1909, VIII + 260 pp.

222 Gaston Duchesne, 'La forêt de Rouvray', *Bullet. Soc. histor. d'Auteuil et de Passy*, vol. II (1895–7), pp. 170–2, and vol. III (1898–1900), pp. 8–11. Cf. Rose Cochot-Laverge, 'Le Bois de Boulogne pendant la Révolution', *ibid.*, vol. III, pp. 11–15.

223 L. Planchouard, 'La forêt royale d'Artie en Vexin délimitée comparativement au XVᵉ siècle et à l'époque actuelle', *Bullet. géogr. histor. et descript.* (1895), pp. 339–78.

224 E. Guillemot, 'Les forêts de Senlis. Étude sur le régime des forêts de Hallatte, de Chantilly et d'Ermenonville, au Moyen Age et jusqu'à la Révolution', *Mém. Soc. hist. Paris*, vol. XXXIII (1905), pp. 89–97; G. Maçon, *Historique du domaine forestier de Chantilly*, 2 vols., 8vo, Senlis, 1905–6, 139 + 155 pp.

225 Melaye, 'La forêt de Montgé en 1778', *Bullet. Soc. de la Vrie*, vol. IV (1907), sect. 5.

226 G. Rethoré, 'La forêt du Mans', *Almanach hist. Seine-et-Marne,* years 1887 to 1896; for another Briard forest, see J. Fortin, 'La forêt de Beaulieu, près Melun, Saint-Leu, Sainte-Assise et le Larré', *Bullet. commiss. hist. dioc. Meaux,* vol. II (1899–1901), pp. 524–45.

227 G. Leroy, 'Recherches historiques sur l'agriculture de Seine-et-Marne, aux XVIIe et XVIIIe siècles,' *Bullet. Soc. archéol., S.-et-Marne,* vol. V (1869), pp. 361–453.

228 8vo, Meaux, 1880, 376 pp. Only one 'lecture' is concerned with the period after the Revolution.

229 8vo, Paris, 1789, 300 pp., cf. particularly p. 20. The history of agricultural societies is important for the study of agricultural technique. Cf. the indications given in Chapter Three, note 2 and add: abbé Denis, *Notice sur la Société d'agriculture, sciences et arts de Meaux, Public. Soc. agricul. Meaux,* 1874, pp. 81–6.

230 Cf. H. Watrin, *Étude sur la nécessité de réviser les usages locaux du département d'Eure-et-Loir,* 4to, Chartres, 1889, 32 pp.

231 Eure-et-Loir. H. Watrin in the work referred to below points out that as the result of a decision of the *Conseil général* in August 1839 the *Usages locaux* of the cantons *Chartres Nord et Sud* were published by M. Bouvet-Mézières, and that following upon a circular from the Minister of the Interior of 26 July 1844, *les Usages locaux d'Eure-et-Loir (rédaction officielle)* came out in 1845. In 1861 J.-B. Hénault brought out the *Usages locaux du département d'Eure-et-Loir, et particulièrement de l'arrondissement de Dreux,* 18mo, Chartres and Dreux, 1861, XXXI + 264 pp.; 2nd ed. circulated by J. Parmentier, 8vo, Chartres, 1889, 380 pp. Finally in 1892 the *Usages locaux,* elaborated by commissions of the canton and *arrondissement,* were published as an appendix to the *Recueil des Actes administratifs de la Préfecture* (1892, no. 28); they have been edited several times since then, notably by H. Watrin, *Départment d'Eure-et-Loir. Usages locaux et Notions de droit usuel,* 3rd ed., 8vo, Chartres, 1910, VII + 535 pp. The *notions de droit usuel* contained in this work include some useful information on agricultural methods. Loiret: The only printed collection I know is the official volume: *Recueil des Usages locaux publié sous les auspices du Conseil général et de l'Administration départementale,* 12mo, Orléans, 1905, XXIV + 112 + 89 + 87 + 80 + XXII pp.; the introduction makes it clear that the reports of the enquiries into local *usages* held in 1803 and 1845 are still extant in the departmental archives. Seine-et-Oise: up to 1905 there were only private publications: L.-G. Sauger, *Du louage et des servitudes dans leurs rapports avec les usages locaux,* 8vo, Fontainebleau, Versailles and Paris, 551 pp.: A. Meunier, *Recueil des usages locaux du canton de Meulan,* 12mo, Meulan, 1885, 40 pp.; *Usages locaux* of the six *arrondissements* published successively in the *Annuaire de Seine-et-Oise,* years 1865 to 1870; Paul Vieille and P. Marais, *Code des usages locaux. Arrondissement de Corbeil,* 8vo, Paris, 1891, 70 pp.; cf. also *Journal de la Librairie, années 1892,* nos. 7891–7893 (but I was not able to find the volumes thus referred to). In 1905, the *Conseil général*

undertook to publish the *Usages locaux*; so far produced are the volumes
dealing with the *arrondissements* of Versailles (8vo, Versailles, 1906,
105 pp.), Étampes (8vo, Versailles, 1907, 108 pp.) and Pontoise (8vo,
Versailles, 1908, 148 pp.). Seine-et-Marne: Paul Quesvers, *Usages locaux de
Montereau-fault-Yonne*, 1st ed., 2nd ed., Montereau 1901; *Département de
Seine-et-Marne, Recueil des usages locaux publiés sous les auspices du Conseil
général et de l'Administration départementale*, 8vo, Melun, 1019, 285 pp.

232 *Mém. soc. agricult. Orléans*, vol. VIII (1864), pp. 59–128. Some
interesting information about Beauceron agriculture at the end of the
eighteenth century will be found in (L. Merlet), *L'agriculture en Beauce en
l'an II; correspondance du citoyen Villeneuve avec l'Administration du département
d'Eure-et-Loir*, 12mo, Chartres, 1869, 77 pp. I have not been able to see
Béthouard, *Histoire du blé en Beauce*.

233 12mo, Corbeil, 1895.

234 8vo, Chartres, 1900, 24 pp.

235 14 March 1903. Vol. II of the work by Henri Baudrillard, *Les
populations agricoles de la France*, 8vo, Paris, 1888, contains a rather mediocre
chapter on 'Les Populations agricoles de l'Ile-de-France' (Seine, Seine-et-
Oise, Seine-et-Marne, and parts of Aisne and Oise), pp. 455–626.

236 Cf. L. Chiffert, *De la vaine pâture* (thèse Fac. Droit Paris), 8vo,
Paris, 1899, 192 pp., and the *Usages locaux*.

237 The *vingtième* lists have been used by M. Camille Bloch in an
interesting though very restricted study; *La répartition de la propriété
foncière à la veille de la Révolution, dans quelques paroisses de la Généralité
d'Orléans, Études sur l'hist. économ. de la France*, 8vo, Paris, 1900, pp. 81–116.

238 *Die Nationalgüter-veräusserung während der französischen Revolution mit
besonderer Berücksichtigung des Departments Seine und Oise (Staatswissensch.
Studien, herausgg. von L. Elster, Bd. 4, H.2)*, 8vo, Jena, 1892, VII + 167 pp.

239 In 1877 the common land occupied less than a half per cent of the
territory in Seine-et-Oise, Eure-et-Loir, and Loiret, one per cent in Seine-
et-Marne; cf. R. Graffin, *Les biens communaux en France*, 8vo, Paris, 1889,
map facing p. 270.

240 See especially Maurice Lecomte, 'La question des biens communaux en Seine-et-Marne, à l'époque révolutionnaire', *Brie et Gâtinais*,
vol. II (1910), pp. 244–7, 294–9, 330–4, 425–7; A. Defresne, 'Partage des
biens communaux dans quatre communes du district de Versailles',
*Recherches et public. des doc. relat. à la vie éc. de la Révol. Comité département
de Seine-et-Oise. Bullet.*, sect. 3 (1908–9), pp. 44–96.

241 Camille Bloch, *Le commerce des grains dans la généralité d'Orléans
(1768), Études sur l'histoire économique de la France*, pp. 1–80 (published
earlier in *Mém. Soc. archéol. Orléanais*, vol. XXVII (1898), pp. 351–519):
Maurice Lecomte, 'La disette des blés en Brie et Gâtinais de 1693 à 1709',
Brie et Gâtinais, vol. I (1909), pp. 134–9, 204–8, 278–83, 342–8; Grave,
'Le service des subsistances à Mantes d'après le registre des délibérations',
Recherches et doc. relat. à la vie économ. de la Révol. Com. départemente. Seine-et-

Oise, sect. 1 (1907), pp. 53–71, and 'Les subsistances à Mantes en 1793 et 1794', *ibid.*, sect. 2 (1908), pp. 60–70; P. Caron and L. Raulet, 'Le comité des subsistances de Meulan à l'approvisionnement de Paris (1789–1791)', *Bullet. Commiss. recherche des doc. relat. à la vie économ. de la Révol.* (1908), pp. 25–66.

242 8vo, Melun, 1897, 88 pp.

243 *Quelques recherches sur le port d'Étampes*, 8vo, Étampes, 1860, 90 pp.

244 'Recherches sur la navigation d'Étampes à Corbeil depuis le XVe siècle jusqu'à sa suppression en 1676, suivies d'un exposé historique des tentatives faites au XVIIIe siècle pour son rétablissement, d'après des documents inédits', *Bullet. Soc. histor. Corbeil*, vol. V (1899), pp. 118–58.

245 *Étude sur les droits de navigation de la Seine de Paris à la Roche-Guyon, du XIe au XVIIIe siècle*, 8vo, Paris, 1889, IX + 139 pp. For the Middle Ages, cf. G. Huisman, *La jurisdiction de la municipalité parisienne de saint Louis à Charles VII (Biblioth. d'hist. de Paris publiée sous les auspices du service de la Bibl. de la ville)*, 8vo, Paris, 1912, ch. III.

246 H. Stein, 'La papeterie d'Essonnes', *Ann. Soc. histor. Gâtinais*, vol. XII (1894), pp. 335–64; Fern. Gerbaux, 'Les papeteries d'Essonnes, de Courtalin et du Marais, de 1791 à 1794', *Le Bibliogr. mod.*, vol. III (1899), pp. 206–15.

chapter five

1 4to, Paris, 1728.

2 Page 3 of the Preface.

3 It goes without saying that I am for the moment leaving out of account such tasks as the editing of texts or the summarizing of historical material, which equip the historian with the tools of his job.

4 Cf. Chapter Four, note 1.

Index

Index

Abbeys, histories of, 33–44, 88–94, 160–1
Administration, 105–12
Afforestation, 19–20
Agriculture, 18, 19–20, 21, 23, 25, 31, 43, 90, 112–16, 122, 173, 174
Altin, 75
Ancien Régime, 10–14, 61, 87, 103, 105–10, 116–17
Appian Way, 70
Archaeology, 47ff., 63–4, 100, 143
Architecture, 95–100; Gothic, 97–100; Romanesque, 95–7
Archives, 51–2, 82, 87–90

Bailliages, 10–11
Barre, Jean de la, 35
Bas-reliefs, 69–70
Beauce, 19–22, 25, 32, 67, 74, 115, 121–2, 131
Beaunier, dom, 88
Belgae, 64ff.
Benedict, Saint, 3–4
Benedictines, 39–40, 88, 138
Bibliographies, 53–5
Bishops, 77–8
Bissy, Mgr de, 41

Bordas, abbé, 42–3, 44
Bouchard, 79
Bouzonville, 72
Briçonnet, G., 100–1
Bridges, 84
Brie, 24–6, 67, 113, 121, 131
Bulteau, abbé, 99

Caesar, 64–5
Cahier, village, 62
Cahiers de doléances, 109
Carnutes, 67
Carolingian period, 1, 2, 79, 81
Cartularies, 42, 87ff., 158–9
Castles, 70–2, 83–7, 156
Caumont, Arcisse de, 47–8
Celts, 64ff.
Champagne, 26
Charles VII, 12; the Bold, 2; the Simple, 28
Charters, village, 60–1
Chartres, 20, 37, 59, 68, 89, 94–5; Notre-Dame de, 98–9
Châteaudun, 48
Châteaux, 104–5, 156, 166
Chelles, 63
Christianity, beginnings of, 75–6
Chronique de Bonneval, 33
Chronique de Morigny, 33–4

Churches, 61, 162–5; histories of, 37–44

Climate, 30–1

Clovis, 2

Coins, 83

Columba, Saint, 93

Commons, enclosure of, 116, 174

Corbeil, 58

Counts, 78–82, 153

Debret, François, 98

Denis, Saint, 8, 75

Départements, 109–13, 122

Dimier, 105

Dioceses, 65–6, 148–9

Documents, 51–2, 55, 62, 82, 87–90

Doublet, Jacques, 37, 40–1

Doyen, 43

Dubois, Gérard, 38

Duchesne, André, 39

Ecclesiastical archives, 87–94; communities, 88ff.; dignitaries, 89; history, 87–94, reforms, 93–4

Édoald, 75, 76

Elephas antiquus, 63

Erosion, 16, 24

Étampes, 18–19, 58, 59, 85

Eudes, king, 3

Félibien, dom, 40–1

Feudal system, 78–83

Fleureau, dom Basil, 35, 59

Fleury, 3–4

Fontainebleau, 104–5; forest of, 24

Forests, 17, 18, 21–2, 27, 104–105, 113, 130

Fortresses. *See* Castles

France, custom of, 5; meaning of name, 1–5

French Revolution, 14, 77, 103, 108–11, 116; and the provinces, 110–11

Froissart, 9

Gallic period, 64–74

Gallois, 9

Ganelon, 86–7

Garnier, 4

Gâtinais, 23–4, 36–7, 113, 131

Gaul, peoples of, 9, 66–9

Généralités, 13–14, 105–9, 122, 168

Geographical characteristics, 16–32

Gothic period, 96–100

Gouvernements, 10–14, 105–8

Gregory of Tours, 2, 3

Guibert, Mgr, 49

Henry IV, 12

Hérupe, 7, 126

Histoire de Melun, 34–5

Histoire du Gastinois, 36–7

Huguenots, 101–2

Hundred Years' War, 86, 157

Hurepoix, 7, 65, 126

Ile-de-France, boundaries, 11–15; meaning of name, 10–15

Industries, 117–18

Inscriptions, 52, 55, 69–70

Intellectual history, 11–12

Intendants, 107–8

Jansenism, 102–3

Juine, river, 18–19

Laurent, Claude, 36

Lebeuf, abbé, 42–4, 60
Lefèvre d'Étaples, 100–1
Lehr, M., 102
Lemaire, M., 51
Ligurians, 63–4
Limon, 18, 22, 24, 26
Lipsius, Justus, 35
Liron, Jean, 53–4
Local histories, 33–44; contemporary, 45–118
Longnon, M., 73, 106
Luchaire, M., 89
Luchon, M., 90
Lucien, M., 89

Marnes vertes, 24
Meaux, 89, 94, 100–1; Cathedral, 100
Meldois, 100
Melun, 34–5, 68
Merlet, Lucien, 89; René, 89, 100
Merovingian period, 66, 74, 77–8, 93
Metric system, introduction of, 112–13
Meulière, 17–19, 24, 27
Meuret, abbé, 103
Middle Ages, 2, 6, 10, 11ff., 26, 37–8, 47, 59, 65–6, 70, 74–100, 103, 104, 162
Modern and contemporary periods, 100–18
Monasteries, 138; histories of, 90–3
Monographs, local, 56–62
Monuments, 47, 53, 69–70, 84, 103–4, 147
Morin, dom, 36–7, 44
Moutié M., 47
Municipal records, 110–11

Nantes, Edict of, 102
Noble families, histories of, 38–39
Normans, the, 79

Pagi, 66, 78–82
Pain de Gonesse, 26
Palaces, 104–5
Pannier, J., 102
Paris, *généralité* of, 13–14
Parisis, 104
Parlement de Paris, 105
Pays, 112
Peasants, 94, 112–13
Pilgrims, 70
Pithiviers, 57–8
Place-names, 72–4, 169
Potentien, 75
Pourpadin, M., 87
Prehistoric period, 63–4
Protestants, 101–2

Rambouillet, 47
Reformation, the, 101ff.
Renaissance, the, 34, 104
Rivers, 29–30, 131–2
Robert the Strong, 3, 79
Rollo, 28
Roman Catholic Church, 38, 152; history of, 102–3; organization of, 65–6, 76–7
Roman period, 64–74, 149–51; roads, 69–72, 149–51; towns, 68–9
Romanesque period, 95–7
Rouillard, S., 34–5, 37
Rousseau, J. J., 102
Rural areas, 112–17

Saint-Denis-en-France, 7–8, 37–38, 59–60, 90–1, 97–9, 126–7

Index

Sanctin, Saint, 75–6
Savinien, 75
Sculptures, 98–100, 163–4
Seals, 83
Seigneurs, 81
Senechaussées, 10
Sens, 77
Societies, local, 45–51
Souchet, J. B., 37
Soyer, J., 73
Statues, 98–100
Stein, M., 88
Suger, M., 71, 97–9

Taillepied, Noël, 34, 43–4
Tanon, M., 95
Tarisse, dom, 39

Tassin, dom, 39–40
Thierri, 2, 77
Toussaint-Duplessis, dom, 41–2, 100, 119
Towns, histories of, 56–62, 94; officials, 94–5

Usages locaux, 114–15, 173

Versailles, 167
Vexin, 5, 27–9, 67, 78, 96, 104, 156; Normans in, 79
Vidier, M., 54–5
Villages, histories of, 60–2
Viscounts, 80–1
Vital, Orderic, 85–6
Viticulture, 23, 25